06/22

WALKING
THE BIG WILD

WALKING
THE BIG WILD

FROM YELLOWSTONE TO THE YUKON ON THE GRIZZLY BEARS' TRAIL

KARSTEN HEUER

M&S

National Library of Canada Cataloguing in Publication Data

Heuer, Karsten
Walking the big wild : Yellowstone to Yukon on the Grizzly Bears' Trail / Karsten Heuer

ISBN 0-7710-4120-9

1. Rocky Mountains – Description and travel. 2. Grizzly bear – Rocky Mountains. 3. Heuer, Karsten – Journeys – Rocky Mountains.
I. Title.

FC219.H49 2002   917.804'34   C2002-903213-X
F721.H49 2002

We acknowledge the financial support of the Government of Canada through the Book Publishing Industry Development Program for our publishing activities. We further acknowledge the support of the Canada Council for the Arts and the Ontario Arts Council for our publishing program.

Maps by Visutronx

Typeset in Minion by M&S, Toronto
Printed and bound in Canada

McClelland & Stewart Ltd.
The Canadian Publishers
481 University Avenue
Toronto, Ontario
M5G 2E9
www.mcclelland.com

1   2   3   4   5   06   05   04   03   02

CONTENTS

For the McIvors, Russ, Leanne, and my parents,
who all introduced me to the mountains

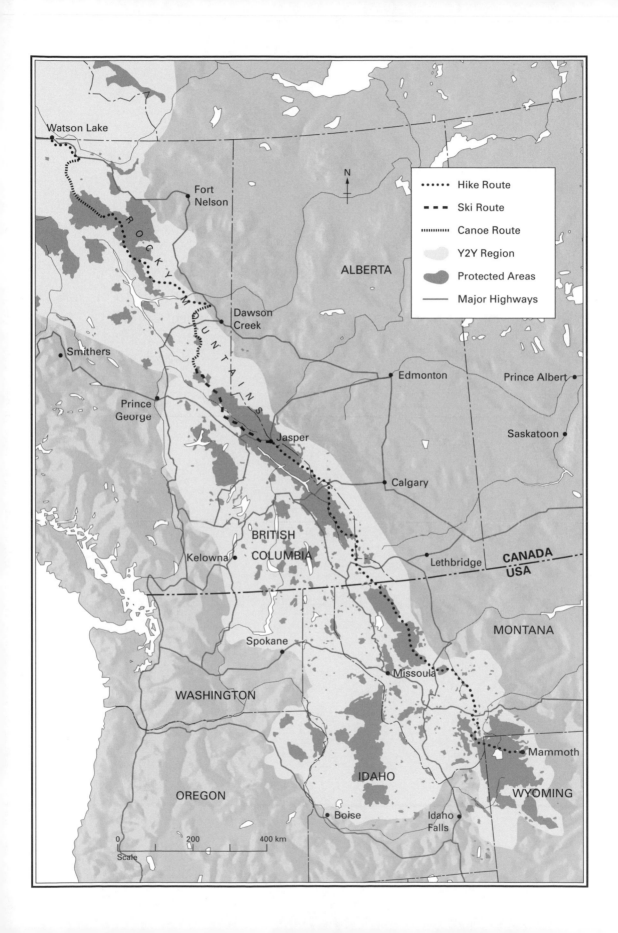

Watson Lake

Fort
Nelson

ROCKY MOUNTAINS

ALBERTA

N

•••••• Hike Route
- - - Ski Route
••••••• Canoe Route
       Y2Y Region
       Protected Areas
—— Major Highways

Dawson
Creek

Smithers

Edmonton

Prince Albert •

Prince
George

Jasper

Saskatoon •

Calgary

BRITISH
COLUMBIA

Kelowna •

Lethbridge

CANADA
USA

MONTANA

Spokane •

Missoula

WASHINGTON

Mammoth •

OREGON

IDAHO

WYOMING

Boise •

Idaho
Falls •

0   200   400 km

Scale

The lives of many animals are constrained by the schemes of men, but the determination in these lives, their traditional pattern of movement, are a calming reminder of a more fundamental order.

– Barry Lopez

PROLOGUE

He had worked hard for this moment: boiling the scent from leg-hold traps, digging them into the ground, then sprinkling each set with urine collected from other packs of wolves. But all that was nothing compared to the waiting – four weeks and two days. Now, finally, the vigil was over. A deep hole lay before him, and drag marks led into the trees.

The wolf went quiet as he approached, her tail tucked completely between her legs. He crept forward slowly in the pouring rain, holding the jabstick in front of him, and in the instant it touched her rump, shoved the needle into her flesh. She winced once, stood shocked for a few moments, then slowly sank to the ground.

The researcher moved quickly once she was down, working with quiet precision as he weighed her, pulled a tuft of her hair, extracted a vial of blood, and carefully fitted a transmitter and battery pack around her neck. Then, in the midst of recording her measurements, he paused to give her a name. "Pluie," he wrote, French for the downpour that had turned her coat black and left him shivering.

It was June 6, 1991, a busy time for the staff in Alberta's Peter Lougheed Provincial Park, and the mess hall where I sat listening to the researcher's story that night was filled with park rangers, maintenance workers, and fellow crew members, all of them as captivated by the story of Pluie as I was.

I had not yet seen a wolf, and just knowing one had been caught and released a few kilometres away was thrilling, a feeling that grew when I stumbled across the tracks of an entire pack the following morning. Abandoning the chainsaw, axe, and my trail-clearing duties, I followed the prints to a hidden lake, onwards to a meadow strewn with the bones and hides of past kills, and finally to the pine forest where each of the six wolves had dug a bed in the shade. The discovery made the Kananaskis Valley come alive for me in ways I had never imagined. I returned to my cabin that evening, phoned Dr. Paul Paquet – the man running the wolf study – and volunteered my spare time.

For the next few months, I shared the duties of recording Pluie's movements with the rest of the research team, tracking her radio signal and collecting bone, hair, and scat samples after her pack had moved off their kills. Judging by the number of elk, moose, deer, and beaver taken, the Kananaskis and Highwood valleys seemed to offer the wolves more than enough food and space. But then suddenly, in late November, Pluie disappeared. We drove hundreds of kilometres in search of her signal, climbed countless ridges, and searched remote valleys beyond her normal range by helicopter and plane. There was no sign of her. Then a month later, long after we'd concluded that either she or her collar was dead, a civilian branch of NASA reported that a satellite had picked up her signal hundreds of kilometres south of the Kananaskis Valley, in the northern United States.

Over the next eighteen months, we tracked Pluie as she travelled thousands of kilometres, criss-crossing parts of Montana, Idaho, Alberta, and British Columbia, covering an area equivalent to the size of Switzerland or, more significantly, 150 Peter Lougheed Provincial Parks in one of the longest wolf movements ever recorded.

I continued to work on the study throughout the remainder of my time at university, and stumbled across more examples of animals that ranged widely in the Rocky Mountains: a wolf that wandered from northern Montana to Mile Zero of the Alaska Highway; a lynx that made it halfway to the United States from the southern

Yukon; a grizzly bear that walked from one side of British Columbia to the other; and a bull trout that swam a thousand kilometres from central British Columbia to the Northwest Territories. In all cases, the the animal had ignored the boundaries between protected and unprotected lands.

It was a lesson that was hard to forget, and its implications came back to haunt me soon after I started my first job upon graduating. My task was to assess the effect of roads, buildings, and other types of development on the winter movements of cougars, lynx, wolverines, and wolves in the Bow Valley of Banff National Park. Not long into the four-winter study, I began to record what other biologists had long suspected: the maze created by the hotels, shops, houses, roads, ski areas, and golf fairways in the area had turned some important wildlife corridors into dead ends.

Recommendations from the study led to a few improvements. Within a year of closing a small airport and removing buildings, fences, and horse corrals from one beleaguered corridor, wolf use in the area increased 700 per cent. And when the local electric company built a wildlife overpass to bridge an otherwise impassable hydro canal, it was used almost immediately by elk, coyotes, cougars, and wolves.

I was pleased with these results, but knew they weren't enough. Like Pluie, many of the animals we tracked moved far beyond the Bow Valley and the boundaries of the park. Without similar initiatives in adjoining areas, wildlife corridors within the park would be inadequate. A larger perspective was needed.

Fortunately, other people were thinking about this problem, in particular Harvey Locke. Only thirty-five years old, the young Calgary lawyer had already led the Canadian Parks and Wilderness Society – one of Canada's largest environmental groups – to a number of victories. But despite these legal and political gains, Harvey saw that wildlife was still disappearing, in some cases even from within reserves and parks. One study by William Newmark, published in *Science*, was particularly troubling. In a sample of four-teen North American national parks, Newmark had documented forty-five cases of species going extinct for the sole reason that the areas protected for them were too small and too isolated. The phenomenon was particularly tough on predators near the top of the food web. River otter, ermine, and mink no longer existed in Oregon's Crater Lake National Park, for example, and since the establishment of Washington's Mount Rainier National Park, fisher, lynx, and wolverine had gone missing. Naturally rare and slow to reproduce, these animals often took decades to recover from catas-trophes such as food shortages, disease, and fire. And, as the evi-dence showed on some of the smaller reserves, they often didn't recover at all.

Amidst all this bad news, Harvey found some hope. In the late 1980s conservation biologists, including Michael Soulé and Reed Noss, were pushing hard for a new approach to wildlife conservation. Studies by Newmark and others showed that the old technique – setting aside tiny parcels of land and calling them parks – wasn't working. The solution Soulé and Noss put forward was not to create giant "superparks" but, rather, to link existing protected areas with wildlife corridors. A network of corridors could provide what none of the existing reserves could on their own: enough room and freedom for wildlife to flourish.

Reserve networks were quick to gain a foothold in parts of the United States. By the early 1990s greenways between Florida's Big Cypress Swamp and the Everglades were being proposed; green belts had been established in parts of Oregon; and wildlife corridors between a few California state parks were recognized. The reality dif-fered from place to place, but the concept was the same: connect iso-lated populations of animals and prevent local extinction.

Harvey had thought about a reserve network for the Rocky Mountains for some time, and in the summer of 1993, after he heard about Pluie's travels, the idea crystalized in his mind. It happened midway through a horseback trip through B.C.'s Northern Rockies, at the end of a day full of wildlife sightings. He had seen elk, caribou, eagles, two dozen moose, and enough wolf and grizzly bear prints to obliterate the tracks his horse had left the previous day. The experience left him with the same kind of energy he'd felt during his childhood in Banff, and later that evening, seated at the campfire, he used a corner of an old map to draw a plan.

He started his sketch with a few circles and squares – Banff, Jasper, Waterton, and other national parks – and followed them with the shapes of B.C.'s Bowron Lakes, Yukon's Tombstone Mountains, Alberta's Willmore Wilderness Area, Montana's Yellowstone and a host of other reserves and national parks. Next, he drew the wildlife corridors prescribed by Soulé, Noss, and Pluie until he had mapped a reserve network that spanned most of the Rocky, Columbia, and Mackenzie mountains. The bottom was the southern edge of grizzly bear range, the top was the Arctic Circle, and in between were the inland rainforests, the mountain slopes, rolling foothills, salmon rivers, trout-filled lakes, and alpine plateaus that made the area so rich and diverse.

That night, the Yellowstone to Yukon Conservation Initiative – or Y2Y, as it was soon dubbed – was born.

I heard about Y2Y, at a presentation Harvey gave in Banff National Park shortly after he returned from his trip. I was initially excited by the concept as it addressed my concerns about wildlife corridors and the lack of regional co-ordination. And yet, as I listened, I grew skeptical. I felt that what he was proposing was too huge and too audacious. There were already too many problems in the region, I thought, and too many political players. I admired Harvey's vision, his ability to think big, but I doubted that Y2Y could actually be implemented.

Travel overseas cured some of my pessimism. While Harvey worked to build support for Y2Y in North America, I headed to South Africa, where, while job shadowing with wildlife veterinarian Markus Hofmeyr, I caught a disturbing glimpse of a possible future.

South Africa's Madikwe Game Reserve is no ordinary state-run wildlife park. Hundreds of years of intensive ranching had wiped out the local ecosystem, and when the economy faltered behind it, the government stepped in with a plan to reintroduce the wildlife that had been lost, build a few game-viewing lodges, and let the influx of tourism dollars begin. Eight hundred square kilometres of land were bought, fires were started to stimulate new plant growth, a ten-foot-high electric fence was erected around the perimeter, and ten thousand large mammals – elephants, zebras, giraffes, and rhinos among them – were imported in the largest and most expensive relocation program in the world. Markus's job was to complete the project, bringing in the lions, hyenas, cheetahs, and wild dogs that would attract the tourists and keep all the other animals on the run.

When I arrived, Markus was preparing to introduce Cape hunting dogs. Every attempt to reintroduce the wolf-sized canids had failed elsewhere, but Markus was confident his efforts would succeed. He had inoculated them against most known diseases, had the fence to secure all avenues of escape, and, against all predictions, had managed to have three captive-bred females form a pack with three wild males in an enclosure where he'd held them for the last six months.

I was excited the morning Markus and I drove down to release the dogs. They watched, their large ears erect, as we dragged a dead antelope to bait them out of the enclosure, then shied away from the fence when Markus approached and swung open the gate.

It took hours for the dogs to muster the courage to venture through the opening, but finally the scent of blood tempted the boldest member forward and the rest soon followed. Markus and I gave a cheer as the last animal disappeared in a cloud of red dust, but in truth, we both knew that the dogs had simply traded one enclosure for another.

At first it didn't seem to matter to the dogs. For the next month we tracked and watched them as they hunted, the wild males teaching the captive-bred females how to bring down impala, gemsbok, and the other antelope. Within a few weeks they seemed to have fully adjusted to their new home, and by the time I left, they were beginning to den.

Over the next two years, the pack grew to twenty-four animals, but just as it seemed safe to celebrate its success, the program met with disaster. A rabid jackal bit the alpha male, and despite all the inoculations, the deadly virus spread. Hemmed in by the reserve's massive electric fence, none of the dogs could escape the epidemic, and within weeks, all but three of them were dead.

By the time Markus reported the outbreak, there was more bad news. One of the recently introduced and highly endangered rhinos had inexplicably died, and recent blood samples from an antelope showed signs of disease. Another rhino would need to be purchased, he explained, more tests conducted on the antelope, and another program started to reintroduce wild dogs.

It wasn't what government officials wanted to hear. Everyone, including the president, was eager to see returns from the millions of dollars invested in Madikwe. They wanted to know whether other wild dogs would survive if another $100,000 was spent on reintroducing them. How about another $35,000 rhino fare? When, if ever, would the tinkering end?

Markus shrugged his shoulders. He didn't have the answers. No one ever would.

I returned from Africa with a new appreciation for the wildness that still existed in the Rockies, and while working as a backcountry park warden in Banff National Park, marvelled at the grizzly bears, wolves, moose, elk, and wolverines I encountered on my nine-day patrols on horseback. There were problems facing all of them – highways to cross, livestock to tangle with, and towns and camps to avoid – but they were minor compared to the issues I'd witnessed at Madikwe. There were no electric fences, no captive breeding programs, no mandatory inoculations, and no engineered migrations. At least, not yet.

I started to think about Y2Y again. I still had doubts about the idea, but I now understood how, without a larger plan in place, the corridors and connections that were so vital to the health of wildlife could so quickly and unintentionally be cut off. I cast off my old skepticism, and, armed with the same questions I'd always had, began to find out whether or not Y2Y was really possible. How intact was the landscape? Where were the barriers to wildlife movement, and how serious were they? Was any restoration needed? And perhaps most importantly, would the people who lived and worked in the area embrace the idea of a Y2Y reserve network?

I spoke to biologists and other colleagues who were working the Rockies and read everything available on the region. It was 1997 and more than 100 scientists and conservation groups from Canada and the U.S.A. had rallied behind the Y2Y vision, and together they had published an impressive atlas of the area. The thick volume held maps that showed the distribution of vegetation, fish, roads, and grizzly bear habitat from Wyoming to the northern Yukon. There was an analysis of the region's changing economy and statistics on oil and gas drilling, livestock grazing, and timber harvesting; and biologists had started to model where some of the best corridors might lie. It was compelling information, but nowhere did it give a hint of what I sought. No one, it seemed, really knew if Y2Y was workable on the ground.

There are journeys that choose you more than you choose them, necessary journeys that demand to be followed more than pursued. And so, my girlfriend at the time, Maxine Achurch, and I considered the prospect of a very long walk. I didn't know exactly what would be involved, only that our journey would start in Yellowstone, end in the Yukon, and, following the wildest and least developed route possible, we would find out whether wildlife corridors existed or could be created among the parks and already protected lands. It was time to unite the theory with the land; to test a dream against reality.

It was time for a hike.

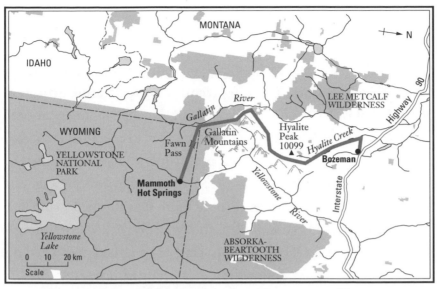

Mammoth, Wyoming to Bozeman Pass, Montana – 160 kilometres

1

You'd expect something at the trailhead of an eighteen-month-long hike, a send-off party, lots of hugs and cheers, but there was no fanfare as Maxine and I prepared to set out from Mammoth Hot Springs on June 6, 1998. There was little to tell us apart from the thousands of people who venture into Yellowstone National Park's backcountry each year. We were out of shape, wore boots and clothing fresh out of their packaging, and carried too much gear.

The departure date had crept up on us, forcing some of the trip's most important preparations into the final few days. We'd hastily assembled food packages for the first six months the night before leaving home, we hadn't even arranged where to cache them before setting off on the two-day drive from Banff to Yellowstone, and much of our equipment – donated at the last minute – hadn't been tested to see if it worked. To make matters worse, Ed Struzik, a writer and photographer from Edmonton had flown down and was busy recording the chaos.

"So what kind of training have you done to prepare yourselves for the trip?" Ed asked, snapping pictures for the feature article on our trek that was to run in *Equinox*, one of Canada's premier national magazines, a month later. Snowshoes, ice axes, headlamps, a tent and tarp, sleeping bags, air mattresses, pots, cups, a stove, fuel canisters, photo equipment, and various pieces of clothing and packages of food were strewn around as if some outdoor shop had exploded. Both Maxine and I tried to look as though we'd packed everything a hundred times before, but in truth, neither of us had even tried on the new backpacks, let alone seen if everything fit inside.

"Training?" I repeated. We were in terrible shape, would have been the honest answer. Maxine was still recovering from a broken pelvis sustained the year before, and I was suffering the effects of sitting behind a desk for the previous six months. I said something about an already active lifestyle but even that was stretching the truth.

The scope of the hike had ballooned with all the interest shown in it before it had even started. Months before leaving, newspapers had started to call, radio stations had requested interviews, and local Rotary and naturalist clubs in Banff and Calgary had asked for pre-sentations. People seemed entranced by my idea of symbolizing wildlife movement along the length of the Rockies and, more often than not, were inspired by the concept of Y2Y. This made me realize, rather suddenly, that there was an opportunity to do much more with the trek than simply satisfy my own curiosity about conditions on the ground. We could use the adventure to increase awareness about the need to think big, across boundaries, and about wildlife corridors.

This realization meant that in addition to mapping the route, planning, preparing, and dropping food caches, we needed to plan a major publicity campaign as well. Neither of us had experience in such matters, but we plodded ahead anyway, scheduling community visits along the route, where we would give presentations and media interviews. We hired a publicist, Justin Thompson, found a vehicle for him to use; developed a slide show; designed posters, press kits, and a web site; and raised money to pay for the whole endeavour. It was an overwhelming amount of work, and although the scientists, economists, and conservationists that had rallied behind the Y2Y vision were keen on our project, they were all too busy to provide much help.

The worst thing about all the preparations was what they did to Maxine and me. In the twelve months leading up to the hike, all the stress had started to show the weaknesses in our relationship. Not only did we have different working styles, but also a different concept of what was realistically possible. My pragmatism clashed with Maxine's boundless creative energy, and it wasn't long before the arguments started. The quarrels worsened over time, until finally, with only two months left before our scheduled departure, we split up.

It was a tough, emotional, and frustrating period. We had lost the ability to communicate, yet neither of us was willing to back out of the project. The relationship was over – there was no denying that – but no matter how much I begged and pleaded, Maxine refused to bow out of the hike. And after so much time and effort, there was no way I was going to give it up. So, only days before our departure, we'd struck an agreement: the expedition and all the outreach work associated with it would be a business partnership. Despite our estrangement, we would work, walk, give presentations together, and even sleep in the same tent, forgetting all the emotions we'd once shared, forgiving all the problems that still plagued us with professional detachment. It was a ridiculous and simple-minded arrangement, but it seemed to be the only way forward.

Yellowstone was the logical place to start the hike, and an appropriate southern anchor for the Y2Y concept. It was home to the largest herds of elk and free-ranging bison in North America; it represented the southernmost point on the continent where all the native large mammals still existed in the wild; and it was one of the few areas where the large-scale, life-renewing wildfires that had cycled nutrients and controlled disease and insect infestations for millennia could still occur with little threat to humans.

But despite its size and the diversity of its resident wildlife, there were obvious signs that the area was in trouble. Because of the disease threat to the livestock that ranged on public and private lands around the park, more than a thousand bison had been shot the previous winter; all the wolves that roamed through the area were direct descendants of a reintroduction program started eight years earlier; and in more than forty years, not one grizzly bear had ever left or arrived in the Greater Yellowstone Ecosystem without being handled by humans. It wasn't quite Madikwe in South Africa – there wasn't a fence around it – but Yellowstone was an island nonetheless.

According to Dr. Lance Craighead and Rich Walker, two American wildlife biologists interested in the Y2Y concept, there was still hope for the beleaguered area and the wildlife trapped on it. With a little work, some of the old connections could be re-established so that Yellowstone wildlife could once again move in and out of the area and be self-sufficient. The two scientists had modelled what they thought were the best remaining routes between the Yellowstone island of wildlife to the larger populations of animals that still stretched down from Canada into northern Idaho and Montana. There were three possible routes: one ventured west from Yellowstone via the Centennial Mountains to the Selway and Bitterroot Wilderness Areas, while the other two went north along the Gallatin Range before splitting into the Tobacco Root and Bridger mountains routes. The latter – up through the Gallatin, Bridger, and Big Belt mountains to the Scapegoat Wilderness Area in northern Montana – was the route we would take. According to Craighead and Walker, it was the best of the three options from a grizzly's perspective and, fortunately for us, was the shortest as well.

It was handy to have the Craighead-Walker report while plotting a route through the American portion of the Y2Y region, and I used similar studies to choose a path through the Crowsnest Pass and Bow Valley areas of southeastern British Columbia and western Alberta. But there was little information available on wildlife movement in the Y2Y region overall, a deficiency that forced me to use my own judgement about the path we would travel. I used the criterion common in most of the studies I'd read: as grizzly bears and other large carnivores preferred areas that were remote and devoid of human development, that's where we would hike.

We'd spent hundreds of dollars to buy the 211 maps for the trip, and at least as many hours poring over them. A jigsaw of map sheets had carpeted the apartment from kitchen to bedroom – forests, glaciers, and towering limestone peaks were traversed in seconds as I raced up and down the hallway, stocking feet trampling down the crisp corners, struggling to pencil in a definitive line. I consulted books, magazine articles, trail guides; even called outfitters, foresters, and local hikers for information, but their answers always led to more questions. Would a trail lead us through a valley in a few hours, or would we be faced with days of bushwhacking? What if I'd misread the contours and one of the ridges or passes I'd proposed to cross was riddled with cliffs? And what if some of the rivers that flowed across our path couldn't be forded? There were always more leads to follow, more information to be found, but only so much time. I finally had to accept the unknowns as part of the trip and, somewhat uncomfortably, traced a bold and presumptuous line across all the maps.

The next step had been to figure how long the trip would take and, from there, work backwards to schedule in community stopovers and food caches. Where I thought trails existed, I banked on an average walking speed of four kilometres an hour with an extra hour for every 300 metres of elevation gained. I halved that speed if it looked as though bushwhacking or trail breaking was involved. It was all guesswork. We had no idea whether we would be following game trails through open pine forests, hacking our way through thickets of devil's club, or ploughing through thigh-deep snow.

I would have been less worried if going a little hungry was all that was at stake, but because we were planning for Justin, our publicist, to ferry us between trailheads and communities, the entire schedule for presentations and media interviews depended on making good estimates of hiking time. I had nightmares of missed appointments, of reporters cursing the Y2Y name and entire audiences waiting impatiently in a community hall while we sat helplessly on the wrong side of a flooding river. And so, when the time came to finalize the dates, I did so with a little prayer.

The entire journey broke down into eight sections, twenty-three food caches, and 190 travel days over an eighteen-month period. In the first spring, summer and fall, we would complete the first three sections: we would hike 1,400 kilometres from Yellowstone to Banff; ride horses for 80 kilometres to the Ya Ha Tinda ranch; and then walk again for another 280 kilometres to Jasper. The following winter we would ski 400 kilometres from Jasper to Monkman Provincial Park. The final four sections would be completed the next spring and summer: canoeing 300 kilometres to Fort St. John; hiking another 570 kilometres to the Gataga River; paddling for 200 kilometres to the Liard River; and walking the final 200 kilometres to Watson Lake, Yukon. In distance, the trip would be the equivalent of travelling from Canada to Mexico and halfway back again. With regard to climbing, the 107 passes would be like ascending Mount Everest from base camp twenty times.

We had the journey figured as best we could, all that remained was the question of how to assess the health of the ecosystem we would be passing through. After all, the purpose of the trip was to judge whether a Y2Y network of wildlife routes was feasible. We decided to use the grizzly bear and wolverine as our measure. Both species are highly sensitive to human disturbance, and because of their position near the top of the food web, they naturally exist at low densities. This double-edged rarity meant that wherever we found signs of either animal – whether it be tracks, scat, digs, scent posts, rub trees, or sightings – we could assume the wilderness was intact.

Despite the odds against us – being physically unprepared, lacking familiarity with much of our equipment, and feeling trapped in the aftermath of a failed relationship – our mood was buoyant as we set off for Fawn Pass and the northwest boundary of Yellowstone National Park. The day dawned bright and sunny, a small herd of elk grazed on a hillside above us, and the dark shapes of bison peppered a storybook scene of meadows tucked into rolling, forested hills and snow-covered peaks.

We hadn't been walking for even an hour when we encountered our first sign of a grizzly – a fresh hole swiped out of a warm hillside as we climbed towards 2,900-metre-high Fawn Pass.

"What do you think?" I asked. Maxine reached down to inspect where the carrot-like biscuitroot had been torn up, and turned over a dislodged sod in her hand. An award-winning interpreter of natural history, she knew how to read the signs left behind by bears. The soil in the hole was still moist, and the blades of grass on the divot hadn't even wilted.

"Today's," she said. "Probably not more than an hour old." Both of us took a good look around the meadow before continuing and gave a few sharp shouts to announce our presence a few moments later when the trail led into a forest of mature pines.

We'd received a lot of advice about bears before leaving, most of it unsolicited. Take a gun, many suggested, while others warned not to venture into bear country at all. The risk of attack was real, especially if a mother with cubs was surprised at close quarters, but it was important to keep the threat in perspective. Of the hundreds of thousands of encounters between humans and bears in the lower forty-eight states over the past century, only fourteen people had been killed by grizzlies, fewer than had died from wasp stings or automobile brake failures, or a host of other causes over the same period. Our own experiences in the backcountry around Banff and Canmore had only confirmed the statistics. Between us Maxine and I had encountered dozens of grizzlies, and each of them had either fled or ignored us. In the unlikely event we did encounter an aggressive bear, we both carried a set of firecracker-like noisemakers and a canister of cayenne pepper-based bear spray holstered to our packs. But we expected we'd have no bear trouble as long as we adhered to a few common-sense rules: stay alert, make noise when walking through areas where bears prefer to feed and travel, keep a clean camp, and if encountered, give them as wide a berth as possible.

We had walked only ten kilometres when we decided to strike our first camp and ease the aches that had already begun to develop in our shoulders, backs, and feet. This was only half the distance we hoped to cover on an average day, but we were still pleased. For a couple of out-of-shape hikers, it seemed enough of an achievement just to have started what we'd been talking about for more than a year.

> JUNE 6, 1998 – *Yellowstone National Park – Setting up the tent, sparking up the cookstove, hanging the food, and writing the day's observations in this journal. Everything seems novel tonight, but over the next few months, these tasks are bound to become as routine as sleeping and breathing. Already there is a strange familiarity to everything, a sense of déjà vu. Perhaps it is the months of writing funding proposals, weeks of media interviews, and repeated conversations with family and friends that are responsible for the feeling. I have planned, explained, and described this trip for so long now that to actually be doing it feels like I'm acting out a script.*

The sense of following a script continued the next morning, for no sooner had we broke camp and hiked to the snow line, than we noticed fresh bear tracks paralleling our route. "Couple to hike in the tracks of the grizzly," local papers had proclaimed a few days before we'd left the Bow Valley. It seemed melodramatic at the time, and yet there we were, Day Two, already fulfilling its prediction.

The snowshoes we had borrowed made travel through Fawn Pass much easier for us than it had been for the bear. Where we sunk a few inches into the six-foot-deep snowpack, the bear had plunged through to its armpits, swimming more than walking its way over the divide between the Gardiner and Gallatin rivers. I couldn't imagine the energy it must have expended, and wondered why it wouldn't simply have waited another few weeks until the last of the snow melted and it could wander at leisure through the rolling meadows of alpine heather and bare rock.

An answer came a few hours later, after we descended below the snow and were walking on dry ground again. In the meadows, elk grazed the green shoots already poking up through the thatch of last year's growth, last fall's berries still clung to bushes coming into leaf, and in the air, swallows, solitaires, and flycatchers were hunting spring's first crop of insects. There had been signs of spring on the other side of the pass, but the season was far more advanced in this new valley. Everywhere around us was a smorgasbord of ripe foods for an enterprising bear: eggs to steal from the ducks and geese that exploded from meltwater pools, newborn elk calves to hunt, biscuit and *Hedysarum* roots to dig, and in the trestlework of decaying logs left by a fire a decade ago, huge colonies of ants to pry out.

It's hard to say why we stopped shouting out to warn bears and other wildlife of our approach, especially as the signs of bear had only increased with each passing hour. Perhaps all the tracks and scat had already become too familiar. Regardless of the reason, we were silent as we descended towards the Gallatin River, walking quietly past fresh tracks, root-filled scats, and logs scratched open by razor-sharp claws. We were setting ourselves up perfectly for a surprise encounter.

I saw the grizzly long before it saw me. It was hunched over, tugging at a rotten stump, and absorbed in the work of searching out grubs. It continued to dig as I stopped short, halting so suddenly that Maxine, head down and following close behind, slammed into my backpack. I grabbed her arm before she could cry out in surprise, and in one silent gesture, communicated our predicament. A grizzly bear was less than fifty metres away, and as of yet, didn't know we existed.

It is one thing to talk of how you'd react to a run-in with a grizzly, and quite another to experience it. Time not only slows, it sharpens. My skin tightened, and as I scanned the surroundings for cubs, a kill – anything that might exacerbate the situation – every moving leaf registered in my mind. The bear looked up from its digging, and I searched its face for the coming reaction. Nothing.

The bear was far enough away that its eyes rolled past us. Something was amiss, but it wasn't sure what. The elk on an adjoining hillside had stopped feeding, a red squirrel chattered its alarm call, and all the birds but a croaking raven had fallen silent. Propping itself up on its hind legs, the bear waved its nose, searching the wind for a message.

It looked to be 200 pounds and young – its head not yet grown into a pair of oversized, cup-like ears. Not a good bear to encounter, I thought to myself. Like teenage humans, subadult ursids are more curious than their full-grown counterparts. And more unpredictable. Too old to accompany their mothers, but too young to know what to avoid, they are roaming time bombs armed with claws and teeth.

We were downwind and wondering what to do when the bear made the decision for us. Having learned nothing from its vantage point atop the log, it dropped back to all fours and set off in search of a better position. The path it chose, unfortunately, led directly towards us, making it impossible for us to stay quiet much longer.

There were no trees to climb, only burnt, branch-less snags; no escape, except for a slow retreat. But even as we backed away, the bear unknowingly closed in. We had to announce our presence, but still I hesitated. A shout at such close quarters could easily trigger a defensive charge. And so we whispered instead, slowly raising our voices as we continued to step back, until suddenly, the bear's gaze locked in.

There was no hesitation once it noticed us. There was a flash of silver motion, and without so much as a crack of a branch to break the stillness, the bear fled across a football field of downed timber and disappeared behind a ridge. I looked at Maxine and gave a smile of relief, then sat down weakly while the sights, sounds, and memories of the rest of the world flooded back. With the immediate threat gone, something softened inside, an edge of wildness faded as everyday emotion returned.

Traces of adrenaline propelled us for the next four hours. We hiked fast and without a break, covering another twenty kilometres with less discomfort than had plagued us after only ten kilometres the previous day. We hiked down to the Gallatin River, and walked along its shore, then followed the road that led over the Yellowstone boundary to a lone ranch wedged between the Gallatin National Forest, the Lee Metcalf Wilderness Area, and the National Park. It was there that we had arranged to pick up two things: a food cache for the next nine days and my dog.

Because of Yellowstone's no-pet policy, Webster – a six-year-old border collie that a friend and I had rescued from the Banff dog pound four years earlier – had been forced to sit out the first two days of the trip. Once we had rendezvoused at the ranch, he was determined not to be left behind again. He watched our every move, whining impatiently as Maxine and I struggled to fit another nine days' worth of food and fuel into already-full backpacks. "Don't worry, you're coming tomorrow," I assured him. He wagged his tail, knowing that something big was about to happen.

He was less enthusiastic when I picked up his pack and called
him over the next morning. It was a custom-made job, ordered and
paid for by the same Bow Valley veterinarian that had donated all of
Webster's food, making him the best-sponsored member of our
shoestring expedition. But he didn't like the idea of being burdened
with his own food and first-aid kit. Normally obedient, he finally
slunk over after some coercing and reluctantly allowed me to strap
the panniers to his back.

As we set out, Webster staggered under his load, struggling to
find his balance down the driveway and up the Teepee Creek trail. I
felt sorry for him but knew that, of the three of us, he had the best
arrangement. At fifteen pounds, his load was only a third of his own
mass, whereas the sixty-pound and eighty-pound packs Maxine and
I were now toting were closer to half our body weights. No wonder
our muscles screamed. No wonder we moved at a crawl. Step, step,
breathe, and rest. Two red-tailed hawks and a merlin soared past,
but I hardly noticed. It took every bit of concentration to stay
upright. We walked until we couldn't keep going, which wasn't far.
That day we covered a meagre eight kilometres.

We were rapidly falling behind schedule, and as we moved north
and onto the crest of the Gallatin Mountains, things got worse. The
high undulating ridge was still under snow, but it was starting to melt.
A wet storm had moved in, and the rain and mist that still lingered
over the peaks had transformed the high country into a half-frozen
quagmire of sticky snow. Even with our snowshoes we plunged up to
our thighs, lurching like drunks, the momentum of our packs exaggerating each loss of balance and sending us face-first into the wet
snow. It didn't take long for Webster to figure out where the easy
walking was. After sinking up to his head a few times, he followed in
our wake.

Navigation proved challenging as well. Only the shadows of the
closest trees and rocks were visible through the thick fog, and with
the ridge branching every few kilometres, I frequently pulled out the

map and compass to deliberate over which way to proceed. We were losing time, and seeing nothing but a grey murk ahead of us, our motivation waned.

JUNE 11 – *Gallatin Crest, Montana – I hadn't counted on this, the snow and wet, this freezing drizzle and fog. Water has found its way into everything: our packs, our sleeping bags, our tent, our boots, and our food. Webster hasn't stopped shivering in forty-eight hours, and the only warm parts of Maxine and me are the blisters on our feet. It's painful to walk, and yet walking is the only way for us to get warm.*

For the first time, the realities of the journey began to set in. We were only ninety kilometres into it – about a fortieth of the total distance – but were already overwhelmed with soreness, exhaustion, and cold. To add to our woes, Maxine and I began to bicker. We plodded on, one moment quiet, the next shouting at each other, both frustrated with the feeling of being lonely and crowded at the same time.

The next day, after climbing a little higher, we came to sections of ridge that were blown clear of snow. Compared to the thigh-deep slop we'd been contending with, walking along the tilted slabs of bare rock and uneven bunchgrass felt like a jaunt along a sidewalk. Every stride rebounded off solid ground and our spirits began to lift.

There were still sections of snow to deal with, but at least we could look forward to breaks in the wading. And as the windblown stretches became longer and the snowy sections less frequent, we saw more and more tracks: a grizzly bear mother paralleled by her yearling cub; the prints of elk, deer, and coyotes; and at one point, the five-toed impressions left by a loping wolverine.

It was a trickle of activity at first, but as we continued north, more tracks merged onto the ridge. Every kilometre brought signs of a few more fellow travellers, animals that had somehow known that a high path of least resistance existed. Side valleys and subsidiary ridge systems joined our path like a series of on-off ramps, east-west secondary routes feeding a main north-south wildlife highway. More elk and deer had climbed up from the head of Cottonwood Creek, the wolverine had climbed down into the Cliff Creek Valley, and another, much larger grizzly had ventured up from Moose Ridge to follow the sow and cub on their journey north.

The amount of wildlife activity perplexed me. Although the Gallatin Mountains have long been recognized by biologists as an important 150-kilometre-long link between Yellowstone and the Bridger Mountains, it seemed odd that animals would travel along the high crest rather than the flat valley bottoms. Why were they traversing a ridge at 3,000 metres above sea level when lower, snow-free routes existed along the benches that paralleled the Gallatin and Yellowstone rivers?

The answer revealed itself with a change in the weather. As the rain and snow gave way to patches of sun, we saw where we stood for the first time in days. Far below, through the holes that formed in the patchwork of cloud, we caught a glimpse of a ski area, of ranches along the Gallatin River, of log homes and a golf course, and of a busy highway glinting with the metallic specks of speeding cars and trucks. And although the cloud didn't allow us a view to the east, the map told us that things weren't much different along the banks of the Yellowstone: more roads, more cleared fields, more dude ranches and executive retreats backing into a John Wayne backdrop of forested mountains and crystal-clear rivers. Sixty per cent of the 110-kilometre-long stretch of the Yellowstone River between the park and the town of Livingston had recently been subdivided for residential development, we later learned. The wildlife weren't walking the ridge because they wanted to, I realized, but because it was one of the only routes left.

The tracks continued for another day to the headwaters of Swan Creek, and then abruptly veered off our route at the exact point where the Craighead and Walker corridor maps had predicted. While the tracks in front of us suggested that the northwest route along the Tobacco Root Mountains was the better used, we stuck to our original plan, following the route that paralleled the remainder of the Gallatin crest before taking us into the Bridger and Big Belt mountains.

Why the animals had veered off the ridge became apparent when we reached Hyalite Peak the next morning. Instead of the gently rounded ridgelines we'd followed for the past five days, the last twenty kilometres of the range unfolded in a jagged, precipitous line. Without ropes or any other climbing equipment, it would be impossible to continue north along the crest, a conclusion underscored by the far-off rumblings and darkening skies of a fast-approaching storm. Not only did we need to find a safe place to descend off the ridge, but we needed to find it quickly.

The only route down was a steep, snow-plastered face that emptied into a huge, snowy amphitheatre cradling two frozen lakes. I crept carefully towards the edge and tossed a few snowballs down to test the snow. One rolled a few metres before disappearing over a bulge in the slope, the other stopped where it hit and set off a small slide.

"I don't know," I shouted up to Maxine. Rain early in the week had formed a smooth, icy crust, and the foot-deep layer of snow that had fallen since lay perched precariously on the surface, waiting for a trigger. Signs of recent avalanches peppered every visible slope, huge vertical bands slashed into the mountainsides, ending in deep, fan-shaped piles of debris. I looked down again, this time focusing on the litter of past slides that yawned up from the bowl far below. Another roll of thunder – closer this time – cracked out of the curtain of clouds, sending Webster cowering against the cliff for cover.

"Quick, give me your pack," I barked at Maxine, who gave a perplexed look, but obliged.

"Why don't you throw your own pack over?" she asked, but there was no time to argue. Grabbing one of the shoulder straps, I tossed everything she carried over the edge and watched as the improvised bomb spun twice and then hit.

It landed with a thump that sent a crack across the mountain, setting an acre of snow adrift in a split second. The whole slope below us moved, sending the pack rolling and pitching with it, riding the avalanche as a leaf might run a wild river, folding in and out of the turbulence, bobbing to the surface and then disappearing again at the whim of larger forces. We watched in silence from the ridge, mesmerized by the energy, until finally, the snow slowed and stopped, leaving the pack half-buried, waiting to be rescued.

There was no time to celebrate the success of our crude avalanche control. The wind ripped at the rocks, howling around us. Plunging the shafts of our ice axes deep into the remaining snow, we eased ourselves over the edge and, coaxing Webster down beside us, quickly kicked steps down the face of the mountain.

The storm hit before we'd even retrieved the pack, a few warm, fleshy drops followed by a blast of wind that pushed us, half-jogging, half-skating, over the ice of the two lakes. By the time we reached the outlet, the rain was falling in sheets, soaking through our clothes, liquifying what was left of the winter snowpack, setting the whole world awash within an hour. The creek we followed turned into a river, the trail into a creek, cliffs on either side of the valley boomed and echoed with the sound of falling rocks. Roots groaned and popped with the strain of the gale; needles, cones, and branches screamed down from the canopy; trunks the size of telephone poles shrieked against one other. Everything seemed alive with protest, everything moved, and for us, caught in the midst of it all, the only logical thing was to keep moving with it.

We walked for two more hours while the storm raged on, hiking late into the evening, unable to find a good campsite before dark. Only then did the winds subside to a point where it felt safe to be in the forest again. By the light of our headlamps, we found a small opening, cleared it of all the branches and small trees that had come down, and scraped out a pad for the wet tent and tarp. Maxine, suffering from stomach cramps and a headache, crawled into her damp sleeping bag while I groped through the dark rain for the stove and pot. Webster, a sorry sight of drenched fur and shivering legs, sought out a dry refuge, but the storm had left nothing untouched. Taking pity, I cut open a garbage bag and draped it around him, then went back to the dinner which, once boiled, I handed to Maxine through the tent door. She looked ragged, sick, and exhausted, and she accepted the bowl without a word.

After eating my own dinner, I cleaned up, hung the food, and crawled into the tent. Maxine lay curled asleep, the bowl of soup, cold and untouched, on the floor beside her. I wriggled into my own damp bag, then lay awake for a long time, listening to the drum of rain on the roof, waiting for my body to warm up.

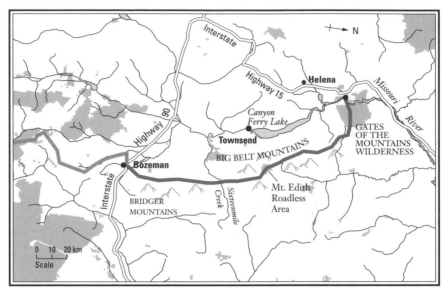

Bozeman Pass to Gates of the Mountains wilderness, Montana – 300 kilometres

2

The Bozeman area was the first major east-west break in the mountains that we had to cross, one of a handful of broad valleys and gentle passes that held some of the region's biologically productive land. Such low elevation habitats are where the bears first emerge from their winter dens, where the majority of birds nest in the brief breeding season, where the elk, deer, and sheep go to escape winter, and the cougars and wolves follow close behind. Warm, fertile, flat, sheltered – the qualities that made such areas vital to the animals of the Y2Y region, had, unfortunately, made them attractive to humans as well.

It had continued to rain hard all that night, the storm finally abating early in the morning as we started to pack up. Maxine's stomach ailments had disappeared, and our mood seemed to have improved with the weather. By the time we descended the last five kilometres of the Hyalite Creek trail to the old forestry road, patches of blue were beginning to show through the clouds. After an hour we stopped to take off our rain suits; the pile jackets and fleece pants soon followed. When we hit the paved road for the last twenty-five kilometres into town, we were walking in shorts and T-shirts for the first time.

What humans have done to the area was scarcely noticeable at first – a few quaint log cabins. But the footprint of development grew with each step out of the mountains. Within a few kilometres we were walking past massive structures of wood, stucco, and glass tucked into the hills. The shiny houses dotted old pastures like an outbreak of thistles, forty buildings parcelled side by side on five-acre plots, forty ranchettes crowding an area that had been nothing but a wooded glen with a lone ranch house only a decade before. It wasn't country living – square corners and garish colours poked out of the landscape wherever one looked – but it wasn't quite the city either. "Too big for the lawnmower, too small for the tractor," someone once said. By the time Maxine and I reached the four-lane Interstate highway, all we'd seen in the way of wildlife were the tracks of a few opportunistic coyotes and half-tame deer. Somewhere between our last campsite and Hyalite Canyon, we had stepped off the Yellowstone island.

Development was sweeping not only the Bozeman area, but through the Rocky Mountain West region in general. Lured by the area's beauty and freed from city living by new communication technologies, urban refugees, retirees, and footloose entrepreneurs were flocking to the area, bringing a demand for housing with them. Between 1990 and 1998, while the rest of the United States grew at a modest 8.7 per cent, the number of people living in counties bordering Yellowstone mushroomed by as much as 60 per cent. And as the semi-urban sprawl we were walking through demonstrated, few of them were interested in living in town.

The good news was that the influx of new people, and the money and business they brought with them, was helping to stabilize and broaden the traditional boom-bust economies of many forestry and mining-based towns. The bad news was that, if left unchecked, the unprecedented urban development could destroy the very attributes – clean air, clean water, open space, and wildlife – that were drawing people to the region.

For the conservationists, who had long extolled the economic advantages of saving wild land to attract tourists and well-heeled settlers, the irony was hard to swallow. The current pace and scale of development had the potential to do as much damage as the wholesale clear-cutting and mining that they'd been fighting for years. The new threats demanded new strategies and so resource economists were now working with ranchers; biologists were conferring with highway engineers; and instead of just lobbying forestry and mining executives, many activists were now meeting with town planners and county commissioners as well.

What was remarkable was that, in some areas, all these people were literally working from the same map: the Craighead-Walker maps of Montana's best remaining wildlife corridors. Because of the maps, the local offices of the National Forest Service had committed to include wildlife linkages in their planning efforts; local Department of National Transport officials were beginning to discuss how to mitigate wildlife bottlenecks across many of the region's roads; a number of counties had recognized previously unidentified wildlife movement areas; and two land trusts were working to stop subdivisions from being built on a number of critically positioned private lands. Easy to read, the simple science-based maps were a powerful tool. The people of the Bozeman Pass were proving that it is possible to implement the Y2Y vision at a local level.

After a week of rain, snow, and dried rice and beans, the prospect of a warm restaurant was too tempting to put off another day, and on protesting feet, we walked over thirty-five kilometres to the highway where we hitched a ride into Bozeman. Once in town, we wasted no time finding the local pub that offered the best beer and greasiest food. I tied Webster outside while Maxine went to find a phone and call Justin. Then we both ordered a tableful of items off the menu.

It hadn't been easy finding a publicist, especially at the pitiful wage we could offer, but we'd somehow lucked upon Justin. Having just graduated with a Master's degree from the University of Guelph in Ontario, he was eager to find meaningful work, but also keen to travel. Roaming the Rockies to promote the conservation of wildlife was the perfect job.

Justin wasn't a publicist by training, but the confidence and diplomacy he'd shown in the interview more than convinced us that he was capable of doing the job. It didn't bother him that he'd be working long hours, travelling alone across a vast landscape, and sleeping in roadside ditches and on people's living room floors. What mattered, he'd said, was that he worked for positive change.

The way we planned the project was straightforward. While Maxine and I walked a section of the hike (anywhere from five to twelve days in duration), Justin would drive ahead and organize media interviews, meetings with local government officials, venues and advertising for public presentations. At a predetermined time and location, he would pick us up from the trail and whisk us off for three to five days of scheduled engagements. Somewhere between all the appointments, we would find time to develop and insert the latest photographs into the slide show, pick up our next food cache, and do our laundry. Then, after Maxine and I had repacked, Justin would drop us back where we'd met days earlier. While we continued walking, he'd prepare for our arrival at the next stop. Nineteen such intermissions had been scheduled for the trip, during which we hoped to visit seventy communities. If either of us missed a rendezvous, the other would get to a phone and check a number we'd set up for messages. If forty-eight hours passed and there was still no word, the authorities would be notified and a search launched.

We'd actually arrived a day early in Bozeman, and so it wasn't until three hours after Maxine left a message that Justin bounded into the pub. Wincing with stiffness as we rose to greet him, I tried not to look ashamed as he laughed at the dishes and half-eaten crusts that still cluttered the table. Together, Maxine and I had consumed two extra-large pizzas, a meal-sized salad, one pitcher of beer, and two slices of pie.

"I gotta be honest, you guys look terrible – like you've been through a war," he said, pulling up a chair. I looked across at Maxine. She looked grey with exhaustion and the clothes she wore – the same shirt, sweater, and pants she'd shivered, slept, and walked in all week – had been so stretched with rain and sweat that they hung off her already-thin frame. I didn't feel as though I looked any better.

"Well, at least you're safe," he continued. "I began to worry when that big storm hit. The local news was filled with stories of people who were caught off-guard and had to be rescued from the rain and hurricane-force winds. What was it like in the mountains?"

Maxine and I offered a brief sketch of the past ten days, touching on the grizzly encounter in Yellowstone, the deep snows along the crest of the Gallatins, the ridge-top animal tracks, the avalanche, and the storm. Neither of us mentioned the arguments.

"How'd you make out with the publicity?" I asked. A mixed look of optimism and concern swept across Justin's face.

"In terms of media coverage – great!" he exclaimed. He'd secured interviews with every local paper and radio and TV station over the next two days. "I don't know about the presentations, though. I booked good rooms in both Bozeman and Livingston, hung posters in all the obvious places, and faxed public service announcements to all the media outlets. But it's all a little short notice. There hasn't been

much time to get word out. It's hard to say how many people will
show up."

Like all performers, we couldn't help but use the size of our audience to gauge interest, and the next night, we dropped excuses to one
another as we set up the slide projector and sound system, trying to
cushion the disappointment if only a few people showed up. It was
too nice a summer evening to be inside; the football game was on TV;
all the announcements had been buried near the back of the local
papers. No matter how real or contrived, however, the excuses didn't
do much to quell the anxiety. A few early arrivals dribbled in, and for
the next half-hour before taking the stage, we watched, hopefully,
for a crowd to follow.

There were no crowds that week, only thirty-five people in
Bozeman, and an intimate but small group of six in Livingston – four
of them from the same family.

"It'll only get better," Justin encouraged, explaining how he'd
already sent posters and announcements ahead to the communities
we would visit in three and four weeks. There would be more time for
word to spread, and as the hike covered more ground, people would
become more intrigued with the adventure. "Have faith," he said.
"The momentum will build."

But it wasn't just the small crowds that left me feeling dis-
satisfied; it was the delivery of the show itself. Maxine and I had
completely different ways of approaching the presentations and a
different concept of how to balance the lessons of wildlife biology
with stories from the trail. Not only did we fight over which images
to include in the slide show, but we battled over how to speak as well.
I talked in a casual, conversational tone, and Maxine liked to work off
a script. Our dysfunctional partnership, already unbearable on the
trail, had taken to the stage.

Fortunately, an unavoidable work commitment meant that
Maxine had to leave the trip temporarily. For the next week, I would
continue walking through the Bridger Mountains on my own. It

wasn't the permanent break we needed, but it was seven days apart, a chance for each of us to regain some calm.

Four days off left me feeling strong and full of energy. My blisters had healed, the soreness in my legs was gone, and I was well rested. But the added load of the tent, stove, pots, and fuel – equipment that Maxine and I had previously shared carrying – had me moving as slow as ever. I wasn't walking for more than a few minutes before a stream of runners out for a jaunt up Mount Baldy breezed past.

"Mornin'," barked one jogger as he ran by. Another four streamed by before the sixth stopped for a second look at Webster.

"Hey," said the Lycra-clad woman as she pointed at his red pack and distinctive one-ear-up-one-ear-down pose. "Hey, isn't that the dog that's hiking to the Yukon?"

Although the presentations hadn't been well attended, we had done well with the local media in Bozeman and Livingston, including front-page articles and pictures in both daily papers. Webster had figured prominently in all of it, and he was well on his way to eclipsing Maxine and me as the Y2Y hiker. Justin had started to call him "Web Star" for his ability to melt the hearts of reporters and photographers. I watched him now as we climbed higher, his tail wagging as he sniffed at every hole in the soil, and once on top of the ridge, how he crept to the edge and looked down every few minutes, nose twitching to extract every story riding in the updrafts. He was a model for living in the moment, for not worrying about the future, and for letting go of the past.

Following Webster's example, I immersed myself in the present, observing my surroundings, and enjoying the beauty. The season's first wildflowers were beginning to bloom: Indian paintbrush, purple larkspur, saxifrage. I chewed a few tender leaves off the yellow glacier lilies that poked from the patches of lingering snow. Up and down I walked, following a footpath along the corrugated flank of the mountain chain, stopping to watch a garter snake lie motionless for half an hour in a rainstorm, and after retreating to a safe distance, a mother black bear with two football-sized cubs scratch down a wind-swaying tree. Light, colour, and life. The hike was becoming the meditation it should be. I walked for the sake of walking; descended only to climb again; and after reaching the summit of Sacagawea Peak, stopped, looked, and listened, hungrily consuming the view.

I was three days out of Bozeman, and the town, as well as the sprawl of development that surrounded it, was now just a hazy gap to the south of a long rib of mountains. From my ridge-top vantage, I could see much of the route we had travelled the week before. I could see that the Bridgers were narrower than the Gallatins, and that the boundaries to either side were sharper. Unlike the wilderness areas that had stretched off to the west of the Gallatins, well-cropped pastures and hayfields pressed against the Bridgers from both sides. I was walking along a sliver of wild land kept straight and narrow by countless farmers' ploughs.

Those abrupt human-defined lines softened over the next two days, while at the same time, the rugged folds and faults that had made the Bridgers steep and cliffy smoothed into gentle, low mountains. Here private and public lands melded one into another. Huge ranches fingered into the hills, and yet I found flower-filled meadows, intact aspen and Douglas fir forests, and abundant signs of wildlife on both sides of the barbed wire. Herds of elk thundered through the trees, and in the odd pasture tucked, I saw antelope and deer grazing among the cows. There was no hiking trail. I saw no people or cars on the scattered gravel roads. In four days I passed five houses. The level and scale of human activity here hadn't wiped out all types of other life. A great horned owl swooped through my camp one night, followed by a newborn fawn that stumbled out of the forest. The next morning, while gathering water from a nearby creek, I found the tracks and scat of a black bear that had gorged itself on horsetail plants for days.

But there was no trace of the grizzly, a fact confirmed later by the local Forest Service biologists. Cougars and wolverines still survived in pockets in the Bridgers, and there were unsubstantiated reports of an odd wolf passing through. But not since the 1960s, not since the last one was hunted down and killed, had anyone spotted one of the great bears.

Perhaps too much development and traffic were preventing them from moving north through Bozeman Pass, or perhaps something I hadn't yet discovered was preventing northern Montana bears from coming south. Or maybe the reason was much simpler; maybe the Bridgers just weren't a good grizzly bear connection.

Exactly what makes a good wildlife corridor is a question scientists have long asked themselves, and the answer is that it depends. It depends on the amount of tree and other plant cover. It depends on the availability of food and water, the amount of human activity within and adjacent to the corridor, on the presence (or absence) of predators and competitors. It depends on the corridor's shape and length, and on the attractiveness of what it connects. Most importantly, perhaps, it depends on the animal using the corridor. A songbird's needs and preferences are different from a frog's, which, in turn are different from those of fish, foxes, wolves, or grizzlies.

Of all the land animals in western North America, the grizzly bear appears to be the most demanding in its requirements. Unlike birds, elk, wolves, or even wolverines, grizzlies need more than a swath of land to move through; they need linkages where they can actually live. Unlike wolves, for example, which move quickly over long distances in search of prey, grizzly bears depend on a detailed knowledge of where and when different foods are available. This difference has important implications for conservation. While wolves can pass through unfamiliar terrain, killing the odd deer for sustenance along the way, bears prefer to stay close to the known while searching out the novel. This is why bears tend to establish territories that overlap with their mothers', whereas some wolves, like Pluie, travel thousands of kilometres. In more than forty years of study, not one of over 400 radio-collared grizzlies has ever moved from one block of protected areas to another within the Rocky Mountains.

The grizzlies' leapfrogging pattern of dispersal results in some large corridor requirements. In order to have enough food, water, cover, and space to live, they may need corridors tens of kilometres wide – even wider where plant and tree cover, flat ground, and security from human disturbance are lacking.

On the Bridgers, I had stumbled across plenty of bear foods, water was readily available, I hadn't seen a person in days, and the band of forested land, although fragmented by pastures in places, was at least ten kilometres wide. What I hadn't sampled, however, was perhaps the single most important factor in determining corridor quality: human tolerance.

Where grizzlies, wolves, or any other wild meat eater come into contact with humans and their livestock, there are bound to be conflicts. There are ways of minimizing them – electric fencing; use of specially trained guard dogs; and keeping the more susceptible animals, such as lambs and calves, out of areas the predators frequent. But even with such preventive measures in place, losses are inevitable.

There were a few predator-friendly ranchers in the Y2Y region, people who, so long as they were compensated, accepted losses to wolves and grizzlies as part of the risk of ranching near the Rocky Mountains. But the agriculture industry in general was implacably opposed to the idea of coexisting with large carnivores. Despite an overwhelming majority of support from the American public for wolf reintroduction, the local livestock producers were causing the federal government to spend millions of dollars defending the Yellowstone and Idaho reintroduction programs and, at the same time, pushing for every wolf found outside of the recovery area to be trapped or shot. Even if wildlife corridors were perfect in every other way, without tolerance and acceptance, only the luckiest carnivores could run the gauntlet and get through alive.

I had talked to many of the ranchers in the area north of the Bridgers before leaving for the hike, seeking permission to cross their land. I'd been honest about what I would be doing, but I'd stopped short of talking about the large carnivores. There were some property owners I hadn't been able to contact beforehand, and as I crossed their lands, I switched to stealth mode, imagining myself to be an unwelcome wolf or grizzly. Travelling only at dusk, dawn, and at night, I moved along the wooded margins of fields, avoided roads and the lights of houses, froze at the sound of anything around me, and crept warily past barns and corrals and over fences.

The ranchers I had talked to asked that a few simple rules be followed while crossing their properties: leash the dog, don't light fires, and don't camp on their land. All but the last request were easy to comply with. Two days short of reaching Highway 12 and my next rendezvous with Justin, I had to walk thirty-five kilometres in one day to reach the only piece of public land for kilometres – a small picnic ground in the heart of Sixteenmile Canyon.

It wasn't an ideal campsite. The only creek was muddy and filled with cowpies, and the winds bounced and knocked off the walls of the narrow canyon, sending smoke from my small campfire in all directions. I didn't like sitting in a wind funnel, in the heart of the only cleft in a kilometres-long wall of mountains, but I didn't have a choice. I went to bed, worried by the sound of approaching thunder.

The storm hit in the black of night, arriving with such a blast that it flattened my tent. I groped to find the door, and crawled naked and blind into a vortex of hail and rain. Lightning flared through the canyon, strobe after strobe hammering frames of chaos out of the darkness, illuminating the leaves, sticks, and water flying past while I stood stunned, half-awake, trying to fathom if such power was dream or reality. A few rocks boomed into the canyon while I stood there, and in another flash of lightning I saw that the creek had jumped its banks. Water rushed past my feet, and within seconds, the collapsed tent began to creep downslope. I lunged for a corner of the wet nylon and, grasping it tightly in cold hands, wrapped it around me. Webster emerged from somewhere in the blackness and crawled between my legs, shaking with panic.

Whether it was my half-awake state or simply the calmness induced by a week of walking alone, I will never know, but through all the chaos, I felt tranquil. There was none of the panic I'd felt during the storms and all the other threats of the previous week. Now I accepted the fruitlessness of any response. There was nothing to do; I had to accept the storm on its own terms. So I sat as comfortably as I could, and patiently waited for it to blow over.

"This is only temporary. This is only temporary" became my mantra as my hands and feet grew numb. My grasp weakened, and a corner of the tent broke free to snap and flap in the wind. "This is only temporary," I repeated, louder this time, as I pulled in the tent and rewrapped it around me and Webster.

How long I sat there, chanting like a shaman, I don't know. A long time passed – maybe hours – before the rain softened and the wind died down. I slumped onto the wet ground, sick for sleep.

It was sunny when I awoke, hot and sweaty inside the nylon cocoon twisted around me. I looked around for Webster, whistled with dry lips before spotting him lying under a tree, his coat still wet and matted from the storm, happily panting in the shade.

"Bad news," said Justin shortly after we met on the highway outside Townsend two days later. "There's a bit of controversy popping up in our wake." He handed me a couple of letters to the editor that he'd clipped from the Bozeman and Livingston papers a few days after the articles on the hike and Y2Y had run. I had to laugh at some of the accusations, especially the one about Y2Y being part of a conspiracy that, along with the United Nations, was bent on removing land-owner rights, as well as the whole notion of private property, from the American West.

"Is this a joke?"

"Afraid not. When it comes to new ideas, there's lots of paranoia out there." Justin's face went serious while I continued to shake my head in disbelief. "Listen, I've been thinking," he began. "There's room for improvement in some of what you and Maxine are saying in your presentations and interviews. Both of you need to be clearer on the point that Y2Y isn't like other, smaller environmental projects. This isn't a campaign to draw a line around an area and have every-thing except hiking and cross-country skiing excluded. There has to be no doubt in people's minds that Y2Y is different."

Within minutes of meeting Maxine at the bus station, it was apparent that the brief respite from one another had done nothing to improve our relationship. We discussed the misperceptions that had cropped up in Bozeman, but both of us were so touchy that it was impossible to suggest that the other person needed to make changes. The presentations and interviews we gave in Townsend and Helena were virtually the same as those we'd offered in Bozeman and Livingston. Justin said nothing, but I could see the disappointment and frustration on his face. Unless something changed soon, the whole project was going to fall apart.

I had asked Maxine to leave the project many times before, and did so again before Justin drove us to the trailhead where I'd left off three days earlier. Her answer remained the same. And so we left together but walking apart, an unhappy partnership venturing up Cabin Creek and into the Big Belt Mountains beyond.

We moved silently that day, plodding up to where an old logging road gave way to a footpath that climbed through low-lying clouds and to the still snow-laden world of peaks and high forests. We crossed the round summit of Mount Edith, and in the murk of a snow squall, plunge-stepped down to a small roadless area of high forests and half-frozen alpine lakes. The snow turned to rain as we descended, and after finding a place to pitch camp, we cooked a quick meal of lentils and rice, then climbed into the tent without so much as saying good night.

JULY 3 – *Mount Edith Roadless Area, Big Belt Mountains – The rain hisses on the leads of open water and strokes down the sides of the tent, gentle, melancholy sounds that only sink me deeper into depression. I feel half dead and dispassionate compared to last week, more lonely than I have ever been on my own. There is no companionship here; we are together in space but otherwise disconnected.*

The next day, only our second in the Big Belt Mountains, the crisis came to a head. We had just crossed Duck Pass and were following a well-worn trail when Maxine missed a corner and stepped onto a wildlife path that led her off in a different direction. I was ahead, and after not seeing her for ten minutes, realized that something must have gone wrong. I sat down and waited, and after she didn't appear, turned back to see what had happened.

I couldn't figure it out at first. I found nothing when I returned to where I'd last seen her; no pack, no Maxine, no answers to my calls. Only after looking closely did I see the scuff marks and tamped-down plants where she'd gone wrong. I pointed them out to Webster, and set off after him as he began tracking her, nose to the ground.

We had made a similar mistake earlier that morning. Ever since leaving the roadless area a few kilometres back, there had been a pro-fusion of paths, jeep tracks, old roads, and unsigned junctions that had made route-finding confusing. But now as the going got tougher, as I had to duck under trees and clamber after Webster through bushes, I began to wonder why she hadn't realized the mistake and turned back. Worried that she might keep going forever, I began to run and shout, yelling into the wind.

It was a kilometre before I caught a glimpse of her and another few hundred metres before I caught up to where she still walked, following the grassy crest of an open hill. I gave out one last hoarse shout, and she stopped suddenly, wheeled around, looking surprised.

"What happened?" I asked. "Why did you keep going?"

"I was only following you," she said. "Following where you disappeared into the trees."

"Maxine, you couldn't have followed me. I was walking through a meadow in the other direction!"

"You led me astray," she insisted. "When I called out, you didn't answer." And then she added, "You tried to trick me."

Everything that was wrong with our relationship – bitterness, self-righteousness, and distrust – was in that statement. My blood began to boil. I have never known such frustration and rage. I cursed at her and shouted as Webster bolted for the trees. Then I stormed off after him, back to the trail.

We hiked the rest of that day without a word passing between us, me moving ahead while Maxine followed at a distance behind. Then, that night, after eating dinner, I gave her an ultimatum.

"Only one of us will continue from now on," I said, "and it's up to you to decide who that will be. We'll walk as far as the next highway together – five more days – and then this absurd farce will be over. You can continue alone or with someone else after that, you can have the whole project, or else I continue on alone. There is no third option. You or me, but not together."

Maxine listened silently and, after staring into the forest for a few minutes, went to bed without saying a word. I stayed up late, writing page after page in my journal by flashlight, while a field of stars emerged above.

The Big Belts rose out of the surrounding prairie as a solitary, thirty-four-kilometre-wide range, loosely connected with the Bridgers and the Little Belt Mountains on either end. Compared to the Bridgers or Gallatins, its peaks were more like hills. Despite the advantage of such moderate terrain, the Big Belts held little sign of wildlife. Over the next three days we saw the tail ends of three deer, five skittish elk, and heard the croak of a far-off raven. Their brief breeding season over, even the songbirds had grown quiet. Only robins and a few other thrushes sang, where sparrows, kinglets, and warblers had filled the spring air with layers of sound only a week before. Nowhere did we see a hint of any of the large carnivores.

Instead we saw people – a few hikers, a shepherd moving sheep across a low pass, pickup trucks bumping along one of the few roads – more human activity than we'd experienced in the Gallatin and Bridger mountains combined. And it got worse. The sound of heavy machinery woke us up the next morning – the drone of engines and squeal of metal scraping over rock. By the time we'd cooked and eaten breakfast, plumes of smoke were drifting out from behind the next ridge.

Our route took us right through the small logging operation. A large machine, outfitted with a circular saw the size of our tent and huge pincer-like arms, felled a tree every thirty seconds on one side of the small clear-cut, while on the other side another contraption stripped each log of its limbs with a huge hydraulic boom and iron diaphragm. A bulldozer and crane worked farther up-slope, stacking what had already been felled into neat piles. It was a small cut, not much more than a few hectares, and except for a handful of lone Douglas firs, nothing much had been left standing. We wound our way through the stumps and branches while the machinery worked on. There was no way of knowing whether the operators – hidden behind smoke and the mesh of their metal cages – answered our waves. Despite all the activity, we couldn't see anyone. It wasn't until we were back into the forest that a truck pulled up and out jumped a man, walkie-talkie in hand.

"What exactly are you all doing here?" A neatly cropped line of white hair stuck out from under his ball cap, and he wore a collared shirt tucked into cleanly pressed jeans. I guessed he was the manager.

"We're just passing through on a hike north," I answered, keeping things vague.

"We're hoping to make it to the Yukon," Maxine added quickly. "We're trying to raise awareness of the need for wildlife corridors along the way." I winced.

"Aren't you too pretty to be doing something like that?" the logger smiled, ignoring me as he talked to Maxine. "That's one helluva trip for a beautiful woman to be making across wild country!"

Bill Kelly, as it turned out, was the owner of one of a handful of logging companies working in the region. His was a relatively small and local operation, inherited from his father who was killed when a tree had fallen the wrong way years before. "It's the little ones that'll get you," he cautioned, pointing to his temple as he told us how the elder Kelly had been knocked in the head.

The cut we were witnessing at the head of Beaver Creek was one of three tenures Bill held in the mountains of both Montana and Idaho. This particular operation, he told us, gesturing to where the crane now moved towards another pile of logs, was a "salvage cut" – one where they had selectively removed beetle-infested pine trees. "And given your love for wildlife, you'd probably be pleased with how we'll be leaving it when we're done," he added, still talking mainly to Maxine. "That backhoe there," he said, pointing to another huge piece of heavy equipment, "is going to be the last piece of machinery that leaves." Once it left, there would be no coming back. It would dig the road under, return the hillside to its original slope, and then workers would come behind to plant trees and shrubs. I couldn't help but be impressed, even more so when Bill explained that the road had been there for over ten years. From the perspective of wildlife security and movement, the small logging operation would be of net benefit – it was removing a road where one had existed before.

"Isn't that expensive?" I asked, remembering all the recent newspaper headlines about timber companies struggling to survive in competitive world markets.

"That's the beauty of being small," beamed Bill. "The company's flexible enough to adapt quickly to changing markets, and right now, right here – even with the added cost of restoring the road – we're going to make money."

Bill Kelly and his method of logging fit nicely into the Y2Y vision. Unlike the wildlife-good, people-bad mentality of many past conservation initiatives, the goal of Y2Y was not to remove but to include human activities. The core reserves – primarily the national parks and wilderness areas – would be protected against resource extraction, but the connecting corridors and surrounding transition zones could offer opportunities for sustainable, small-scale forestry, for hunting and fishing, even for tightly controlled exploration and drilling for oil and gas. "Try to imagine it as different *levels* of protection," someone had told me at my first Y2Y meeting.

The last two days had been hot, and as we followed Bill back to his truck to say goodbye, I noticed a jug of water sparkling on the back seat.

"Say, are you going to need all that?" I asked, pointing at the four-gallon container. He was out of his seat before I'd finished the question, pouring until all our bottles were full.

"Now you take good care of that fine lady friend of yours," he called out to me after we'd said our farewells.

JULY 6 – *Maxine has said little since the ultimatum. I still have no idea who will continue and who will be out. Not knowing has made the days even more silent. With nothing to share and no common future, it seems more pointless than ever to rest, relax, or otherwise sit together around camp. And so we are*

walking long distances, moving through the silence and awk-
wardness, steadily working our way to where it will finally be
over. Yesterday we walked thirty kilometres; today we covered
thirty-five more.

The long days helped to deal with the emotional stress but
exerted a toll on the body: headaches, muscle cramps, and nausea
plagued us every day in the Big Belts. The heat and drought-like conditions were more challenging than the distance. In the span of three
days, we'd walked from creeks that spilled their banks to dry stream
beds. The parched ground popped and crackled underfoot as we
walked, and the plants that brushed against our shins were already
brittle and cured. The greens of spring and early summer had fled the
arid landscape; it was early July and already we were walking through
the browns and yellows of fall.

In the space of fifty kilometres, dehydration had replaced hypo-
thermia as our chief concern, and we switched from moving along
our planned route north to searching for water. Using the map to
identify springs, we zigzagged across the northern Big Belts, detour-
ing to the rare oases where water bubbled like a miracle from the
parched ground.

Shade was at a premium in such heat, but for much of the time
there was no forest cover. Old clear-cut blocks, tangled with dry
underbrush, littered our route, and more square or rectangular scars
dotted every hillside of every valley in sight. None of the clear-cuts
was that large, but each still had an attached and fully functioning
road. Fresh tire tracks and spent oil cans littered every road we
encountered. In the Big Belts, the conditions under which Bill Kelly
was logging seemed to be the exception, rather than the rule.

The failure to deactivate or otherwise close off the many forestry
roads had resulted in a flood of motorbikes and 4 by 4s in every
valley north of Mount Edith. And judging by the profusion of rutted
trails marking every pass and hillside, in all directions, few that

reached road's end had turned around. Every moment that we walked through the Big Belts was filled with the buzz and roar of gasoline engines. Even on the narrowest of ridges, in the most rugged and rough corners of the range, we encountered vehicles.

I heard the grinding of metal on rock before I saw the truck, an old brown Ford crawling along the divide towards us, fighting to stay on the precarious route while it lurched in and out of the deep ruts. I couldn't see much through the dust: young trees snapping out from the undercarriage, rocks spitting out and disappearing down off the ridge, two silhouettes bouncing in the cab, and a motorbike shifting in the box behind. It looked a whole lot less comfortable than walking.

"Where you all headed?" the middle-aged driver barked as the vehicle rolled to a stop. His unshaven face dripped with sweat from wrestling the steering wheel, and he seemed unconcerned that in taking up most of the ridge, the full-sized pickup had pushed Maxine and me towards the steep drop-offs on either side.

"Gates of the Mountains Wilderness . . ." I started, referring to the protected area that we hoped to reach in another two days.

"Hey, I saw you guys on TV," interrupted a woman peering at us from the passenger seat. She pointed to where Webster lay in the shade. "I remember the dog." That seemed to be all she remembered about the project though, for there wasn't a hint of shame in her voice as she continued to talk. "We love coming up here, to fish the lake just over that ridge." I looked to where she gestured – a steep, rocky slope that couldn't possibly be driven. "The final half-mile is too rough for the truck but fine for the dirt bike," she said, as though reading my mind. The man revved the engine, then gave a wave as Maxine and I edged back to let them pass. The truck bounced a few times and then disappeared over a rise.

Metre for metre, roads are among the top ways in which humans damage natural systems. The quick and easy access they afford leads to an increase in legal hunting, poaching, collection of rare plants, and disturbance of wildlife. And there are the less obvious effects as well: the paths of animals, even birds, can be disrupted by the narrowest single-lane road; roads act as conduits for weeds and exotic species; and road building – along with the soil slumps and land slides they invariably cause – silt spawning beds, suffocate fish eggs, and wipe out whole communities of aquatic insects.

The goal of the Y2Y project is not to eliminate roads but to limit their number. Recently the U.S. Forest Service announced its goal to keep road densities in all areas still occupied by grizzly bears to less than 0.3 kilometres per square kilometre. The goal sounds admirable until you realize that the target applies only to lands currently occupied by the endangered animal. Despite their potential as a corridor then, the Big Belt Mountains, where the road density is three kilometres per square kilometre of land, are excluded from the targets, as are the Bridgers, where the grizzlies have already been pushed off the land.

Road hiking is the most punishing form of walking. The ground is hard and unyielding, and the lack of dips makes every step a bone-jarring repeat of the last. So we were relieved to step onto the uneven footpath that begins abruptly at the boundary to the Gates of the Mountains Wilderness Area, an aptly named protected parcel of rolling peaks and plateaus sliced by deep canyons. We followed the path into Refrigerator Canyon, a channel of water-sculpted rock so narrow that I could touch both sides as I walked. A tiny creek bounced down between the walls, only a sliver of sky shone above, and for a few moments I hopped blind in the dim light, stumbling while my eyes adjusted to the shadow. Alder, moss, and ferns replaced the juniper and pines that had surrounded us only moments before. For the first time in five days, I needed to put on a sweater.

It seemed the thin cleft would only lead to a dead end, but after an hour's walking, the walls became less sheer and a bottleneck of trees forced us up and out of the canyon. We were hit by a blast of heat that made the climb harder than any we'd done all week. Eventually we made it to a tableland of trees, where we pitched camp, our last camp together, while the evening sun etched the canyons below us in gold. Beyond them, the mountains rose out of the dark like islands of light. To the south the summits of Mount Edith, Mount Boulder Baldy, and the rest of the Big Belt Mountains were drenched in crimson light, and to the west rose the cutout ridge of the Continental Divide. It was a dramatic view of where we'd come from, and a fitting backdrop to a discussion of where we were going. It was a difficult, wrenching talk, but we managed to hold back our emotions long enough to address the facts. Maxine didn't have the wilderness experience to be able to continue alone into the north. And there wasn't enough time for her to find a new partner. It would be me who continued on.

Maxine sobbed and I fought back tears. I apologized, or tried, but after all the fights and arguments, nothing sounded right.

The next morning, after dropping down into Meriwether Canyon, we walked across the boundary of the wilderness area and onto the alluvial fan that spills into the Missouri River.

Here the Missouri was a wide slip of muddy water that whirled and boiled in lazy currents around spire-like walls of rock that rose sharply from either bank. Except for the odd twisted tree there was little in the way of vegetation. Everything was either stone or sun-caked earth. The scene was stark but awe-inspiring, not unlike that which greeted Meriwether Lewis and William Clark, the Europeans who paddled upstream through Shoshone Indian territory in search of a route to the Pacific on a similarly hot summer day almost 200 years earlier.

JULY 19, 1805 — *we are almost suffocated in this confined valley with heat. . . . We entered much the most remarkable clifts that we have yet seen. These clifts rise from the waters edge on either*

*side perpendicularly to the hight [sic] of 1200 feet. Every object
here wears a dark and gloomy aspect. The towering and pro-
jecting rocks in many places seem ready to tumble on us. . . .*
— Journal of Captain Meriwether Lewis

A few things had changed since then. The once-free Missouri
had been channelled through a series of reservoirs and hydro dams
both above and below the canyon, and the boats that now plied its
tamed waters were powered by motors and steered by vacationers,
not paddle-weary explorers. We waved down one of the boats and
were ferried down and across the river to where the canyon walls
gave way to sagebrush flats. Ranches and houses occupied the dry
meadows, and as we pulled up to the marina, I could see traffic
speeding north-south along a distant highway. After leaving a
message for Justin, I left Maxine napping in the shade of the boat
buildings while I wandered around.

It was a busy day at the docks. Throngs of tourists were pouring
through the turnstiles for the hourly boat trips up the canyon, while
those returning from the tour filed into the concession for chips,
pop, and ice cream. I bought a cone and then drifted into the café,
drawn to an impressive collection of Indian arrowheads in one
corner. A number of points were on display, including a perfect
flake of triangular obsidian that must have been traded from the
Yellowstone Plateau.

"I figure most of them are Blackfoot," said a scratchy voice over
my shoulder.

"You found all these?" I asked, turning to face an old man in
a Stetson.

"A man finds a lot of things when he looks for more than eighty
years." He pulled out a chair and invited me to sit down. A dog-
eared photo album was propped behind a line of rocks on the
table, and a number of historic news clippings hung framed on
the wall behind.

He was Bryan Hilger, the son of the man who, in the 1920s, had started the first boat tours on the river. It had been a side business to the family's beef ranch, but it had never paid off. Hard hit by the Great Depression, the family had had to sell off the boats, along with most of their 10,000-acre spread. "Us kids never really got over that," said Bryan. For the rest of their lives, his brother and sister and he worked to buy it back.

It was a story he'd told many times before, and one well illustrated by the photo albums he pushed across the table towards me. I flipped through images of branding parties, barn raisers, fall hunts for antelope, and more sombre times when drought, storms, fire, and disease brought heavy losses to the herd. "There were lots of ups and downs," said Bryan, "but we finally made enough to buy it all back." His big smile faded with his next words. "But that was only a few years ago and it all came too late. My brother and sister died. I'm eighty-five. We all worked so hard that none of us really dated, much less married. There were no children or grandchildren, no one to inherit what we spent our lives to regain.

"A few years ago I decided I was getting too old to ranch, and despite everything that we'd done to get it, it was time to sell the place." He shook his head. "But first, I wanted to make sure of one thing. No matter what, the place would never look like that!" He pointed out the window. The small farms and vacation homes dotting the landscape were a far cry from the cancerous growth of houses I'd witnessed outside Bozeman, but they signified the beginnings of a similar trend.

Fortunately, Bryan had been able to negotiate a conservation easement for his land. Working with the Montana Land Reliance, a local nonprofit group that recognized the wildlife value of his 10,000-acre property, he'd contracted to give them the subdivision rights to hold in trust while he, in return, received a tax break and other financial incentives. No matter who owned the land or how many more times it was sold, it could never be subdivided.

Conservation easements have emerged as one of the most popular and powerful tools for the preservation of open space on private land. Bryan's agreement was just one of an estimated 700 that already protected more than 850,000 acres from future subdivision in the Montana portion of the Y2Y. And the Montana Land Reliance was only one of dozens of land trusts already working across the entire region. The Nature Conservancy is working to secure easements for a number of privately held parcels of prime grizzly bear habitat along the Rocky Mountain Front; the Southern Alberta Land Trust – a group run by and for ranchers – is helping to conserve large, traditional ranches across the Canadian border; and the Land Conservancy of British Columbia is doing similar work in British Columbia. Bit by bit open space is being preserved, and a plan like Y2Y will only help to coordinate the process.

It was late afternoon by the time I thanked Bryan for the conversation and got ready to leave.

"Now where you say you walked from again?" he asked.

"Yellowstone," I said pointing south, "and hoping to get to the Yukon. I'm trying to look at how wildlife might make the same trip," I explained, going on to give him a brief sketch of Y2Y and how conservation easements like his fit into the bigger picture.

"Yes, yes, wildlife," he nodded, locking up the arrowhead case as he talked. "We still get lots of deer, along with some predators. Last year, one of the neighbours saw a cougar swim the Missouri just upstream. I've seen all sorts of wildlife swim that river – black bears, deer, elk, mountain sheep – but never a cougar." He paused for a moment, fixing me with a stare. "Lots of wildlife and lots of wild country still left." He reached out with gnarled fingers and shook my hand. "Lots right now, that is."

It was difficult to believe that all the bad times with Maxine would actually be over in a few days, that we had finished walking together and, after a few more presentations and interviews in the small city of Missoula, we would go our separate ways. Only when she opted out of some of the interviews did it begin to sink in.

When it came time to drop her off at the bus station, Justin wished Maxine luck then stayed in the van with Webster while I walked with her to the station door. We both stood there for a moment, trying to muster up a last-minute conciliation, but all we managed was a flat goodbye. Then she turned, climbed up the stairs, and was gone.

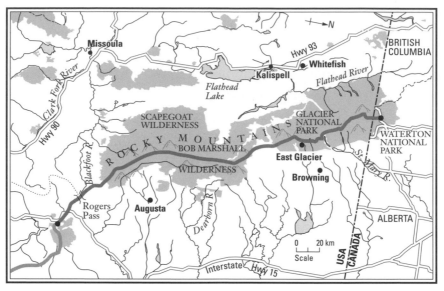

Gates of the Mountains, Montana, to Waterton, Alberta – 465 kilometres

3

I stepped off the Interstate highway into wheat grass that came over my knees. To my right, a line of irrigators swirled rainbows into the sky; to my left, a line of dust billowed in the wake of a pickup.

The Sieben Ranch Company Lands felt far from wild at first, but as I walked westward, the non-native grasses disappeared, and the number of signs prohibiting motorized vehicles increased. It wasn't an ideal corridor. There was no wildlife-crossing structure across the busy highway where Justin had dropped me off and the area was devoid of the trees and bushes that would offer shy animals secure cover. But it wasn't bad. Together with Bryan Hilger's old property, the Sieben land (much of it also in conservation easements) had saved most of the dry, fifteen-kilometre-long link between the Gates of the Mountains and the Continental Divide from further development.

It had been midday by the time I got going, and by late afternoon, I was deep enough into the hills that heart-shaped antelope and deer tracks began to replace the ubiquitous round domestic cow prints. The wind and the temperature both dropped, and in the shade, the vanilla-like aroma of ponderosa and whitebark pines hung low to the ground. Two deer bolted from a thicket as I stepped over the last barbed-wire fence; by early evening I was back on public land.

I climbed until it was almost dark, up and over the round summit of Mitchell Mountain, and then down an old mining road into Canyon Creek. There, past the old tailing piles that had been overgrown by thistles, the road came to an abrupt end.

"Closed to all Motor Vehicles for Wildlife Security," read the wooden sign at the locked gate. I peered closer and read the fine print in the dim light, "To encourage use by Endangered and Threatened Species."

It wasn't a grizzly track or dig, but it was the most hopeful sign of their presence that I'd seen in 320 kilometres.

The rounded, gently undulating crest I scrambled onto the next morning was similar to many of the other ridges I'd followed through the Big Belts except for one thing: those ridges divided a few creeks and rivers; this one divided two ocean catchments. In climbing out from Canyon Creek, I had worked my way to the crest of the Continental Divide. To the east, behind me, flowed the Missouri, which, after draining into the Mississippi, spilled into the Gulf of Mexico. To the west ran the beginnings of the creeks and streams that fed into the Blackfoot, Clearwater, and Columbia rivers, which, eventually, emptied into the Pacific.

I followed the ridge north, straddling the backbone of the continent as I walked, right foot in what drained to the Atlantic, left foot in the Pacific, kicking the odd rock from one side to the other for the sheer thrill of altering the billion-year-old destiny of ocean sediment. There were places in the ridge that were too flat or broad to pinpoint where, exactly, the dividing line existed, but that would soon change. Looming in the distance, barely visible through the high-altitude haze, was wave after wave of rugged peaks – sharp, triangular summits of rock and ice stacked one against another in a broken grey and white skin. Soon, the issue would be less about locating or following the divide than about finding a route through a maze of tight valleys, high passes, and steeply tilted rock.

The prospect of walking in real mountains – cliffs, waterfalls, raging creeks and rivers – excited me. The Bridgers and Big Belts had been beautiful, but too gentle and forgiving. Their shallow slopes and low, broad valleys had allowed them to be so tamed, so overrun with human activity and settlement. Ahead was a different kind of mountain range, too rugged to settle and too wild with avalanches and floods to make roads or railways feasible. Ahead, I hoped to find a landscape that still held adventure, mystery, and one of the last strongholds of grizzlies left in the lower forty-eight states.

No sooner had the thought of grizzlies entered my mind than the small excavations began to appear, shallow digs where biscuitroot plants had been swiped from wind-sheltered pockets.

> JULY 12 – *Continental Divide, Rogers Peak, Montana – Grizzly! More than thirty digs spotted today in the shallow gravels atop the ridge, not more than a day or two old. In among the clipped roots and half-chewed tubers are the distinctive claw marks – round holes set inches from the imprint of five toes. It has been fourteen days since I have seen such tracks or any other sign, and it sets off a response I never realized had waned. My heart beats faster, my eyes scan ahead more intensely, and I keep Webster close, watching him for any change. Here, tonight, inside this tent, I lie awake with both ears wide open.*

Left: Starting out, June 6, 1998, at Mammoth in the Yellowstone National Park, Wyoming. Ed Struzik, Maxine Achurch, Karsten Heuer, and Webster.

Right: The path of least resistance: Following the (sometimes) windblown ridge of the Gallatin Mountains, Montana.

Top: Karsten and Webster, relaxing before entering the ranchlands north of the Bridger Mountains, Montana.

Left: Bill Kelly and Maxine.

Opposite: Karsten and Webster in Refrigerator Canyon, Gates of the Mountains Wilderness Area, Montana.

High up on the ridges of the Continental Divide in Scapegoat Wilderness Area, Montana.

Flying the Y2Y flag atop Crow Peak, Scapegoat Wilderness Area.

By mid July, fleabane, arnica, vetch, Indian paintbrush, and other flowers begin to dot the alpine meadows of the Scapegoat Wilderness Area.

Top: The Chinese Wall in the Bob Marshall Wilderness, Montana.

Left: The arrowhead that Karsten found below the Chinese Wall in Montana.

Opposite: Headwaters of Red Shale Creek, Bob Marshall Wilderness.

Top: Washing in Dean Lake,
Bob Marshall Wilderness.

Left: A rainbow after a thunderstorm
at South Fork, Two Medicine River,
East Glacier, Montana.

There were more signs the next day: I spotted blond hairs snagged on pine tree trunks along Teepee Pole Creek, and torn stalks of cow's parsnip beside a wet seep above Rogers Pass. The signs petered out when I crossed a two-lane highway, but I soon spotted them again on the other side. By the time I reached the southern boundary of the Scapegoat Wilderness Area the next day, grizzly bear digs, tracks, scat, and rub trees had littered every one of the last fifty kilometres.

The Scapegoat is part of the Crown of the Continent Ecosystem, an impressive conglomerate of wilderness areas, tribal lands, national parks, and private property that encompasses more than 23,000 square kilometres of prime grizzly and other wildlife habitat. Straddling the Continental Divide, it is where the moisture-loving plants of the Pacific butt into the drought-resistant grasses of the Great Plains, giving rise to one of the most diverse environments that I would walk through on the entire trip. Here, mountain goats and bighorn sheep feed on alpine plants while wolves and cougars shadow moose and elk through the valleys below. Long-toed sala-manders live in the many marshes and wetlands, and one of the purest strains of the rare cutthroat trout swim in the rivers and lakes. Living in the rich mix of forest, alpine, wetland, and streamside habi-tats are more than a hundred species of birds and as many, if not more, grizzly bears as are thought to live in and around Yellowstone.

I had scheduled twenty-four days to walk the chain of protected areas – three for the Scapegoat; ten in the Bob Marshall Wilderness Area; nine in Glacier National Park; and in Canada, two days to cross Waterton National Park. My plan was to follow the Continental Divide Trail, a footpath that travelled within view of the divide from Mexico to Canada, but at the last minute I decided to travel cross-country. The ridges of red, broken rock and alpine forget-me-nots were too much of a lure, so when the trail dropped into the Dearborn Valley, I stayed high, climbing up and over Caribou Peak and onto the line of low summits that stretched north.

It was hot in the Scapegoat, hot enough that I took a cue from the wildlife that surrounded me and changed habits. Now I rose before the sun and was walking by five o'clock, ate breakfast around eleven, slept from noon until four, ate dinner, then walked from five until it grew dark. It was an odd schedule but felt natural. I could rest for as long as I wanted, move when it seemed appropriate, bathe in creeks and shallow lakes when the opportunity presented itself, and lie naked on sun-warmed rocks before crawling to nap in the shade of trees. I felt liberated and free, guided by my body and the temperature, not by a clock. There were no bugs, no people; the only demand was a gentle urge to keep moving.

The shade I sought for my midday breaks was at a premium. Valley after valley of the Scapegoat had burned when lightning struck after a record drought in 1988. Even ten years later, at first glimpse, the landscape seemed dead. But on closer look, among the charred and weathered wood, life was returning. Deer and elk grazed on the lush grass that grew out of the nutrient-rich charcoal and ash; countless bears had left a wake of splintered logs where they'd searched out ants and termites; and in the woodpecker holes bored in the snags, a whole community of swallows swooped down on the insects that flew and buzzed amid hip-high blooms of bear grass and fireweed. Soon fungi would follow the ants and bears and turn the ash to soil. Soon the fireweed would fix enough nitrogen to attract less hardy plants. And soon the knee-high pine seedlings would be big enough to house and feed birds and squirrels which, in turn, would attract marten, weasels, and other predators.

But for this to occur there needed to have been a refuge from the flames. That seemed to have happened in the Scapegoat fire, which, although burning a large part of the wilderness, had affected only a fraction of the entire 20,000-square-kilometre chain of protected areas. But what if the fire had been bigger? Was the Crown of the Continent Ecosystem large enough to ensure species survival in the event of something so catastrophic?

The answer to the question of how big is "big enough" remains elusive. One study calculated that 500,000 square kilometres were needed to support a long-term population of wolves in the face of natural change. Another suggested that, for 2,000 grizzlies to survive, 130,000 square kilometres of good-quality habitat were required. These are massive areas, ranging from three to eleven times the size of the Greater Yellowstone Ecosystem, and six to twenty-two times the size of the Crown of the Continent Ecosystem. Such a huge block of undisturbed land no longer exists in North America and, if it did, couldn't reasonably be protected. But protecting corridors of land between the existing parks and wildlife reserves would achieve the same end.

"Wildlife corridors? Why don't you guys take your ideas and all those letters behind your names and go back to the city where you came from?"

I glanced briefly at Justin, then back at the thin rancher who, along with the two men either side of him, had walked in just after the show had started. We usually opened the floor to questions and comments afterwards, and in the dozen or so presentations we'd done so far, we'd had nothing but positive feedback. Not in the small ranching town of Augusta, though. The wiry cowboy took a breath and continued his rant.

"Who do you think was managing the wildlife before the government came and messed things up?" He waved a bony arm in the air and then brought it back to point at himself. "Us, that's who! And by all measures, we were doing a far better job."

"Sir, I understand where you're coming from but we're not suggesting for a minute that the gov –"

"If you want corridors, then go build them out in the prairies!" blurted out the man on his right before I could finish. The rest of the audience – about fifteen people – shifted uncomfortably in their chairs. "Wolves and grizzlies weren't meant to be in the mountains anyway. They're meant to be in the prairies."

You can't reason with such logic, and so I thanked the men for their comments, answered a few more questions, then gave some closing comments and started to pack up. My adversary and his two buddies filed out into the parking lot and quickly drove off while the rest of the small crowd milled around the dirt parking lot wondering how a slide show about a hike had turned so ugly.

We learned later that the man's name was Ray Krone and that he had his reasons for being so bitter. A few years earlier, one of his neighbours had allowed wolves to den on his property, and before long, the pack had moved onto Krone's ranch. "Killed a calf a day," Krone claimed. With the wolves protected under the Endangered Species Act, he had felt powerless to do anything and, in the end, was reimbursed for only two of the many calves he said had been lost. The experience had left him fiercely determined to protect the landowners' right to manage their own properties and the wildlife that ventured onto them.

Controversy was bound to hit the project sooner or later, I just hadn't expected it to be in Augusta. Everything about the small town had been welcoming when I first arrived. The thirty-kilometre drive from the trailhead took Justin and me through a spectacular sweep of open hills rippling with grass, wildflowers, and clear creeks. Lass Dudley, the woman who put us up for the night, lived in one of the well-kept wood and brick houses that typified the picturesque town, and like her neighbours, kept a horse to mow the lawn out back. Friendly dogs roamed freely in and out of shops, artists' studios, and the bar; and the local diner and ice-cream parlour served as the unofficial town hall. It was everything we had imagined small-town America could be: a quiet, friendly enclave set in beautiful sur-roundings. But the comments of Krone and his friends showed us another side, a segment of the community that was quick to discredit outsiders, viewed conservation as a threat rather than an opportunity, and refused to believe that the development sweeping across every other beautiful area in the west would ever affect them. Meanwhile, at the local realty office, David Letterman, America's most popular late-night talk-show host, had just closed a deal on a ranch, and other top-paying millionaires were following suit.

"We thought we had a window of about five years before prices escalated out of reach," said one Montana Fish and Game Department official who was working to secure conservation easements in the area. "With all the speculation that's started now, though, that window has probably narrowed to less than a year."

We moved on to the neighbouring town of Choteau the next day and, after a few interviews and a much less controversial presentation, raced back to the trailhead for an early morning start. It had been a whirlwind two days, and it left me scattered and forgetful. As Justin pulled away, I realized I'd left the tent poles and most of my lunches back at Lass's house, and with the sound of the engine still audible in the distance, it dawned on me that I'd left more food, and my flashlight, in the van. The sudden transitions between fleece-clad solitary hiker and Oxford-shirted spokesperson were proving to be as taxing as the publicity itself. All the stresses usually faded with the first few kilometres on the trail, but not this time. No sooner had I entered the Bob Marshall Wilderness Area than I was being yelled at by well over thirty bright yellow signs posted on trees down the trail: "Warning. Be Alert. Bear Frequenting Area." I wondered whether the sheer number of them reflected the severity of the danger. Within minutes, I had a chance to find out. Trotting down the trail towards me on horseback was the local forest ranger.

"You should be all right," said the clean-cut man as he brought the horse to a halt. A small black bear had found food in an unattended backpack a few days before and had been harassing hikers and campers ever since, he explained. "I hit him good this morning though," he said, describing how he'd shot the bear with rubber slugs. "He shouldn't be bothering anyone for a while."

Another kilometre down the trail, I heard quite a different story from the couple marching hurriedly past me.

"It's interested in anything that moves and carries a pack," gasped the man. Just half an hour earlier, he and his wife had warded off the curious bruin by throwing rocks.

The next news came ten minutes later from a group of Boy Scouts: "We had to throw sticks at him," said the leader. "Be careful. He's somewhere around the next corner."

There was no corner, just one three-kilometre-long curve in the Sun River valley and I walked it with every one of my senses on edge, keeping Webster close as I clapped two rocks together and shouted out every few seconds. I saw tracks and fresh droppings of half-digested leaves, berries, and even some plastic food wrappings. I heard the snap of something move through the forest. But I never saw the bear. After another five kilometres I came to a small beach along the river and sat down. It was the first time I had stopped long enough to think in four days.

> JULY 25 – *South Fork of the Sun River, Bob Marshall Wilderness Area – Irate ranchers one day, marauding bears the next. I feel like I'm living two lives, bridging separate worlds. What I have to realize, however, is that what I hear and experience in the towns and cities are the values that will determine the future of these narrow strips of wildness through which I walk. It is too easy to forget how human and natural history have always been intertwined. Wilderness as a place devoid of human influence is a mythical concept, an idealistic notion at best.*

Two days later, in the heart of the Bob Marshall Wilderness Area, the history behind this realization hit home. It was before dawn, and looming above me was the Chinese Wall, a 450-metre-high,

25-kilometre-long sweep of limestone cliffs. At that hour, it was nothing but a black mass blotting out the stars, but I began climbing by the light of my headlamp up the scree slope anyway, determined to be sitting at the base of the lichen-splashed rock when the sun hit its great curve.

I wanted to be there to photograph the dawn light, but what I found was something else, something dark and triangular dislodged by one of the camera tripod's legs. I reached down, brushed the gravel aside, and there, staring back at me, was an old Indian arrowhead.

The line of the dawning sun came and passed while I marvelled at what I held in my hand. Obsidian, I guessed, thinking back to Bryan Hilger's collection. It had the same grain and jet-black colour. The edges were still razor sharp, the faces covered with small dimples, each one marking where a tiny flake of rock had been patiently knapped away.

It may have belonged to a hunter from the South Piikani (Blackfeet) nation which, along with the Kaina and Siksika, had formed one of the world's most complex communal big-game hunting cultures. For the most part, they had followed the vast herds of bison that roamed the prairies and foothills, but every once in a while, hunting parties had made forays into the Rockies in search of mountain goats and bighorn sheep. Alternatively, the arrowhead could have been dropped by a passing trader. There is ample evidence still today of the extensive trade network that once linked native peoples along and across the Rockies. Obsidian points from the Yellowstone Plateau have been found as far north as the Peace River in northeastern British Columbia, and the vestiges of Indian trails still crisscross the mountain corridor for its entire length, linking the old buffalo- and salmon-eating ways of life.

I looked up from the arrowhead and into the valleys below. Slowly, the world was emerging from the shadows – other cliffs, forested hills, and on an open slope in the distance, something silver glinting in the sun.

It was a grizzly bear – far enough away for me to be safe, but close enough to watch with binoculars as it wandered upwards. I watched its progress, wondering whether a similar scene had greeted whoever had dropped the arrowhead hundreds of years earlier. Probably. The odd bend in the creek might have curved left instead of right, more hillsides might have been burned from forest fires, but the rest of what I saw would have been the same. For the first time since leaving Yellowstone, I could see no roads, clear-cuts, or seismic lines (swaths through the forest, cut to facilitate oil and gas exploration). Except for bison and caribou, all life that had been there before Europeans still existed.

It was beyond the horizon where things were now different. People still travel, but at speeds and altitudes that allow a missing species or razed forest to go unnoticed. There are still traders too, but today they live and work far enough from their transactions to be ignorant of their effects. The sad truth is that most of what once bound people to the land has been lost in the time the arrowhead was dropped and now found. This realization brought home to me that as much effort needs to go into re-establishing the psychological connections between people and the wilderness as is needed to restore and maintain the connections between parks for wildlife. Without the first, however, there can be no support for the latter.

JULY 28 – *Dean Lake, Bob Marshall Wilderness, Montana –*
Still five days and 120 kilometres before the next cache and
already I'm rationing because of the food I left behind. Today
there are three passes to traverse, and by the time I start climb-
ing the last one – a 2,200-foot ascent up Kevan Mountain – my
energy bottoms out. The last of my hot chocolate mix – three
spoonfuls of sugary powder – is what gets me to where I camp
and cook a half portion dinner. Fifteen minutes later I'm
hungry again, so hungry that I sneak a few pieces of Webster's
food. It doesn't taste bad – like fish crackers – but I still have to

*chase it down with a bottle of water. I make it up to him by
spending an hour pulling apart his coat and extracting a week's
worth of burrs.*

I encountered three groups of people over the next two days, and
hunger shaped my interactions with all of them. I didn't spend much
time with the first, a man heading to a high plateau for some solitude
and a week-long fast. The second, a college professor and his wife,
were nearing the end of their trip and, except for half a loaf of
crushed and mouldy bread, needed all the food they had left. The last
party, a group of friends halfway through a week-long horseback
trip, offered the most promise for a handout, and when they waved
me over to their tarp, I almost ran.

"You walked from where?" asked the oldest cowboy again,
handing me a cup of tea.

"Yellowstone," I answered a little louder so as to be heard over
the stamping and ringing of the hobbled horses grazing around the
rustic camp.

"Hell, we come about the same distance – over from Idaho near
the Frank Church country," laughed the man, "but we *drove*."

The Frank Church Wilderness is part of the Salmon-Selway-
Bitterroot Ecosystem, one of the other "large islands" in the southern
Y2Y region. Wolves had recently been reintroduced to that part of
Idaho, and pending a favourable outcome at public hearings, grizzly
bears would soon be reintroduced as well. I asked the group what
they thought of the grizzly returning to their neck of the woods.

"No such thing as a good bear," spat out one of the younger men.
"All those animals they eat, especially the young. They're nothin' but
competition for us hunters."

"Wolves are bad news too," said the round-faced man who lay
propped up on one elbow under the far corner of the tarp. "They
were doin' just fine in Alberta until the goddamn government went
and moved them to Idaho!"

I smiled, got up, helped myself to an open package of cookies, then sat back down, wondering whether to say anything. Taking a chance, I broached the subject of why I was hiking all the way to the Yukon, using stories of a few far-ranging animals to highlight the need for wildlife corridors.

"You mean one of them wolves moved more than 900 kilometres without help from the government?" joked the oldest cowboy with a wink. Everybody laughed and asked more questions: How wide would these corridors need to be? What about the ranchers? And what about hunting – how would it be affected? I much preferred this informal outreach to the slide presentations and fancy map displays that Justin and I used in the communities. There was no stage under the grubby tarp, and with everyone sitting on the ground, there could be no pretensions.

The next three evenings were rainy, leaving the mountains cloaked in mist until late in the morning. Every day, I started out with dry feet, but they didn't stay dry for long. The evening thundershowers turned the trails into mud and the sticky earth globbed onto my boots in layers that soon gave them three-inch heels. Half-sliding, half-walking, I crashed into the bushes on either side of the trail, sending the water that had gathered in all the leaves pouring into my socks.

The trail leading down Clack Creek from Kevan Mountain was just such a mud trench, and in addition to the task of staying upright was the challenge of avoiding all the spider webs. I had never seen such a profusion of webs, curtain after curtain of gummy silk that stuck like glue in my hair, beard, and eyes. I soon switched to walking with a long stick ahead of me, waving it like some crazed dowser in search of water. There weren't any webs below hip-height, though, and where the rain hadn't washed out the tracks, I soon saw why: a grizzly had headed down the trail not long before me. I hollered into the trees and then carried on, rounding out my sliding, stick-waving shuffle with a few songs that set off a chorus of squirrels, chickadees, and flycatchers.

The grizzly tracks veered off the trail a few kilometres later, but soon there were others that led north. The next day, I walked out of the Bob Marshall Wilderness where a grizzly had walked in. I back-tracked it across the unprotected Badger-Two Medicine basin, then lost its trail a few kilometres short of the two-lane highway at the southern boundary of Glacier National Park.

The highway was busy with campers, holiday trailers, and other traffic headed through Marias Pass, so I walked the last few hours to the town of East Glacier on railway tracks that paralleled the road. A few years before, a huge grain spill had attracted and killed thirteen grizzlies on those tracks. In one instance, two of them were hit by trains in the same hour. The first was a cub, followed not long after-wards by its angry mother, who, at the sound of the next oncoming locomotive, had dropped her head and charged.

The railway tracks made for difficult walking. The awkwardly spaced ties matched neither the stride of man nor dog, and the sharp rocks between them wreaked havoc on both feet and paws. By the time we reached the town of East Glacier, both Webster and I were limping badly.

There weren't many streets to the small gateway town, but because of nearby Glacier National Park, the few that did exist were crawling with tourists. Despite the crowds, I didn't have any trouble making my way along Main Street; the streams of people parted magically to let me pass, and when I caught a glimpse of myself in one of the shop windows, I saw why.

I couldn't really afford the ten dollars, but I booked into the local hostel for a hot shower and clean bed. I would save the money on food, I reasoned, and after a good scrub, I dug the last meal of dry lentils and rice out of my pack and walked with the trail stove into the yard.

The hostel was a collection of dormitory-style cabins tucked behind a popular restaurant, and it wasn't long before the sound of patio laughter and clink of beer bottles got to me. By the time my water boiled, I'd inhaled enough burning grease from the kitchen fans to reawaken the memory of every juicy steak and burger I'd eaten. I looked at the dried beans and rice grains soaking in the water and almost retched. Pitching the half-cooked dinner into the toilet, I flushed and, with an already over-extended credit card in my pocket, made my way to the restaurant.

The place was packed but after chatting with the hostess, I found myself bypassing the long lineup of people to be seated beside someone else who not only was eating alone, but was on a long solo walk as well.

Richard was an unlikely long-distance hiker. Ruddy-faced and with a body that seemed more softened than hardened, he was a far cry from a picture of health. Having hiked up the Continental Divide Trail from Mexico, he'd spent the last few days in East Glacier, drinking beer and wondering if he would continue after an experience with lightning a few days earlier. "It was like fireworks up there, you know what I mean, man? Everything buzzing."

Apart from the intricate description he gave of his near-death experience on the ridge, Richard had little to say about the rest of the landscape he'd walked through. Instead, he steered the conversation to one of my least favourite subjects: trail statistics and equipment.

"So what sort of mileage you clockin' each day?" he asked, and followed with a string of questions and comments about boots, tents, packs, stoves, and other backpacking equipment. I thought about excusing myself to find some better dinner conversation, but couldn't; I was hostage to my own appetite. No sooner had I thought about leaving the table than the food I'd ordered began to arrive: two salads, a soup, a twelve-ounce steak, a piece of pie with ice cream, all washed down with two pints of beer. Even Richard was speechless.

I met Justin the next morning and continued to binge for the next four days, seeking out the greasiest restaurants as we toured the towns of Whitefish, Kalispell, and Browning.

"Will that be all?" asked the server in one roadside diner.

"No, no, I'll have another Trucker's Breakfast, please."

"Another one?" The cigarette smoke was so thick that the air streaming up her nose reappeared as blue-grey words. Justin laughed at her reaction, then sat back to watch me eat for another half-hour.

Working with Justin was proving to be a pleasure. In addition to drumming up more media interest than we could possibly satisfy, he would sniff out and brief me on the local issues that made every interview and presentation I gave more relevant. The late-night drives and early-morning breakfasts were his time to talk strategy; the days and evenings were my time to talk to reporters and audiences, struggling to remember everything he'd said. It was hard work, but my ability to think and speak under pressure was improving, and, as a result, so too was the coverage. Newspaper and TV news features talked as much about the Y2Y concept as they did about the hike, and national magazines such as *Sports Afield* and *Audubon* were running cover stories that reached millions of people. Only the public presentations still suffered. Despite our best efforts to advertise them weeks in advance, the turnouts were still dismal. Four people showed up in Browning, and only three in Kalispell.

Northern Montana's Glacier National Park is best known for three things: spectacular mountain scenery, steep but well-engineered hiking trails, and a disproportionate number of North America's fifty or so fatal bear maulings over the past hundred years. The last of those fatalities had occurred earlier that spring on the trail I was about to take into the park. A young hotel worker had been attacked and dragged off by a sow grizzly and her two cubs while hiking alone. When the park rangers had gone looking for him, all they could find were his eyeglasses and one chewed-off finger.

Partly because of all the past bear problems, Glacier (like Yellowstone) had a no-pets policy on their trails, and once he'd clued in, Webster was sorely disappointed. Despite all the sorrys mixed in with the stays, he still glowered at me as I packed up. The long rambling days had become as much a way of life for him as they had for me, and he looked pretty dejected when I closed the van door and left him with Justin.

Although the park rangers had killed the trio of marauding bears, I was still a little edgy as I struck off down the trail alone. There were other bears around, and always the possibility of an attack. Nonetheless, I tried to remain calm, reminding myself that such incidents were rare. I hadn't gone more than a kilometre, however, before a cowboy leading a pair of tourists on a trail ride told me that what I feared lay just ahead.

"Bear just up the next rise," he said, not even slowing his horse as they passed me in the open pine forest. I stopped dead and wheeled around.

"Pardon me?" A half-smoked cigarette hung from his mouth as he turned in the saddle.

"I said there's a grizzly up the hill." He pointed towards a slope of aspen trees that fluttered in the breeze. "You might want to be careful where you walk."

The first of the two clients wasn't any more forthcoming.

"Bear?" I asked, at which he nodded, smiled and then shrugged his shoulders. He didn't speak English. But the woman riding behind him had more to say.

"A bear! A bear! A big bear, a grizzly bear," she babbled.

"Where?"

"Just over there." She gestured with a nod of her head, not wanting to let go of the horse. She needn't have worried. The animal, which had probably walked the same one-hour loop its whole life, was plodding on without any change of pace as she simultaneously kicked its sides and pulled on the reins. "Whoa!" she commanded, eager to stop and tell me more. The horse was oblivious, and the woman, along with any information she might have had about the bear, disappeared with the others down the trail.

I'd left Yellowstone two months earlier knowing that at least a few bear encounters were likely. I had even thought about how I would respond. If charged by a bear that had cubs, I would probably play dead. If it was a lone bear that approached slowly and seemed curious – even predatory – I would probably fight back. Probably. Sometimes a charge was only a bluff; other times it turned into a deadly attack. One never knew for sure. A large part of dealing with bears was staying alert while keeping calm, but an equally large part was to simply accept fate.

I didn't move until I had spotted the bear with my binoculars – it was a healthy and heavy-looking grizzly, about 300 metres away. It either didn't notice me or didn't care, and the way it was feeding hungrily on a patch of saskatoon berries made me think that if I gave it plenty of room, everything would be all right. I dropped off the trail and traced a wide arc around it, softly calling out as I worked my way through the aspens, stopping, listening, straining to hear a hint of an approach or retreat. Nothing. Safely around it, I continued calling out for the next few hours, climbing up the trail until I was above the trees and there was no need to make noise any more. I could see for kilometres across the alpine landscape of rolling tundra and bare rock that lay ahead.

The sight that greeted me once I was through the pass descending to treeline again would become familiar over the next two weeks: sun-bleached relics of old, wind-gnarled trees were scattered across the subalpine like ghosts. The whitebark pine trees had been hit hard by a parasitic fungus known as white pine blister rust. It had spread throughout the park, and with the trees dead, so too were the nut crops that fed birds and squirrels. There were fewer Clark's nut-crackers flying around now, and because the nuts had also been a major part of the grizzlies' diet, I reckoned there were probably fewer bears as well. Fortunately, nature had provided an antidote: pockets of the five-needled pine outside of the park had been found to be resistant to the rust, and if the connections for their dispersal remained, seeds from those hardier trees might be carried back to this spot, and a whitebark pine forest in Glacier Park might grow once again.

AUGUST 13 – *Morning Star Lake, Glacier National Park, Montana – The wild animals aren't obvious but the people sure are. It's strange to pitch my tent among so many others in these designated backcountry campgrounds. After two and a half months of travel, Glacier is the first place I've had to share a campsite, let alone share it with ten or twelve other people. There are backpackers from all over the world here – Germans, Swiss, Texans, students from Maine, Belgium, and Australia – and although it's nice to be social for a change, so many people is a little overwhelming. Tonight I leave the evening gathering around the communal firepit, wander for a few hundred metres through the bush, and sit by the lake. A golden eagle flies out from the cliff after a few minutes, and moments later, the white dots I'd assumed were far-off snow patches become a herd of goats. Just as I start to leave, a water vole shoots out from a clump of moss, drinks from its own reflection, then disappears into the lake.*

The stretch of perfect weather I'd enjoyed since the Big Belt Mountains continued as I made my way through Glacier: starry nights followed by warm, sunny days. Although it wasn't quite as hot as it had been in the Scapegoat and Bob Marshall areas, I continued to rise before dawn and set off – as much to avoid people as the heat.

Most days I had the passes to myself while the majority of other hikers were only just starting out from the campsites below. It wasn't so at the pass above Morning Star Lake though, for no sooner had I settled down on the rocky ground and pulled my water bottle from my pack, than the first of eight Boy Scouts appeared from the other side. One by one the young teenagers emerged from below, followed, many minutes later, by their breathless leader.

"Now ain't this something spectacular! Eh boys?" he wheezed, collapsing beside his troop on the ground. Dark semicircles of sweat stained the sides of his Boy Scout shirt, and he coughed between the words of exultation. "I mean real wilderness, boys. Real wilderness!"

None of the kids answered. One had spotted a group of six goats, and the rest were busy debating how the shaggy beasts could be midway on what looked to be a vertical cliff.

What surrounded us was spectacular. Slabs of ice tens of metres thick hung over red-brown cliffs, and the meltwater pouring from under them plunged in a series of cascades that dropped over the cliffs in ribbons into turquoise lakes. But wilderness? True, everything within view was protected from development. True, there weren't any motorbikes, jeeps, or other kinds of off-road vehicles. But the Scout troop was only the first of many groups I would encounter that day. Down both sides of the pass I could see people toiling along the trails, and judging from the map, a similar scene was playing out in almost every valley of the park. All but two of the major valleys had trails in them, and because of the rugged cliffs and glaciers, the benches and passes they wound over were the only ones available for anything else that needed to move from one area to the next. The area was being loved to death, and I was starting to understand why, every once in a while, one of Glacier's grizzlies got a little pissed off.

The problem of too much human use wasn't unique to Glacier National Park. Just about every core protected area in the Y2Y region was suffering from an increase in visitors. Some were even bursting.

Banff National Park had seen an eleven-fold increase in the number of visitors over the previous eight years, and during that period, had scrambled to deal with the problems in ways that only made them worse. Highways had been twinned, sewage plants upgraded, more hotel and motel rooms built, and ski areas expanded. Glacier National Park on the other hand had adopted a different approach. A permitting and quota system had been set up for all backcountry campgrounds, and over the same time period, not one additional restaurant or hotel room had been built in the park. Unlike Banff, the park managers at Glacier had decided to impose limits rather than accommodate more people, and judging by a draft management plan that was out for public review, those limits were about to get even tougher. The scenic flights that buzzed over the park every few minutes would soon be regulated, and a number of the trails that could be accessed by day hikers from one of the park's many busy roads would soon fall under the permit and quota system as well.

It was easy to think that the park managers should take an even tougher stance – to close off entire areas to human activity of any sort – but there was a problem with that too, a problem that stared me in the face when I emerged at the Many Glacier trailhead to pick up my next food cache two days later. In the parking lot were hundreds of people, pushing and squirming past cars that had been abandoned at all angles and with doors wide open, making their way to where a uniformed ranger stood behind a telescope trained on the slopes high above. People of all shapes and sizes stood in the long lineup, blinking and laughing in the late evening sun, waiting for their turn behind the eyepiece. When it finally came time to look through the scope, what they saw high above, standing almost on the top of Grinnell Peak, was an unlikely pair of animals grazing in the shadows. Side by side, feeding on the bright green plants on a narrow cliff ledge, were a grizzly bear and a mountain goat.

I lowered my binoculars and watched the crowd. The animals were a sight to behold, but it was the people and their reactions that fascinated me most. Kids shouted out in excitement while looking through the telescope, then ran to tell strangers what they'd seen. Stoic, blank-faced adults looked through the eyepiece, then walked away, giggling like teenagers. The bear and goat, clinging to the side of an impressive peak, were touching and transforming people in a way that wasn't possible through a magazine, slide show, or TV. Sure, there were times when human use in parks needed to be limited, I thought, but they had to be balanced against opportunities like this – people seeing animals in the wild. Without the chance to reconnect with the land and its wildlife, there could be no hope for people to support national parks, never mind the corridors needed to connect them.

I was still basking in all the hope and encouragement I'd felt in that parking lot when I sauntered over to the Park Station and met a much less friendly ranger behind the counter.

"Hi, I'm here to pick up a food box I dropped off a couple of months ago."

"We don't have any food boxes here," he answered curtly.

"No, no," I insisted. "I put it in the basement myself with another ranger in May." He clumped down the wooden stairs to the cellar of the old log cabin and, after a few minutes, clumped back up, emerging with the box and a sour look on his face.

"Here's your box," he said, brushing at his pants and shoes. "I don't know what kind of powdered food you have in there, but it leaked all over my uniform."

I apologized and left, carrying a box that seemed much lighter than I remembered. Once outside, I opened the flaps and looked inside. Half-chewed raisins and loose grains of rice sat in a mixture of rodent droppings and gnawed plastic bags. All the nuts, oats, granola bars, and dried fruit so carefully packed three months earlier were gone. Only the beef jerky – green and fuzzy with mould – and the lentil and chickpea dinners had been left untouched. Luckily, there was a store next to the local campground, but it was pricey. I spent fifty dollars before striking out for the trail again, and the four days' worth of instant oatmeal, cheese, crackers, and noodles it bought were the last things I charged to my overextended credit card before the bank closed my savings account.

AUGUST 18 – *Canada-United States border – There are no stoic border guards here, no gun-toting Americans on one side and painfully polite Canadians on the other. There is no one. All that marks the line between the two countries are a few rock cairns, a metal sign, and a five-metre-wide swath cleared straight through the forested slopes of these mountains. The pine trees, bearberry, and juniper bushes are identical on both sides; coyote, deer, and black bear tracks continue along the trail from one country to the next without pause.*

It was an imaginary boundary I crossed, a human construct without ecological meaning, and yet so powerful a line for many of the animals that unknowingly wandered from one jurisdiction into another. In the United States, anyone found killing a grizzly was subjected to fines as high as US$50,000 or six months' imprisonment, and any development that might affect their habitat inside designated recovery areas was prohibited under federal law. In Canada, there was no legislation to protect their habitat, and an average of 150 of the slowly reproducing animals were killed for trophies in a tightly controlled but highly controversial hunt each year. From the perspective of wolves and grizzlies, the notion that Canadians were more gentle and conservative than their well-armed neighbours could not have been further from the truth.

Despite its negative connotations for grizzlies, the border was good for the hike's publicity. The people of Montana had not thought it any great feat to walk across their state, but in Canada, a hike from Yellowstone was suddenly a trek of international significance. That night, more than 200 people crammed into the hall in the tiny tourist town of Waterton, Alberta, the first of dozens of standing-room-only crowds that came to most of the hike's remaining presentations.

There were disadvantages to the rising interest, though. The next day, I spent two hours with television crews, then another eight crammed into a phone booth giving back-to-back interviews with reporters, answering the same questions over and over again. It got to the point that I had trouble remembering what I'd said to whom, and before long, felt as though I spoke like a machine, repeating the same answers in some trance-like state. It wasn't until one reporter asked me if I was worried about all the bear attacks and forest fires that I snapped to attention.

"Forest fires?"

"Yeah. Lots of fires are burning far to the north. One or two in the country where you're headed."

"And about the bear attacks?"

"Just one I know of for sure. I think it happened somewhere in the mountains west of Calgary. Someone got mauled pretty good and the area's closed until further notice."

After the interview, I called the forestry and wildlife departments for Alberta and British Columbia to ask about the dangers ahead. One blaze, I learned, was burning in the Height of the Rockies Wilderness Area, along the route I hoped to hike in another three weeks. North of that, just south of the Bow Valley, a grizzly bear had attacked a lone hiker in Banff National Park. The next morning, as Webster and I set off on the Cameron Lake trail, a plume of smoke rose out of the mountains behind us. Lightning had struck overnight, and the heat of the morning sun had set the valley where I'd walked two days before ablaze.

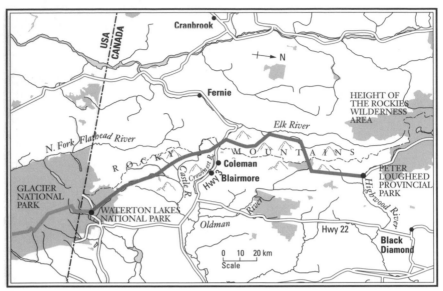

Waterton to Highwood Junction, Alberta – 150 kilometres

4

The wolf was the third in a trilogy of hopeful signs I spotted after leaving Waterton Park, and a surprise given all I'd heard about the area. Stay high and expect little, I'd said to myself as I stepped across the boundary onto a ridge of broken rock. For the first time in four weeks, seismic lines, oil and gas wells, and the odd clear-cut surrounded me. I had crossed from one of Y2Y's largest core reserves into one of its most endangered connections.

Before the wolf I had seen a peregrine falcon, then wave after wave of Clark's nutcrackers surfing past on ridge-top curls of wind. Forty, sixty, maybe eighty birds had come up the lee slope, and I had stood a long time watching after them as they dropped, like bombs, down the windward side. Then I saw the wolf, no more than a smudge of jerky movement, edging its way across a meadow hundreds of metres below. Its stop-and-go motion caught my eye, minutes of stillness followed by explosive leaps and bounds. I leaned into a rock to steady the binoculars, while Webster found a cliff ledge out of the wind. Within seconds he was asleep, opening his eyes only when I laughed at the comedy unfolding below. An animal built to hunt moose and elk was pursuing mice and voles, and its long, lanky legs and oversized paws were poor tools for the task. It took more than a dozen clumsy pounces for the wolf to catch its prey, and no sooner was the mouse in its teeth than it tossed it into the air again. Wagging its tail, the wolf pounced after it, bounding through the mats of grass and dry leaves. More throws ensued, more dives and lunges, until, finally, the hapless rodent no longer moved. The game was over. The wolf walked off into the trees, leaving the dead mouse to feed whatever found it. For the wolf, only the chase had mattered.

I looked east to where the rock walls that hemmed in each of the tight Front Range valleys ended abruptly in a golden haze. There were no foothills, only the prairies slamming headlong into the mountains, a sharp line where two worlds collided. And to the west, woven into the thin range of mountains that made the Continental Divide, were the twin folds of the Castle and Flathead valleys, the sole valleys in a chain of peaks only three ridges wide. In addition to being endangered, it was one of Y2Y's narrowest connections as well.

With few barriers to obstruct them, the winds blew strong here, and the gale-force chinooks could raise the temperature of a mid-winter day by as much as twenty degrees, forcing animals that had been caught in a blizzard one day to seek cool shade the next. It was a land of extremes but it nurtured a vast range of life. More than 150 species of rare plants grew in the Castle drainage area, and its extensive high-elevation grasslands fed large herds of elk and mountain sheep. On the west side of the divide, life was no less diverse. Horsetails, cow's parsnip, glacier lilies, and a myriad of berry bushes grew in the Flathead, which hosted the highest density of non-coastal grizzlies in the province of British Columbia.

But industry was beginning to threaten the Castle and Flathead drainage areas. Fording Coal, Canada's largest coal company, was actively exploring new deposits in the heart of the Flathead, while Crestbrook Forest Industries, one of British Columbia's major logging corporations, was cutting in the same area and would be for the next decade. Past logging had already left an extensive network of more than 800 kilometres of dirt and gravel roads in the Flathead alone. On the Alberta side, oil and gas extraction had pushed a road up every Front Range canyon, and logging operations in the 1970s and 80s had left roads up both the South and West Castle valleys. It hadn't taken long for the off-road machines to follow: vehicle trails were carved down seismic lines, horse trails, and old mining tracks. Any trail that was driveable had been driven.

I descended one such track from Spionkop Ridge into the South Castle Valley, searching for a flat campsite out of the wind. I was amazed at the persistence of whoever had driven up the steep, over-grown slope. The driver had actually ridden over the shoulder-high tangle of bush, leaving behind a trail of broken stems, skid marks, and oil. Whatever hadn't been possible to drive over had been chopped out.

The destruction left in the wake of all-terrain vehicles was just as bad at the bottom of the valley. Well-used trails disappeared up creeks, into the river, and through forests at every drainage and old cutline. The problem had been recognized – a number of junctions bore signs that announced seasonal and permanent trail closures – but without gates, steep ditches, berms, or the threat of enforcement, the lure of open country was too strong. Fresh tire tracks led into every voluntary closure I passed.

Despite all the off-road activity, there were signs of at least one grizzly bear having recently passed through the valley. As I searched for a campsite, I came across overturned rocks, torn-open logs, and tracks pressed into the riverbank. All the signs were encouraging until I saw the garbage. Aluminum cans, smashed beer bottles, charred steak bones, and tin-foil packages of half-eaten food. In a few of the campfire pits, the bear had dug a hole or two, raking through the old coals in search of an easy meal. I kept moving when I saw that. A bear that had learned to associate humans with food was the worst kind to encounter.

It took another two hours to find a site I was satisfied with – two hours of getting drenched by an evening thunderstorm only to have to pitch camp, cook, clean up, and hang the food in the dark. Still tired from the previous day, I went to bed exhausted.

"Now you know this valley's closed, don't you?" slurred the driver of a pickup that bumped up behind me the next morning. Both he and his passenger looked rough, eyes bloodshot and watering, and I could hear empty beer cans clinking, under a load of coolers, camp chairs, barbecues, foamies, and duffel bags in the back. "Friend of ours was killed by a grizzly yesterday. Wildlife cops want everyone out of the valley."

I was so badly shocked I could hardly breathe. It explained the helicopter activity that morning, landing and lifting out of the trees a kilometre upstream from my camp while I cooked breakfast and packed up. I'd assumed it was something to do with firefighting, perhaps a new strike that had flared up in the storm the night before. I dropped my pack and leaned into the truck, suddenly sympathetic about the alcohol and teary eyes.

"What happened?"

The two men glanced at each other. "Kim here was just coming back from a walk with his wife when they saw the bear standing over the body," said the driver gesturing towards his passenger. "Whole thing happened no more than 500 metres from where the rest of us were sitting round camp. None of us heard a thing. No screaming, no yelling. Nothing. Been camping here for five years and none of us had ever *seen* a bear here, let alone one that was acting aggressive." He stroked at the stubble of his tanned face and stammered on. "Hard to say what happened. Lots of them cow's parsnip growing around the water," he said, pointing past me to a carpet of broad-leafed plants growing along the road. "Bear probably eating away and then along come Chris, nothing but the whiz of his flyfishing rod to warn of his approach, and then suddenly both of them are real surprised."

"No, no, that's thimbleberry, not cow's parsnip," said the passenger as he climbed out of the truck and fingered the plant while relieving himself. "It looks a lot like that though," he mumbled over his shoulder, doing up his fly. When he was finished, he walked up to me with an outstretched hand and introduced himself. "My name's Kim and this here's Otis. Where you coming from?"

"Waterton," I said, "but from Yellowstone earlier this summer."

"Yellowstone?" Kim wrung my hand harder. "Shit, Otis, you hear that? This is the guy we read about in the paper." Kim' s eyes moved down my legs and stopped at my feet. "Those aren't the same boots you left in, are they?"

I nodded, holding up the light leather hikers for them to have a look. The inexpensive boots were doing well considering all the snow, rocky ground, and rain I'd been through. The usual questions about my route, pack weight, the dog, and bear encounters ensued.

"Any of them acting weird?" asked Otis when I'd listed the four grizzlies I'd seen so far. I shook my head.

"Only two were close and neither of them showed any aggression. But what about this bear that killed your friend, what finally happened?" The smiles vanished from both men's faces as Otis continued the story.

"Soon as Kim and his wife saw what was happening they come back to camp and told the rest of us. You never saw people move so fast, gettin' all the kids in trucks and shipped off to town. When most everyone was gone, me and Kim walked back upstream with the rifle. I'll never forget it," he said, half-choking on the words. "Just a little baby bear, no more than 200 pounds, on top of poor Chris, feedin' away. It was like some horror film, chewing on his head while, off to the side, the fishing pole floated in the water. I was so shocked I couldn't even think about shooting. It was Kim here who let the air out of him."

The two men stared into space for a few minutes until Kim broke the silence.

"Nobody knows what happened or why." He tilted back his head and sighed deeply. "It just don't make sense."

"The Fish and Wildlife Officers and cops that came in to take away the bear and Chris didn't have any explanation either," piped in Otis. "Near as they could tell the bear was fat, well fed, and perfectly normal."

We stood in the middle of that old forestry road for a long time, all of us kicking at the ground while Otis and Kim tried to put words to their emotion. Neither of them were in a hurry to go to town and fill out the police reports or talk to reporters, so I listened, nodding as they reeled off one bear story after another, everything from personal experiences to third-hand accounts from TV and friends. And when they learned that I'd worked on a bear study as a park warden and biologist, they peppered me with question after unanswerable question.

There is no typical bear and no typical bear behaviour, I explained. Like humans, each bear has a character, formed by its own experiences. There are calm, timid bears; aggressive, dominant ones; and everything in between. The one thing that can be generalized, I allowed, is that every bear is intelligent. Both men shook their heads in wonder when I told the story of how one grizzly had robbed our trapline for more than a month before finally being caught. No sooner had we fitted it with a radio collar than it had wandered off, found a suitable tree, bitten off a branch, hooked the leather strap on the remaining stub, and pulled the transmitter off its neck and over its head. "What we found when we walked in on the stationary signal a few days later," I laughed, "was a battered spruce sapling with a collar hanging halfway up its hair-covered trunk."

"Now don't get me wrong," said Otis after the stories wound down. "It was terrible what happened to Chris. But at the same time, I'd never want to see bears gone. Life means more with them around. You look around more, hear more, see more." He paused, cocking his head to watch a flock of crossbills fly overhead. "I like how having bears makes me feel wild."

> AUGUST 23 – *South Castle River, Alberta – Given all that they've been through, I can't help but be impressed with Otis and Kim's continued respect for bears and their place in this world. I know exactly what Otis is talking about, how in a world filled with hubris, it is good to have a place where we're reminded of the eat-and-be-eaten ordinance of all living things. No person would wish for Chris's fate, and yet it is valuable for us to know that there are places where such a fate is still possible. As humans, we need situations where fear and humility pound in our hearts.*

Unfortunately, Otis and Kim's attitude was rare in the region. I later learned that in 1997 fifteen grizzlies had been removed from the area because of conflicts with humans and their livestock. And the relationship with wolves was no better. In 1995, forty-four of an estimated sixty wolves ranging in southwestern Alberta were shot, trapped, or poisoned for much the same reason.

Those alarming statistics had brought the Alberta Cattle Commission and local wolf biologists together to search for solutions. And the same statistics, in part, had prompted the Alberta government to establish a new grizzly strategy for the southwest corner of the province. Among the initiatives to come out of the projects were the use of scare devices and specially trained dogs to condition bears away from potential problem areas; fencing off bone pits, grain sheds, and other attractants with live wire; and moving cows and calves out of pastures that were close to dens, rendezvous sites, and other wolf habitats.

As I walked north, I saw that the problems facing wildlife in the area went far beyond the age-old standoff between predators and ranchers. Moving out of the Castle and into the Carbondale drainage, I dodged more and more campers, clear-cuts, dirt bikes, bulldozers, and backhoes; and where I emerged in the Crowsnest Valley a day later, I skirted a sawmill, numerous smallholdings, railway tracks, and a two-lane highway that linked the mining towns of Coleman, Blairmore, Elkford, and Fernie.

Highway 3 was the seventh and by far the busiest paved road I'd crossed since leaving Yellowstone. Trucks laden with logs, gravel, coal, and fuel streamed past in both directions, while lines of cars and vans stacked with mountain bikes, kayaks, and windsurfers pressed impatiently behind. It took a few minutes, but finally there was enough of a lull to rush across the traffic and into the opposite ditch where I lay in the shade, waiting for Justin to arrive. Two more trains laboured past in the next hour until, finally, the familiar blue van, riding low and listing off to one side, pulled out of the blur of vehicles.

"Man, am I happy to see you alive and well!" he said, all smiles as he got out and gave me a hug. "It sounds like it's getting pretty dangerous out there for bears." He bent down to unclip Webster's pack, then called him into the ditch for his usual welcoming romp while I pulled open the side door, bracing for the avalanche of paper and gear I had come to expect.

Bags of chips, 7 Eleven cups, and a couple of half-eaten burgers spilled out with the business cards, phone messages, gas receipts, press kits, fishing flies, and muddy boots. At first I'd worried about the disorder in which Justin worked, but his record had more than allayed my concerns. Despite the chaos, he never failed to organize more meetings and interviews than I'd thought possible. After a few minutes of hastily pushing papers towards the back of the van, I climbed in, sighed as I sank into the soft bucket seat, and waited as Justin searched for the briefing notes on the next round of talks.

"I hope you're well rested," he began as we pulled into the heavy traffic, "because you've got seven intense days ahead of you, including a full luncheon presentation for the Elk Valley Chamber of Commerce."

He looked over for a reaction, but I was too mesmerized for the news to sink in. There hadn't been a need to drive anywhere during our last stop in Waterton, and as a result, more than two weeks had passed since I'd moved faster than a brisk walk. The pace at which birds, trees, and entire landscapes sped by was overwhelming.

"Heuer! The Elk Valley Chamber of Commerce! Miners, forestry companies. You better be ready."

With some coaching from Justin, I was ready three days later. By then, we'd already driven more than 600 kilometres, visiting communities in the foothills, learning how rancher conflicts, a boom in smallholding development, and the naturally open, arid landscape had combined to squeeze most grizzly and wolf movement across the Crowsnest Valley to a single gauntlet near the Continental Divide.

"It's not that they're not trying to get across elsewhere on the Alberta side," explained one biologist, walking me through a recent World Wildlife Fund report on local grizzly linkages. "It's just that they're not having much luck." He reeled off the alarming statistics for grizzly removals and wolf kills as his finger roamed from ranch to smallholdings to highway on the map. "And up here, where there's less private land and trees grow in the sheltered and wetter mountains," he said, sweeping his hand close to the Alberta-British Columbia border, "wildlife have better cover but all the coal mines and logging operations edge into the equation." He paused, looking up at me with concern before pointing back at the map. "This is about the only place we figure anything big and wary of humans can still consistently make it across on the Alberta side." I looked at his finger. It pointed to where Star Creek met the highway, right where I'd emerged a few days before.

Things didn't look much better in the B.C. portion of the Crowsnest Pass. In a 120-kilometre drive the next day, Justin and I passed signs for five open-pit mines and saw logging roads branch off up every side valley. The World Wildlife Fund report had identified three grizzly linkages on that side of the Rockies, but there were worrisome problems that plagued each one. One led directly into mining developments to the north and south, another included a large chunk of private land slated for logging, and the last skirted Fernie, a rapidly growing resort town. New golf courses, scenic hiking and biking trails, blue-ribbon fishing, good winter snow, and the fastest-growing ski area in western Canada, had all helped to fuel a development boom in the once sleepy town.

Justin took me for a quick tour before the Chamber meeting. Trees were being cleared and condominiums built on benches above the downtown core, while in the valley, historic houses and mining offices were being bulldozed to make room for fourplexes and new hotels. It reminded me of similar pressures around Bozeman, along Montana's Rocky Mountain Front, and in my own hometown, Canmore. What was different, though, was that in addition to the influx of retirees and recreationists, the historic logging and mining activities were still going strong. The new tourism economy that was replacing resource extraction elsewhere was an addition, rather than a substitute, in the Crowsnest and Elk valleys.

The repercussions for wildlife from such development were severe. According to scientists, high road densities and habitat loss from forestry and mining operations already exceeded levels tolerated by most large predators, and there was little, if any, room for the area to absorb more people, houses, vehicles, resorts, or off-road recreation. The issue was international. Without a connection linking the Crown of the Continent to the Central Rockies, the isolation of grizzlies and other wildlife in the United States would only get worse. The entire southern quarter of the Y2Y region was at stake.

There were simple solutions. Backcountry road closures, private land conservation easements, and animal-highway underpasses or overpasses would help wildlife, but even more pressing was the need for a plan to guide everyone involved – government officials, landowners, conservation groups, and concerned citizens – on where to focus their time and money. In effect, the southern Canadian and U.S. portion of the Y2Y vision needed to be defined quickly, before it was too late.

But even with a good plan in place, the politics of implementing it would be complex. Most of the lands fringing the main road and railway corridor in the Fernie and Elkford area were privately owned parcels held by a number of large forestry and mining companies. Representatives from all of them would be at the Fernie Chamber luncheon.

"Now remember, keep it simple," advised Justin as we pulled into the parking lot. "Ten minutes, max. Focus on the conservation initiative, and go easy on the hiking and dog stories." His tone was friendly but serious. "Your purpose is to make sure nobody walks out with misconceptions about Y2Y. There's already rumours floating around the area of Y2Y being a U.S.-funded conspiracy to remove humans from the landscape – I heard it more than a few times on my way through last week. Go in there thinking your audience is a group of suspicious skeptics and you'll probably do a good job." I nodded, silently reorganizing the talk in my head as he spoke. There was still a half-hour before show time, yet already my heart was pounding. Justin gave a reassuring slap on my back then opened his door. "Remember to keep it short. This is an audience that needs time to ask questions and voice concerns."

He'd done a good job of assessing the situation. No sooner had I shown the last slide and the lights came up, than a dozen hands shot up in the crowd of forty people.

"How do you see logging and mining fitting into this plan?" asked one of the foresters from Crestbrook. "I mean you'd be hard pressed to find anyone in this valley – a logger, miner, ski area developer, anyone – who didn't agree that we needed to do everything possible to keep wildlife around. But where exactly are these corridors? Who will they affect? How wide do they have to be?" A number of heads nodded as he fired the questions across the packed room. It wasn't the first, nor would it be the last time people asked for specifics about the Y2Y vision.

"What I'm speaking about here today is a concept," I began, "a new way to approach wildlife conservation. Unfortunately, there is no one-size-fits-all solution. Corridor widths will vary with topography, vegetation, human use, distances between patches of habitat, and target animals. Some researchers have recommended corridors ranging from half a kilometre wide for deer to something in the order of twenty kilometres wide for grizzly bears and wolves." A few gasps broke out around the room. "Of course there would be bottlenecks within those wider corridors," I quickly added, "rare squeeze-points where animals might be forced to funnel through a much narrower gap for a short distance – a highway underpass, for example."

"Okay, but where exactly will those corridors run?" asked another man sitting at the same table. A number of his colleagues beside him scribbled down everything I said.

"There are some ideas for this area," I said, and referred to the World Wildlife Fund report, "but those ideas need to be validated by local people. Biologists working here in this valley, local First Nations, trappers, hunters, and naturalists – these are the people who need to get together and decide exactly where those corridors and core reserves need to be, not some outsider like me. The role of Y2Y is to help start, coordinate, and support such work, not actually to do it."

I saw Justin nodding his head, pleased with how the discussion was unfolding. But just when I thought everything might end on a productive note, a woman sitting near the front, who had glared at me for the whole presentation, let the accusations rip.

"What about the years that preceded Y2Y and your little walk? What about all the hard work of local volunteers who have spent thousands of hours sitting in meetings to hammer out a land-use plan for the area? We've already done our planning here, and now you're telling us we should just ignore it and start over?"

I swallowed hard and smiled.

"Not start over," I answered, "but reopen it to include something important that wasn't previously considered. Something that wasn't known before – that wildlife need more than islands of habitat to survive. They need to move from one island to another."

"And what if one of these wildlife connections includes an area with top-quality minerals or wood? Are you saying Y2Y will have no economic impact on the mining or forestry industries?" Her dark eyes burned like embers.

"There would undoubtedly have to be limits and restrictions –"

"Aha!" she interrupted. "So there will be financial impacts!" Her head twisted around the room, inviting others to join the attack. "This is a pathetic diatribe," she exclaimed, waving a copy of the Y2Y atlas above her head. "Groups like Y2Y and the foundations that support them are out to ruin small-town economies."

I'd been warned about her before starting, a less-than-diplomatic public relations officer from Fording Coal who hated anything or anyone with a Green tilt, but still I was surprised. I felt like I'd been confronted by a storybook villain. She even looked the part – dressed in a black suit, feet strapped into oversized high heels, dark rings of eyeshadow, and a stringy mop of unkempt hair. I let her

finish, thanked her for her comments, then addressed a few friend-
lier questions.

"Most people consider her to be harmless," said one of the
foresters who came up afterwards to chat. "Just shrug off her comments." Which I did. But unfortunately, it wasn't the last we would
hear from her or her company. In the months to follow, Fording Coal
would spearhead the first of two industry-led anti-Y2Y campaigns
that, by fall, dogged us everywhere we stopped to talk.

There comes a point on all long-distance treks when the body
revolts, when muscles cramp instead of strengthen, and joints begin
to break down. That point, for me, came a few days north of
Crowsnest Pass.

Problems with my hips were to be expected. In childhood, I'd
been diagnosed with Legg-Calvé-Perthes disease, a degenerative
condition where the ball of the hip joint fits poorly in its socket. I'd
endured terrible, chronic pain at age six and seven, then nothing but
a slow, hardly noticeable decrease in my range of motion. By age
twenty, enough cartilage had been worn away so that I could no
longer sit cross-legged. Now it had progressed to the point that it was
difficult to plant my feet much more than shoulder-width apart. The
back-and-forth motion of walking and skiing was fine though, and
the doctors had actually recommended staying active to keep blood
flowing to the area. All in moderation though, and the pains I felt as
I worked my way over Deadman Pass and into Alexander Creek was
my body's way of saying enough.

"Let me put it this way," a specialist had said before I left on the
hike, "you've got the hips of a sixty-year-old, and no matter what you
do, they'll both need replacing within twenty years." He'd pushed
some drug samples my way, painkillers and anti-inflammatories, but

after reading through the possible side effects of long-term use, I'd
stuck them in a bathroom drawer at home along with all the other
drugs I'd never used. On the trail, I would rely on stretching and
massaging my joints.

> SEPTEMBER 1 – *Alexander Creek, British Columbia – These
> hips are more of a discomfort than a pain, a dull ache that keeps
> me awake at night, wishing for a soft bed. Instead of feeling
> young and unstoppable, I now feel old, as though I'm seizing
> up. No matter how much I stretch, the fist of tension remains,
> a deep, inaccessible knot above both legs that spreads down to
> the arches of my feet. I am stiff in the morning and sore at
> night, making the first and last hour of each day more of a
> hobble than a walk. At night I sleep fitfully through the dis-
> comfort, worrying. I worry that I've only covered a third of the
> distance to the Yukon and already I feel like I'm falling apart.
> And the toughest sections – the trailless mountains of northern
> British Columbia – are yet to come.*

Of course all the road walking didn't help. I'd walked on roads
for a few days before reaching the highway at Crowsnest Pass, and
after Justin dropped me off again, I walked north on roads for four
more. Allison Creek, Alexander Creek, and the Elk River; every valley
held a network of both active and old logging roads, which surprised
me, given that the World Wildlife Fund report had labelled the route
I was following as one of four potential pathways for grizzlies. I'd
hate to see the worse options, I thought as I trudged past a subdivision, a few scattered clear-cuts, and a group of free-range cattle.

To make matters worse, hunting season had just started, which
meant a sharp rise in the amount of traffic on the backroads. Figures
with rifles strapped over their backs raced past on all-terrain vehicles
in the early morning and evenings, and pickups cruised the roads

midday, searching for anything that moved. I carried a yellow pack, Webster a red one, and although it would have been difficult to mistake either of us for a wild animal, I shouted and sang out anyway, for fear of mistakenly being shot.

"I was wondering what was making all the noise," said a voice near the headwaters of Alexander Creek. I jumped with surprise, turning in time to see somebody move out from the edge of the forest holding a crossbow. The man, dressed in camouflage greens and face paint, had been invisible against the pine and spruce trees. Even Webster had walked past, oblivious to his presence only a few metres away. He stretched out a hand in greeting. "You're the guy that's come up from Yellowstone, aren't you?"

"Have we met?"

He looked over his clothes, and smeared a finger across his cheek.

"Yeah, I guess it's pretty hard to recognize me," he chuckled, wiping the paint on his pants. "I was at that talk you gave to the Chamber in Fernie – an excellent talk, by the way. I work for Crestbrook." He paused for a moment and as an afterthought added: "In fact, it was me that wrote the prescriptions to have a lot of this country logged."

"It seems like a lot of logging has gone on," I said. "This whole place is riddled with roads." My concern didn't register with him, and he went on to explain which cut-blocks he'd mapped and when, as though it was a matter of prestige. I tried a different tack.

"Has hunting changed any because of all the forestry?"

"Some," he admitted. "It's getting tougher to find an animal to shoot every year." He paused as a gust of wind brought the sound of more vehicles coming up the valley. "And harder to find spots where other people aren't out messing up your hunt." He was my age – in his late twenties – and from his confused expression, I thought perhaps he'd finally stumbled on the contradiction between his work and passion. He stroked at his beard for a few moments, fingered the arrows strapped to his bow, then dismissed the paradox with a quick shrug. "So long as you know where to look, you can still find them." He pointed to an avalanche slope and told me he'd watched a six-point bull elk feed there all morning. "Bedded in the trees now and not much chance of him movin' for the rest of the day." He glanced at his watch. "I'll probably head home for lunch, have a nap, then come back and continue the hunt this evening."

By this time, we'd reached his truck, and I gave a half-hearted wave as he honked and drove off. It wasn't the hunt that bothered me, but how motorized access had reduced it to an act of convenience. Before roads, a hunting trip to the head of Alexander Creek had been a week-long endeavour filled with horse wrecks, freak snowstorms, cold river fords, and dead-end creeks. Hunters in those days had returned with more than meat and a pull-the-trigger story; they'd returned with better respect for the wilderness, and more often than not, a little humbled. But vehicle access had changed all that. Always having a truck or all-terrain vehicle nearby meant an easy escape from any suffering, and the shortened travel times lessened the opportunity to learn from the land. And for the few who still did hunt on foot or horseback, a roadless valley was getting difficult to find.

SEPTEMBER 3 – *Kept awake through the night not by my hips, but by the clang and drone of machinery working the terraced pits of Line Creek coal mine. Trucks, diggers, earthmovers, working around the clock to dismantle a mountain. This morning, I hear different engines on top of those working the mine, and ones that are closer. A chainsaw, and by the time I'm packed up, a bulldozer scraping, pushing in another road 200 metres away. Boulders, bushes, and trees scrape and snap under the blade. Behind it, the pungent musk of fresh soil and broken roots mixes with the acrid smell of diesel. I'm depressed when I*

head up towards North Fork Pass, but hopeful for a better view.
What greets me on the other side, however, is Alberta's version
of the same kind of devastation. I count eighty-eight clear-cuts
quilting the Oldman River basin, with a web of roads sewing
the slashed patchwork together. I stop and sit down. I want to
be free of this madness, to be clear of the dragnet of develop-
ment, to see fresh and abundant grizzly signs instead of the odd
dried-out dig. I want to walk in forests, not tree farms; past
pristine meadows, not more cabins and houses. I want to walk
on game trails – even to bushwhack – just no more of these
bone-crushing roads.

Respite came a day later, just over Tornado Pass. All the roads seemed to creep back from the divide then and an old foot trail, heavy with deadfall but well marked with orange diamonds on trees, emerged. I had stumbled on a section of southern Alberta's little-known Great Divide Trail.

Unlike the United States, Canada had no formal long-distance hiking route along the Continental Divide, a shortcoming that, in the early seventies, a group of friends had set out to correct. "Our intent wasn't to build a trail so much as it was to conserve a landscape," Dave Higgins had explained to me the previous winter. It was Higgins who, along with three fellow students, had started the Great Divide Trail Society two and a half decades ago and built 150 kilometres of trail. "We wanted to create a route that people would fall in love with," he'd explained, "something that would move them to call on the government to give the area between Waterton and Banff national parks some level of protection."

They'd succeeded in their first goal. After only a day of winding up and down from valley-bottom wetlands to alpine meadows, I went to sleep hoping the next day would hold more of the same: wind-swept ridges, subalpine larch forests and valleys deep in shade. Their second, more political goal, however, had met with more resistance.

Initially, both the Alberta and B.C. governments had seemed receptive to the idea of surrounding the trail with a one-kilometre-wide development-free buffer, but the forestry and oil and gas industries had lobbied against it. Many of the problems I had walked through over the past week – the clearings, cutlines, and roads that had obliterated parts of the old trail – were a part of the wave of development that had ensued. It was hard not to wonder what the place would have looked like had the four students won protection for the trail. A vital link in the Yellowstone to Yukon region would have been conserved two decades before the Y2Y acronym was first uttered. Instead, the landscape through which I had just walked was so sliced and shredded that even a raven would need provisions to cross it.

The legacy of the Great Divide Trail Society was relatively unspoiled north of the Oldman, and for the next three days I followed markers and good sections of cleared trail across Cataract Plateau, Rye Ridge, and through the forests fringing Etherington and Baril creeks. Disturbances were fewer – the odd old seismic line seemed almost nothing compared to what I'd just been through – and the wildlife activity increased. Herds of bighorn sheep and elk grazed across alpine slopes, while in the valleys, I saw moose, deer, and wolf trails tracking through meadows dotted with yarrow, goldenrod, and other late-blooming flowers. There were bear scats too, big, red, seed-filled excretions of half-digested berries, some of them almost lost in the other splashes of early-September colour. The birch and willow leaves trailed red and yellow across riverside meadows, and the alpine meadows and subalpine larches glowed gold and orange among bands of evergreen trees. Even the sky announced a change in the seasons, shifting from the pale tones of summer to a deep, autumnal blue. Only the mountain peaks were indifferent to the shortening days. Their grey slabs stood, day and night, unaffected by the threat of sun, sleet, snow, or rain.

The possibility of snow was beginning to preoccupy me. I still had more than 750 kilometres to walk before reaching Jasper – about forty days – and knew it would be a race against winter.

I tried not to think too far ahead. The scale of the trek still held the power to overwhelm me, and as I descended Baril Creek, I limited myself to the kind of thinking that had brought me this far: one step, one day, one section at a time. Tomorrow was what I focused on. Two boxes of food awaited me at the Highwood Ranger Station, and after a rendezvous with Justin and a few more presentations, I would return there to meet my sister, Erica, who planned to walk with me on the next section.

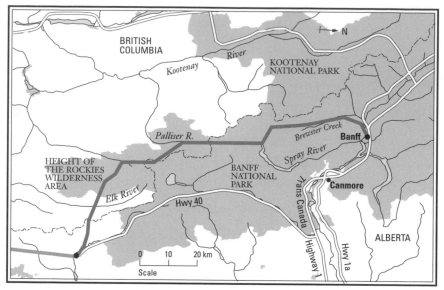

Highwood Junction to Banff, Alberta – 190 kilometres

5

It was three and a half months since I left Yellowstone, long enough that all the walking, sleeping outside, and carrying a heavy pack seemed normal to me. Too normal, in fact, for when it came time to give interviews and presentations in the ranching communities of Alberta's foothills, it became apparent that I'd lost perspective.

"This long-distance walking is no great feat," I suggested to a local newspaper reporter whom Justin and I met for breakfast in one of Black Diamond's two eateries. "Simply a matter of putting one foot out in front of the other, step after step, day after day."

"Yeah, but . . ."

"No, no," I interjected, gesturing with my toast to include every cowboy in the smoky room. "Anyone can do it. All they need is time and a little energy. The map and navigation skills are simple, living is cheap, and after a painful first week or two, you get fit and strong." Her pen stopped, the notebook closed, and the interview was suddenly over. Without any of the long-distance hiking bravado, there wasn't much of a story.

"Listen, Heuer," Justin scolded after we were on the road again, heading back to the trailhead where he'd fetched me the day before, "I can appreciate all this walking is beginning to feel common for you, but we have a hook to keep in mind here – a tool to capture public attention. What you're attempting to do *is* remarkable in the modern era. These days, few people hike, or even walk to the corner store. For the sake of the project, give the modesty pitch a rest."

I could always count on Justin for a quick and blunt assessment, but it was my sister who would really bring his words home. An hour and a half after the interview fiasco, we pulled into the parking lot at Highwood Junction and there she was, waiting as we'd arranged, ready to join me on the next six-day section through the Height of the Rockies to Banff National Park. It was hard not to notice her enthusiasm. She wore brand-new hiking boots, a hodgepodge of borrowed clothes, and a huge smile. I wondered if it all would be enough. An asthmatic, she hadn't been on an overnight hike in her life.

Erica had different memories of the family camping and fishing trips that had so impressed me as a child: mosquitoes, blisters, and the cold were what she remembered. When she had left home, she had not replaced the outgrown skis and hiking boots, and had left the tents, fishing rods, and backpacks stuffed in the rafters of our parents' garage. She hadn't ventured far from a road or building in the last fifteen years.

Despite this, Erica had taken an intense interest in the Y2Y Hike from the start, and when it had become obvious that Justin and I couldn't do everything from the road or trail, she'd jumped in and volunteered to run a part-time office for the project from her home in Calgary. We talked regularly – discussing which newspapers and magazines needed to be sent pictures and dispatches, and how to design the next print run of press kits and posters. And with each successive conversation, her eagerness to join me on the trail grew.

We started late and didn't get far that day. Although Erica hadn't needed to pack more than her own bare essentials, the backpack she wore was heavier than anything she'd carried before, and it wasn't long before the hip and shoulder bruises were beginning to form. We stopped many times that afternoon, readjusting loads, snacking, taping blisters. Ten kilometres from the road, at the head of McPhail creek, I pitched camp while she contemplated the cliffs that loomed on three sides around us.

"Is that where we go tomorrow?" she asked, pointing to a thin switchback through the bands of rock.

"Don't worry," I assured her, "it'll be easier than it looks." I pointed to an elk that had emerged from the forest 300 metres away, the first of five cows, followed by a massive bull. Already in the throes of the rut, the big antlered male was oblivious to anything but his harem, trotting from female to female, nosing one in the rump then moving to the next, checking and rechecking each of them for breeding condition. The cows were more interested in feeding than anything he had in mind, though, and after being repeatedly rebuffed, the big bull succumbed to his hunger and began to graze as well. By then, a spectacular sunset had faded, the elk were ghostly shapes in the blue twilight, and most of the concern on Erica's face was gone.

It was probably a good thing Erica was asleep when a grizzly bear sauntered past camp early the next morning. I wasn't much more awake, groping around in the semi-darkness, cooking breakfast. If it hadn't been for Webster, I might not have even noticed the bear at all. But seeing Webster snap upright, ears cocked and eyes set into a burning stare, was enough of a clue for me to shut off the stove. When the last flame sputtered out, I could hear what had caught his attention: branches breaking and heavy footfalls heading our way.

There was no time to react before it emerged from the trees, no time to move. What had been a sound only a moment before was suddenly a 300-pound grizzly only a stone's throw away.

It seemed impossible for it not to have noticed us at that distance, and yet everything in its manner suggested it hadn't. Casual and unhurried, the bear ambled forward in a loose, pigeon-toed gait, moving on a course that passed less than twenty metres away. Breathless, I prayed for Webster not to bark, and for Erica, still sleeping in the tent, not to stir.

I was half mesmerized, half terrified as the grizzly walked past, every detail searing itself into my mind as its long claws brushed through the grass. Only when it continued to our downward side did I begin to breathe and recoup the sense of time that, for a few seconds, had come unhinged. When I was sure the bear had gone, I called for Erica to come out quickly.

"It walked past right here," I told her. I was still reeling from the encounter and needed to convince her – and myself – that it had actually happened.

"Really?" She sounded both sorry and relieved as she bent to inspect the ground. The signs were subtle: some tamped-down grass, and a dark path traced through the morning dew. Not enough evidence to convince my sister. "A grizzly bear, huh?"

Her doubts were soon put to rest as we began climbing the crease up through the cliffs. Fresh paw prints, skid marks, and still-wet splashes of red berry scats all told of the bear's rapid descent. And the bear was just the latest animal that had used the trail. The cloven prints of elk, goats, and sheep lined every pocket of earth on the steep path; and hanging off every protruding rock was a flag of fur. I was surprised by all the signs of wildlife but shouldn't have been. We were going through the only break in a line of cliffs that guarded the whole valley. The narrow gap was a wildlife portal from one side of the Continental Divide to the other.

"How's it going?" I called back to Erica as we scrambled through loose stones, lichens, and moss.

"Not bad," she answered, sounding less than confident as she double-checked each hand and foothold. "It's a little steep, a little high."

Her voice trailed off and was replaced with the rattle of asthma in her chest.

SEPTEMBER 10 – *Weary Gap – The first mountain pass of Erica's adult life; my fiftieth of the summer. For me, another forested valley beckons in the distance while, behind, everything but the grizzly encounter is lost in the memories of so many other valleys walked on similar days. Erica, meanwhile, points to every meadow where we stopped to rest, every creek junction where she overcame a few more doubts, every place we saw a bear print or game trail. And in the distance, the expanse of glaciated peaks and shining cliffs is stunning to her, the space and freedom exhilarating. Before dropping into the next valley, she lets out a few whoops and hollers, all but her skinny legs and waving arms lost behind the bulging mass of her backpack. I can't remember the last time I saw a mountain pass bring someone so much joy.*

That joy was dampened briefly by what greeted us along the upper Elk River three hours later: more roads, and a handful of hunters driving from clear-cut to clear-cut in search of game. But I knew we were leaving it all behind when we forded the knee-deep river and stepped into the old-growth forest of Cadorna Creek. I breathed a sigh of relief. Unlike the other forests I'd entered in the last two weeks, this was more than an intact fragment surrounded by development. There would be no clear-cuts around the next corner, no mines over the next rise, no cottages or houses visible from the next pass. In crossing the Elk River, we had stepped into the Height of the Rockies Wilderness Area, the southernmost in a conglomerate of thirteen protected areas that straddle the Continental Divide for 750 kilometres. In Y2Y terms, we had made it to the next great island, a 40,000-square-kilometre core reserve that would take me the better part of two months to cross.

The next challenge was the aptly named Pass in the Clouds. Towering 1,200 metres above the valley floor, the rocky defile looked more like a mountaineering route than a pass, a cleft of light carved into cliffs of limestone and glacial ice. I flashed Erica a smile that said it would be tough but possible, and she flashed one back saying she'd give it her best shot.

We were far from the first to attempt the strenuous climb. For thousands of years, the pass had served as a valuable, if unlikely, route for the Kootenay and other mountain Indian nations to reach the wildlife-rich prairies. It was the ruggedness that made it so attractive. While the notoriously fierce Blackfeet jealously guarded the low elevation routes like Crowsnest Pass, the Kootenay sneaked over Pass in the Clouds and nabbed a few bison and antelope before retreating home, undetected.

I don't know if it was the original Indian trail that we followed up Cadorna and then Abruzzi creeks, but it faded as we climbed, disappearing under the mats of cow's parsnip and false hellebore already flattened by the first hard frosts of the coming winter. As the slope steepened, it only got harder to imagine a line of people, horses, and dogs laden with buffalo meat making the same journey.

Erica and I stopped to rest before tackling the last steep traverse. There was a good game trail to follow, but it was over an angled field of loose boulders that shifted with each step. Mist swirled, and a cloud-bank swept in, obscuring the view of where we'd come from. Erica stole a look above. Then she looked again. "Is that where we're going?" She pointed to a wide but uneven ledge that skirted a steep dropoff.

I nodded. "Think you can do it?"

She took a deep sigh. "Well, I guess I'm going to have to. We can't leave me here." We both laughed but I wasn't sure she thought it was funny.

Erica started out upright behind me, but a few steps later, dropped to all fours. I paused, and she tried to face me, forcing her hunched body to straighten.

"You go ahead, Karst, I'll be right behind you."

Webster dashed off like a mountain goat, and I followed for a few seconds, then turned to check on Erica again. She'd made progress but was just creeping along, getting slower and slower until she reached an outcropping where her hands walked her to a standing position and she stopped. Her face crumpled and she began to sob.

I knew better than to push her, so I sat down, gently rubbing her back. Darkness was descending, and we still had to get up, not to mention down the other side of the pass. Reaching into Webster's pack, I pulled out his leash and tied it around her waist.

"Don't worry," I said, tugging her to her feet. "Step exactly where I do, and I've got you if you fall."

It did the trick.

There was another pass the next day, a low saddle between the White and Palliser rivers, and this time Erica was ahead instead of behind, continuing to lead even when the path faded, hardly slowing as she picked up an elk trail that led into the trees and eventually down to the braided outwash of the Palliser River. Once on the gravel flood plain, it became more obvious where we needed to go. A fresh set of grizzly prints led from one crossing to the next, pointing like an arrow to where the glacial river's many channels were best forded.

Once we were off the flood plain and back in the forest, we came across a well-used horse trail, an outfitter's cabin, and a few kilometres later, the outfitter himself, leading a pair of hunters on horseback. He was a wiry character, weather-beaten and hard compared to the two awkward-looking clients who sat uncomfortably on their saddles. When he spoke, the words came out in a mumble from behind his wispy moustache.

"Where you two comin' from?"

"From the Elk River three days ago," I answered, choosing not to tell the whole story. From the way the horses were fidgeting, I knew it wouldn't be a long conversation. We'd hardly started talking, and already the animals were trying to push past, stamping circles in the duff beside the trail. They smelled of smoke, and I could see rings of charcoal around their hooves. "Where's that fire at?" I asked, pointing at the black streaks as one of the ponies spun and reared.

"She was burning up Queen Mary Creek, but she's out now," the outfitter said, reigning in the horse and adjusting his hat at the same time. "Where are you headed?"

"Palliser Pass, first thing in the morning."

He glanced back at his clients. "First thing, huh? Well, my friends here have their eye on a few elk up there so if you can help it, don't go pushing them over into the park."

Unlike Banff National Park shouldering its northern border, the Height of the Rockies Wilderness Area allows hunting. In fact, it had been a coalition of hunters and hunting outfitters that got the ball rolling on the successful campaign to protect the area. That had been back in the 1980s, a time when small logging companies were being taken over by a handful of corporate giants, who streamlined the industry with computerized mills and log-eating machines. The result was a double blow for many small forestry towns in British Columbia. The number of jobs plummeted while the number of felled trees jumped. More raw materials and fewer labour costs; the owners must have been laughing all the way to the bank.

There had been nothing funny for the people who made their living off wildlife, though. As each valley was roaded and razed, there was one less place left to trap, guide, and hunt. When the forestry companies reached the wildlife-rich headwaters of the Elk, White and Palliser rivers, local hunters and outfitters drew the line. And in 1987, after almost a decade of fighting, the Height of the Rockies was established as British Columbia's first-ever Wilderness Area.

We never did see elk at Palliser Pass the next morning, but we didn't spend much time looking. I was too excited. For the first time since leaving Yellowstone, the ridges and valleys that lay ahead were familiar. After a long journey, I was finally coming home.

"Hey, slow down!" Erica barked from behind. "I'm half-jogging just to keep up to you."

After the rough trails in the Height of the Rockies, I couldn't help lengthening my stride on the clear, well-defined paths of Banff Park. Each turn in the trail brought a memory and a hunger for home. I had made more than a dozen trips up that pass as a park warden on poaching patrols, doing wildlife surveys, and clearing trail. I could almost feel the heft of the axe in my hands as I marched past the greying ends of logs I'd cut years earlier, and lower down, where the forest gave way to open wetlands, I recalled the time I'd counted dozens of frogs, the morning I'd encountered eight moose, the meadow where I'd come across fresh tracks of a wolf pack, and the innumerable times I'd passed that same pool in the upper Spray River and seen bull trout streak under the cutbank, just as they did now.

The ridges held their stories too, and while gazing at Mount Leman from the porch of the Palliser warden cabin that evening, I told Erica about the great flyway of the golden eagle.

"There," I said, pointing at three dots hundreds of metres above the rocky ridge.

Erica tried to follow my fingers but even through binoculars the birds were almost invisible. It was because of how high they flew that the migration had gone unnoticed for so many years. If biologist Peter Sherrington hadn't stumbled upon it, the phenomenon still might not even be known. While trying to identify a bird in a treetop, during a spring bird count in Kananaskis, Sherrington had inadvertently turned his focusing ring the wrong way, blurring the bird in the foreground and sharpening the specks in the sky behind. The specks, he realized, were golden eagles. Over the next few seconds, five more had flown into view, all of them heading south. By the end of the day, Sherrington and a friend had counted 102 flying past, a new record for Alberta. Intrigued, he'd returned a few days later and counted 250. Sherrington now estimates that more than 6,000 golden eagles make the migration twice a year.

The migration, which spans the Y2Y region from Wyoming to the Yukon, is impressive, but it is the fact that it went unnoticed until 1992 that keeps me wondering what else we don't know. The golden eagle is one of the largest, most studied birds in the world. Tens of thousands have been sexed, weighed, fitted with transmitters, and followed by researchers. And yet, prior to Sherrington's accidental discovery, there had been not a hint about a 4,000-kilometre-long migration across North America. Identifying the migration was important, but perhaps the more valuable lesson is the realization that we are still a long way from understanding even the most basic things about the earth's most obvious inhabitants.

Justin arrived later that night at the warden cabin, after hiking in with Leanne Yohemas-Hayes, a CBC Radio journalist, over Burstall Pass. The plan was for Leanne to continue to Banff with Webster and me the next morning, while Erica and Justin returned to Calgary. After a fine dinner of fresh vegetables and meat, Erica called me out to the porch while Justin and Leanne cleaned up.

"Karst?"

"Yeah?"

"Thanks."

"Thanks for what?"

"For everything. I see now how it's supposed to be."

I had a sense of what she meant but wasn't sure. And so we stood there for a few seconds in silence. Then I found her hand in the darkness and gave it a quick squeeze.

It was a good thing that Leanne was a fit, young triathlete as well as a journalist, for Erica and I had taken an extra day to get through the Height of the Rockies, leaving only two days to walk seventy kilometres to Banff and the next presentations. We packed and headed off before Justin and Erica even stirred in their bunks the next morning.

SEPTEMBER 15 – *Upper Spray Valley, Banff National Park – I hate this hiking to a schedule, but there are merits to moving before the land begins to thaw. A skin of ice fringes the creeks, the Spray River steams in the early morning light, and in the skiff of snow that fell overnight, the tracks of two wolves veer on and off the trail. I think of the outfitter and his clients we met two days ago and wonder if today's the day they'll make their move. Hunters edging in from the south, wolves closing in from the north, it could be a tough day for an elk at Palliser Pass.*

Over the next few hours, the sun turned the trail to soft muck, then dried it completely, and we changed from gloves and wool hats to shorts and T-shirts in the span of a few hours. It was a glorious fall day: crisp but warm; no bugs, no people, and a sky ringing deep blue. The only person we encountered was Ian Syme, my old boss in the warden service, riding down Bryant Creek and headed for Palliser cabin on a fall boundary patrol. After catching up on news of friends and happenings at work, I asked him about the lack of people on the normally popular trail.

"The valley's closed to mountain bikes until further notice," he said. "Part of a new effort to create secure areas for large carnivores."

Just over a year earlier, I had patrolled that same district and monitored a radio-collared grizzly bear while more than 100 mountain bikes zipped up and down the trail. The steady stream of cyclists had prevented the grizzly from crossing the valley for three hours one afternoon, and, on another day, had forced her to abandon her route altogether.

"And the recent bear attack has turned off a lot of the hikers," Ian added, almost as an afterthought. "The guy's still in the hospital with stitches after the bear followed him up a tree." I felt Leanne stiffen beside me. "We only lifted the closure on the Allenby Pass trail a few days ago," he continued, with just the beginnings of a sardonic smile, "and I do believe you two will be the first to hike through since the mauling."

I was used to Ian's dark sense of humour, but found it a little unsettling when, four kilometres later, we came across fresh grizzly prints pressed into the tracks left by his horse. It made sense that the bear was still there. The low-lying grouseberry bushes were laden with the best batch of fruit I'd seen all trip, an oasis amid the widespread berry crop failure that had left many bears in the Rockies hungry that fall.

"Daaaaaayoh!" I shouted as we approached the pass.

"Daaaayoh!" repeated Leanne, so loudly that Webster cowered beside me. Seconds later, both our warning calls echoed back from the nearby cliffs. Only a deaf bear wouldn't know that we were coming.

It was late, but we took a deserved rest at the top of Allenby Pass. While I scrounged for a snack in my pack, Leanne turned on the microphone and conducted an impromptu interview – something about fatigue and endurance, I think – then left the tape running for ambient sound. A breeze whispered through the branches of a small tree, but it was impossible to capture the silent dance of evening light. I took a few photos, then packed up and led the way into deepening shadows.

Half an hour later, darkness fell, leaving us stumbling as we felt for the trail. At least there was the comforting babble of Brewster Creek, which I used as a guide. When the stream hooked left, I knew to veer right, up the side trail that led to the warden cabin. It was midnight when we finally arrived, and both of us were too wobbly-kneed to do anything but pull off our packs and collapse on the bunk beds. There was no dinner, no fire, that night, just sleep.

Both of us were stiff and sluggish the next morning, the kinks and knots from one thirty-five-kilometre-long day not working out of our legs until we were a few hours into the next. By then, we could already hear the sounds of the Bow Valley another ten kilometres away. The deep drone of trains seemed to reverberate through the ground more than through the air, and the hum of cars and trucks on the Trans-Canada Highway penetrated the thick stands of trees. It wasn't quite the sound one would expect upon approaching the centre of Canada's first and most celebrated national park.

With a summer average of 21,000 vehicles driving it in a single day, the Trans-Canada Highway through Banff was, by far, the busiest road I would cross on my trip. It, along with the railway, a golf course, numerous hotels, ski areas, conference centres, tourist shops, and two towns, clogged what was not only the most productive valley in the whole park, but a key corridor in the Y2Y system as well. During five years of intensive monitoring of grizzly bears in and around the valley, for example, not one adult female had crossed the Trans-Canada. For them, Banff Park and the rest of the Y2Y region had been split into two islands.

It was partly geology that had made the situation so dire for wildlife in the area, for the limestone in the central Rockies had folded into knife-edge ridges and mile-high headwalls, creating some of the most constricted valleys I'd come across so far. If a valley didn't dead-end, it often offered only one route to the next, and so much of the park was covered in rock and ice that only about half of it was available to bears and wolves. Add some of the highest levels of human development of any national park to the equation, and you begin to understand the problems behind all the grim statistics: twenty wolves killed on the highway and railway in the last ten years, an average of two grizzlies relocated or killed because of conflicts with humans every year, 238 elk captured and removed from the park because their natural predators could no longer get at them, and the local moose population all but gone extinct.

Drastic problems had forced some drastic compensatory measures. To reduce the number of animals killed on the highway, the four-lane road had been outfitted with a three-metre-high fence and twenty-two underpasses for animals to cross to either side. And when the seven-metre-wide underpasses had proved too small and noisy for wary wolves and grizzly bears, two fifty-metre-wide overpasses had been constructed, the first of their kind in North America.

But for every step forward, there were two slips somewhere else, said Mike McIvor, a close friend and mentor, who, with his wife, Diane, walked the last few kilometres with us down Brewster and Healy creeks. The couple had been involved for almost thirty years with the Bow Valley Naturalists, educating people about the area's diverse array of plants and wildlife. But not much teaching had happened lately. Instead, they, and a handful of other volunteers, spent their time in the library and courtroom defending the area against further development. While we walked the final kilometre into the town of Banff, Mike offered a grim update on the latest proposals: a four-season resort was slated for a tract of prime lynx habitat in the middle of the park; a seven-storey conference centre was proposed for the outlet of Lake Louise; and another three pods of development planned for the booming town of Canmore, just outside the park's eastern boundary.

I stared into the turquoise waters of the Bow, trying to quell my anger. There were already so many problems facing wildlife outside of the parks system. How could we afford to have so many within? For the Y2Y vision to work, parks needed to be places where wildlife prospered, reproduced, and spilled out into the surrounding land-scape, not places where they struggled against the tide of development that plagued them everywhere else. All the laws were in place for such protection to happen, but the political will was lacking. And so, instead of enjoying their surroundings, the McIvors, like so many other activists, were spending their time trying to make sure govern-ments and corporations fulfilled their legal obligations.

It was a shock to drive through the town of Banff later that evening. Streams of teens filed into the local Cineplex for Hollywood's latest thriller, lineups stretched outside the doors of the many pubs and dance clubs, while, out on Main Street, people laden with huge shopping bags weaved from one brand name store to the next: Roots. Gap. The Body Shop. Ralph Lauren. It was hard to remember we were inside a national park, let alone one that was in trouble.

"What do you say we go for a beer?" Justin suggested, trying to cheer me up.

"No thanks," I said. "I think I just better get some rest." I wasn't feeling at all happy to be back home.

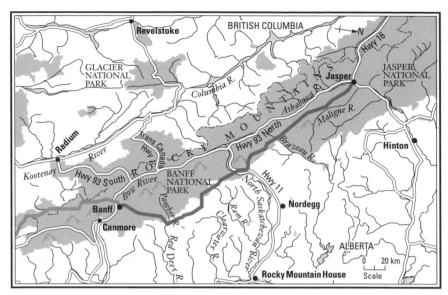

Banff to Jasper, Alberta – 260 kilometres

6

The Bow Valley was our most successful publicity stop yet. Two hundred people came to the presentation in Banff, more than 400 to the one in downtown Calgary, and in the days between, there were more requests for interviews, press conferences, meetings, and presentations than Justin and I could possibly handle. We stopped to speak to town councils, national television crews, land managers, school children, and hunting groups in a five-day, 500-kilometre whirlwind tour of four towns and one city. It was a ridiculous, overwhelming pace, made all the more hectic by the visits with friends and family we crammed in between. I arrived back at Banff tired and frazzled, still thinking about home more than the trail ahead.

SEPTEMBER 25 – *Elk Pass trailhead, Banff, Alberta – From Yellowstone to home, and now from home to the Yukon. Not too*

*long ago, those were both far-off places at the end of plane trips
or multi-day drives, not destinations for someone travelling on
foot. But the act of walking into the Bow Valley from Yellowstone,
and to now be leaving again to walk to the Yukon has unseated
all notions of home and distance. I now understand the movements of wide-ranging animals in a way that isn't possible from
studying reports and maps. They are less fantastic than they
once were, less extraordinary. I have walked those connections
– from valley to valley, state to state, province to province, from
one country to the next – and I understand how Yellowstone
affects the Crowsnest Pass, and how Bozeman influences Banff.
I'm not leaving home, only setting off to explore its boundaries.
Home, for me, has expanded.*

Trying to communicate such thoughts to people who hadn't
actually walked the trail would be challenging, I realized, but I had a
chance to practise over the next four days. Travelling with me over
Elk and Dormer passes would be a four-person crew making a radio
documentary for *National Geographic*.

How to transport so many people and so much gear was solved
with seven horses: two for carrying equipment and five to carry a
wrangler, me, and the show's host, technician, and producer. It meant
a different style of travelling, and as I watched the crew tiptoe around
their horses, repacking and adjusting their stirrups, I knew there
would be no quick and early morning starts that week.

That was all right because our plans weren't ambitious: ride
eighty kilometres in four days from Banff to the government-owned
Ya Ha Tinda Ranch, a huge end-of-the-road spread where a trio of
cowboys trained and wintered a herd of 180 horses for use by backcountry wardens in the nearby national parks.

I was riding one of those horses when we finally set off, bracing
myself for the explosion of farts and hooves that typifies the start of
any horse trip, praying that the outfit would hold together while the

skirmishes that establish the pecking order of the animals sorted themselves out. There were a few mute kicks, a bite or two, but no serious injuries in the fifty-metre dash to where the forest closed in. There, squeezed into single file by the trees, the horses grudgingly accepted their places in the hierarchy and plodded up the stony trail.

The rain that started an hour later turned to wet snow as we climbed higher, the kind that clings and soaks through every bit of clothing. Even the horses suffered as the snow balled under their hooves, sending them stumbling and skating along the trail. We dismounted and walked ahead of the lurching animals, fighting to stay upright in the same slippery muck. Curses rang out and there were periodic complaints about the cold, but mostly we walked in silence, through a world muffled by winter's first snowfall. It was a beautiful but unappreciated transformation, as everyone on the crew was feeling too cold and wet to look around.

The next day dawned clear, and by the time we got up, the sun had rolled back the snow to reveal a valley of freshly washed colour. It was fall again – however briefly – and the taste of winter the day before made us all value it more than ever. The horses seemed happy too. When we stopped to record interviews in Dormer Pass, they grazed quietly around us, and when it came time to move again, they peacefully complied. Goats looked down from the surrounding ridges as we wound down the steep switchbacks on the north side of the pass, cutout silhouettes against an ocean of peaks still white from the day before.

"If this is earth," said the producer from Washington, D.C., "I'm not interested in what heaven has to offer."

Ya Ha Tinda, a Stoney Indian phrase, translates to "prairie in the mountains," a fitting description for the scene that greeted us as we splashed into the Red Deer River the next afternoon. After the tight valleys and looming peaks of the previous three days, the open sweep of grassland appeared as a mirage to the Washington crew, an unlikely oasis amid the surrounding forests and grey cliffs. It was a magical valley, one where two hundred horses and more than a thousand elk shared the open range each winter, shadowed by cougars and wolves. As we pulled up and dismounted beside the barn the ranch's lead hand told us there were two wolf packs hanging around the property, but in the decades he could remember, not one had bothered a horse.

"Snow eater" was what the Stoneys called the warm winter breezes that make the Ya Ha Tinda such a great winter range for elk and their predators. The chinook wind, which often gusts at speeds greater than 100 kilometres an hour, can send the February thermometer climbing 30°C in a few hours, consuming not only the snow, but the ice off ponds and creeks as well. It dries the landscape and shapes the vegetation, creating one of the sharpest transition zones in the temperate world. In the span of a few miles, blankets of coniferous trees give way to open stands of aspen and vast hillsides of grass. While a moose wallows in shoulder-deep snow in a Main Range valley, mountain sheep and elk can be blinking in the warm, dusty wind of the foothills less than thirty kilometres away.

Despite their value as a wildlife winter range, the eastern slopes of the Rockies aren't well protected. The density of roads, pipelines, seismic cuts, and power lines is among the highest of any area in the Y2Y region. Rich oil and gas reserves and accessible timber have resulted in a cross-hatching of roads, cut-blocks, and seismic lines as bad as in Montana's Big Belt Mountains.

It hasn't always been like that in Alberta, and there are some small pockets of land, especially around the national parks, where the situation is improving. Although still scarred with seismic lines and old roads, the upper reaches of the Dormer, Panther, and Clearwater rivers, for example, are now restricted to foot and horse travel. It is an improvement from the 1970s when vehicles could be driven up every valley right to the park line, but far from what it was

when all those areas – the Ya Ha Tinda ranchlands and the town of
Canmore included – were part of a much larger Rocky Mountain
National Park. But in 1930, in the face of provincial pressure to
develop natural resources, the park was shrunk from 9,920 square
kilometres to its current 6,500-square-kilometre size. As a result, the
large mammals that inhabited the park in summer now spent much
of the winter on unprotected lands.

We had passed a few hunting camps just outside the park boundary as we rode into the ranch, but it wasn't until I headed off alone
on foot again that I met the hunters themselves. A father-and-son
team scoured the low pass at the head of Scalp Creek the day I followed a seismic line north of the ranch, and at the mouth of Skeleton
Creek the next morning, I watched two Texans and their guide close
in on a bugling bull elk. Both Webster and I cringed a half-hour later
when two shots rang out, followed by the ravens and crows flying to
the site soon after, telling me that the bullets must have hit their mark.

There was one last camp along the Clearwater River before I
crossed back into a corner of Banff Park, an inviting wall tent steaming from the heat of a wood stove after a day of rain. Soaked to the
skin and cold, I happily accepted the inviting wave of a bearded man
who peered through the door flap as I approached. Within minutes,
I was seated beside three men and a fire, sipping a mug of hot tea.

"You're walking from where to where?" asked Glen Wilsey, looking
under a makeshift table to size up my muddy boots. I had met the
heavy-set but soft-spoken guide before, during fall boundary patrols
I'd made as a park warden, and I remembered him wearing the same
wool pants and thick suspenders that he wore now.

"Yellowstone to the Yukon." I laughed, aware of how preposter-
ous it must sound. "But tomorrow I just hope to make it to White
Rabbit Creek."

"Yukon, huh?" said the small Asian man who seemed dwarfed by
Wilsey and his assistant guide. "I was up in Alaska hunting brown
bear just last year."

"Any luck?"

"Oh yes!" He proudly traced the outline of a huge head in the air. "A really big one."

"And what about here?" I asked. "Any sheep so far?"

"Not yet. We've seen a few small rams," he said. "But I'm not leaving until I get a big one."

Wilsey grinned. The Philippine banker was the perfect customer for him: hungry for big animal trophies and rich enough that money was no object. With fees in the thousands of dollars per week, October was going to be a lucrative month.

Henrique was typical of the foreign trophy hunters who feed Alberta's $48-million hunting industry. The year before, a Texan had paid $650,000 for the right to hunt a bighorn sheep a month after the normal hunting season had closed, speculating that the privilege might bag him the biggest bighorn ever shot. Wilsey had been one of many guides he'd hired to help him find the ultimate ram, but the team had come up empty.

"We found lots of sheep but not the right one," said Wilsey. "The guy must've spent another $10,000 on guiding fees and gas by the time it was all over, but because he never found the sheep that would've given him number one in the books, he didn't fire a single shot."

The "books" Wilsey referred to are the international Pope and Young score card registers that list horn, antler, and body measurements for the largest animal ever killed in each of the big game species. I've always had a difficult time with the ethics of trophy hunting, and Wilsey's story of someone possessed with killing an animal to secure top spot on some obscure list didn't help.

Yet it was the trophy hunters who had helped to protect the Height of the Rockies, the Willmore Wilderness, and other areas from development. Large tracts of habitat had been set aside from industry, leveraged by large amounts of hunting money. In many cases, the economic and utilitarian arguments of hunters had worked better than the value-laden reasoning of environmentalists. And now that the hunt for a single animal could fetch almost a million dollars of revenue, government officials and politicians – especially the business-minded Conservatives in Alberta – took even more notice. I had philosophical differences with trophy hunters, but I could count most of them as friends in the fight to protect habitat in the Y2Y region.

I saw plenty of bighorn rams as I crossed the northeast corner of Banff Park the next morning, over eighty on one hillside, many of them sporting the thick, full-curl horns that would have made Henrique and the other hunters in the adjoining valley tighten the grip on their rifles. Fortunately for the sheep, it didn't look as if they would be moving out of the national park soon. A mile-wide canyon lay between them and the boundary, and the way they lolled and chewed their cud on the sunny, grassy knoll assured me that they might stay put for the rest of the hunting season. Satisfied, I pocketed my binoculars, grabbed Webster's leash, and headed for the Ram River.

In crossing out of Banff Park and into the Ram Valley, I moved out of familiar territory, and also back into terrain where motorized vehicles were allowed. No sooner had I waded across the river than the roar of an engine drifted from somewhere downstream. I stopped, listening to the sound, trying to decide which of the many rutted trails forking away from the bank to follow. But the labyrinth of tracks proved too confusing, and I had to dig out the maps and compass from deep in my pack to find the treed pass that led into White Rabbit Creek.

OCTOBER 3 – *White Rabbit Creek, Alberta – The sun doesn't hit all morning in this dark, treed valley, and the sound of snow sloughing off the sides of the tent makes it easy to roll over and sleep in. Not since the Gallatin Crest outside of Yellowstone have I been so cold. Even Webster, who normally sleeps sprawled at the*

base of the tent, moved to a corner of the sleeping bag last night.
When I finally do get up and venture outside, it's to a world of
white. Not quite enough snow to warrant putting on the gaiters,
but plenty to register the tracks of something that walked past
since it stopped falling an hour before. I walk over to inspect the
fresh trail, then call for Webster, who has already left in hot
pursuit. I whistle, then scream, fearful for what he might bring
back. I breathe a sigh of relief when it's just him that comes
bounding out of the trees and not the grizzly that can't be far off.

There had been other grizzly sign since leaving Banff: rub trees and
dried-out digs, and while walking up the Clearwater Valley, iced-over
prints. Nothing nearly as fresh as these crisp impressions, though. I
packed up slowly, and when I did finally set off, made more noise
than usual.

I relaxed when the bear tracks veered off into the forest about a
kilometre later, but no sooner was that threat gone than a new challenge appeared – a rapidly deteriorating trail. By mid-morning I was
crawling as much as I was walking, ducking and climbing through
tangles of deadfall and windthrow. It had obviously been some time
since someone had cleared the trail, a few years judging by the
amount of new plant growth and the alternative paths that had been
worn by wildlife through the forest. I followed those rough trails,
stumbling where elk and deer hooves had worn rutted trenches
around fallen trees, dropping to all fours when a tunnel of broken
branches beckoned. It was an effort to crawl through such spots, my
pack and clothes catching on branches already festooned with elk,
moose, and bear hair.

I'd fought more than walked down that valley when I finally
emerged onto the Kootenay Plains, a peaceful land of cured grasses
and rattling aspen trees. Members of the Stoney nation still congre-
gate here every year, near the confluence of the Siffleur and North
Saskatchewan rivers, to celebrate the once-banned Sun Dance. The

Top: Spionkop Ridge, looking towards the high ridges in the north of Waterton National Park, Alberta.

Right: Erica Heuer walking across the steep ground below the cliffs that guard Pass in the Clouds, Height of the Rockies Wilderness Area, B.C.

Left: Leading horses over the Dormer Pass, Banff National Park, Alberta.

Below: Grizzly bear in Banff National Park.

Top: The hunters' camp near the Clearwater River, Alberta. *Left to right*: Glen Wisley, Henrique, park warden Art Laurenson, and Karsten.

Right: Fresh grizzly bear tracks at Maligne Pass, Jasper National Park, Alberta.

Top left: Don Gardner hanging one
of the food caches in a tree on the
upper Morkill River, B.C.

Top right: Roy Howard preparing
to take a food cache up the Holmes
River, B.C.

Top: Jay Honeyman and
Leanne Allison edging their
way through the Moose
River canyon, a skywalk of
snow and air.

Right: Bushwhacking is a
whole lot easier for a
two-foot-high wolverine
than an five-foot-something
skier on seven-foot-long
skis. Jay forces his way along
the Smokey River, Jasper
National Park, Alberta.

Top: Wolverine tracks paralleling our route along the Continental Divide near Holmes Peak, B.C.

Left: Jay descending into Spider Creek, Willmore Wilderness Park, Alberta.

Opposite: Launching the canoe below Kanuseo Falls, Monkman Provincial Park, B.C.

Heading back into the mountains along the banks of the Peace River, B.C.

Karsten and Webster making their way past one of many oil drilling rigs near Halfway River, B.C.

Siffleur was little more than a large creek in the late autumn, and its clear waters poured over a beautiful cataract just metres before flowing into the much larger North Saskatchewan River. The falls were lovely, but what I really appreciated was the footbridge built for tourists. It saved me a cold swim to the highway. Thin panels of ice were already floating in the swift current, and the bottom was lost in the deepest tones of blue.

Justin pulled into the Siffleur Falls pullout within minutes of the prearranged time, and, after the usual greeting, stepped back to consider me with concern.

"You look exhausted."

"I am," I admitted. It wasn't the walk from the Ya Ha Tinda that had done it so much as the whole trip. Despite the easy days on horseback, an increase in trail rations, and an average of ten to eleven hours sleep a night, I was feeling sluggish and run down. The cumulative wear and tear of the last 1,800 kilometres was finally catching up.

"One more section," Justin encouraged. Once I reached Jasper, there would be a rest before I continued a few months later on skis.

Justin had been working hard since I'd last seen him in Banff, organizing not only the presentations and interviews we did in Nordegg and Rocky Mountain House over the next two days, but also the ones we would give in Hinton, Jasper, Edmonton, Dunster, and Prince George the following week. With all this work out of the way, he would finally join me for a few days on the trail. But before that, we had some appointments.

We didn't pass a single vehicle on the hour-long drive to Nordegg, and when it came time for the show to start, there were only six people in the audience, including two enterprising kids who had shown up to sell popcorn. It had been a long time since we'd had such a small audience, and Justin and I looked at each other, disappointed.

"Just a minute," said one woman as she walked to the phone and began calling friends and family. In less than ten minutes, the audience had tripled – almost half the residents in the small community.

It was altogether different the next night. Getting people to attend wasn't the problem in Rocky Mountain House; the challenge was trying to keep the fifty or so people who had crammed into the basement of the local veteran's club from fighting. The audience was a mix of trappers, high school students, housewives, and foresters, and when the subject of local logging patterns came up in the question period after the slide show, I suddenly found myself mediating a very heated discussion.

"Folks, folks, the purpose of this meeting is to be constructive," I said, trying to dampen the emotions that had flared between community activists and representatives from the local sawmill. More barbed comments flew before people quietened down enough for me to close the meeting on the hopeful note of Y2Y.

"Sorry you had to deal with that," said Patsy Haupt, the woman who had helped organize and advertise the evening. "Ever since the Sunpine deal went through, things have been pretty polarized around here."

The Sunpine deal, as Patsy explained it, sounded similar to other deals we'd heard about from frustrated Albertans in the past weeks. After holding a number of open houses and public hearings in the area, the Alberta government had ignored residents' concerns and had granted a single corporation exclusive rights to cut most of the local public forests.

"The open, transparent process that was promised at the beginning of the hearings turned into just another cozy backroom deal," said Patsy with bitterness. "Instead of the democratic process we were promised, we got a wholesale giveaway of publicly owned land."

Patsy's trapper husband, Steve, had the most to lose. It had been hard enough to make a living from the trapline he'd inherited from his father, but this finally forced him to give up. Now he was a plumber.

"So much of the line had been logged that there just weren't any animals left," Steve said later that evening in the couple's kitchen. "I mean, have you seen it? Have you really seen it?" His voice rose as he waved off what I'd talked about earlier that night. "I'm not talking about the little disturbance you saw next to the national parks. I'm talking about here – in the foothills – where every time I head to my favourite valley there's another logging road, another clear-cut, another few seismic lines scraped into the ground." He paused for a moment. "I just can't believe how fast it's going. It's like the world's gone nuts!"

The easiest thing would have been to do nothing, but instead Steve and Patsy had formed Friends of the West Country, a local conservation group that organized the growing number of concerned locals into a united voice for responsible planning and conservation.

"It's not like the tight-knit communities of enviros in the big city," said Patsy as she poured us all a cup of tea. "Out here you can't be anonymous. We live next to loggers and have brothers and sisters in the oilfields. Heck, the parents of some of our kids' friends work for Sunpine!" She chuckled at the absurdity, then grew serious again. "You have to put up with the name calling and hate mail, but after a while you don't notice it. You just accept it as the way some people choose to express their fear."

"You know, we're afraid too," Steve added. "Not about paycheques and jobs like you hear in the news, but about the pace and extent of the impacts. It doesn't take a degree to see that what's going on isn't sustainable."

The van pitched with every curve in the highway as we drove back towards Siffleur Falls, me swaying silently in the passenger seat while Justin piloted us through the night. It was a clear sky, the kind that draws the eye into the depths of the Milky Way and the mind into thought.

"Well, I don't know about you, but I can't help but feel as though we're a part of something much larger," said Justin, "like we're messengers, travelling from place to place, finding the key people to tell about a new and inspiring vision."

I knew what he was talking about. The project was becoming an affair of people as well as wildlife, and the hope I held for Y2Y was rooted as much in the Haupts, McIvors, Hilgers, and Kellys that I'd met as it was in signs of grizzlies along the trail.

"We're connecting people to connect a landscape," said Justin, smiling at his own clever phrase, "but even more than that, we're helping to spawn a movement."

It sounded arrogant when he said it, but it was exactly what I was feeling: an intoxicating mix of excitement and responsibility. All the hopelessness and frustration I'd felt when so few people showed up at our stops in northern Montana was a distant memory. We had momentum now, and it was growing.

We weren't the only ones to notice the attention the project was getting. Unbeknown to us, the final touches were being made on a number of industry-led anti-Y2Y campaigns, the most powerful of which was to be launched across British Columbia by a consortium of multinational logging firms in just a few days.

There was an air of finality to our preparations at Siffleur Falls the next morning. The last box of food in the van was divided between our packs, the last set of maps removed from the grubby file folder, and the last of Webster's dog food stuffed into his now tattered panniers. In another week and a half, the first section of the hike would be over.

"C'mon, Web," I cooed, showing him the bulging set of packs. He skulked over to receive the inevitable load. "Atta boy," I said, reaching under his belly to fasten the straps. Like the hip belt on my own pack, they pulled easily through the buckles past the last holes. "They'll just have to be looser than they once were," I said, kissing the top of his head and releasing him with a pat. He stumbled for a few steps before finding his new balance point, then trotted across the parking lot and into the forest, leading us to the start of the trail.

Our plan was to hike about 100 kilometres to Maligne Lake in six days, after which Justin would leave to make final arrangements for the next stops while I continued for three more days to Jasper. An easy enough hike, but made risky by the time of year. It was mid-October and there were still a number of high mountain passes to cross, any of which a hard-hitting snowfall could render impassable in the span of a few hours. Already walking through a skiff of snow, Justin and I set off up the Cline River, hoping that there wouldn't be much more in the week to come.

Despite the gamble, there were advantages to being out so late in the season. Even though our route would follow some of Jasper National Park's most popular backpacking trails, we were unlikely to run into another person. And so long as it didn't get too deep to walk through, a little snow on the ground would make for some interesting tracking.

"Deer!" said Justin, pointing at a line of crisp, heart-shaped prints soon after we started. "Marten," he barked a few minutes later, and "Moose!" a kilometre after that. He was like a bloodhound, and I struggled to keep up, silently cursing myself for refusing his offer to carry most of the weight. It was Justin who spotted all the details: the bear rub trees, the slow-moving tadpoles in an ice-covered puddle, and an abandoned bird's nest in a thicket of willows. Not only was I hiking with a great publicist, but with a gifted observer as well.

"Mouse!" I said smugly, pointing to a tiny line of dots along the river cobbles that had escaped his attention. It was about the only thing all week that would pass by Justin unnoticed. The next day, he picked out the white ptarmigans against a backdrop of snow at Cline Pass, and then, shortly afterwards, stopped dead when he saw crescent-shaped tracks the size of a man's hand.

"What are they?" he asked when I caught up to him. They looked a lot like cattle prints but it was unlikely a cow had made them. We were in a high alpine meadow inside a wilderness area. Besides, the prints were too big and round.

We followed the line of tracks, looking for more clues: a few raisin-sized pellets, and after a while, spots where something had brushed the snow aside to tear clumps of lichen from the ground. We looked at each other, then back at the evidence in front of us.

"Caribou?"

Neither of us had seen a caribou before, and we were thrilled to find their range brought them this far south.

OCTOBER 9 – *Cline Pass, Alberta – We're possessed with the idea of seeing caribou, and stop frequently to look with binoculars at every caribou-sized rock, bush, or tree. Images of the light brown animals fill our heads as we climb up every hill and pass, but all that greets us is another wintry view of grey forests and white peaks. It's as though the brisk cold winds that washed the songbirds south have also pushed the caribou out of these smoke-coloured mountains. Day after day we search, but all we find are a few grey jays, a lone moose, and at one campsite, a couple of hungry red squirrels.*

It wasn't until a few evenings later, after Justin and I had all but given up the search, that the caribou showed themselves – two mature bulls on a high plateau overlooking a trio of lakes already half frozen. We were only twenty-five metres away when we noticed them, but the wind was in our favour. I put Webster on the leash, and we quickly moved farther downwind, settling behind a clump of wiry subalpine trees to watch the show.

The bulls were half-heartedly sparring, gently approaching one another with bowed heads until their antlers locked. Then the shoulder-flexing and neck-twisting began. Back and forth they pushed one another across the tundra, the rattling of antlers drifting to where we sat huddled in the biting wind. It seemed to be more of a ritual than a real contest; the two stags disengaged and fed for a few moments, then resumed their gentle jousting. Rehearsal or not, what happened in front of us was real, not a performance, and when the sky opened enough for a few shafts of evening light to brush across the snowy peaks, I felt my heart skip. No one could have imagined a scene so beautiful and wild.

Webster eventually broke the trance, not with a bark or chase, but by straining against his leash so much that I had to check him with a sharp, shouted whisper. It was too loud though, and the larger of the two bulls abruptly abandoned his dance to charge towards whatever had made the sound. Towards us.

A dip in the slope concealed most of his approach, but the drum-beat of hooves told of a dead run. We had a few anxious moments before he burst over the rise and stopped ten metres in front of us, snorting and huffing. Webster shook uncontrollably as the bull pranced closer, while Justin and I sat rigid, fearful of making a move. The bull ventured closer, so near that we could hear the click of leg tendons over his raspy breath. Then, suddenly, he turned and fled, blowing our scent from his nose as he galloped across the spongy tundra and, with his companion following, disappeared from sight.

Justin and I were still high from the encounter two days later when we parted at the Maligne Lake parking lot. He would be making last-minute preparations for the next lot of presentations and interviews while I hiked three more high passes along the Skyline Trail to the town of Jasper. I wasn't heading off alone though, for waiting to take Justin's place was Ed Struzik, the Edmonton-based writer and journalist who had joined Maxine and me for the first night of the trip in Yellowstone that spring.

"How the hell are ya?" Ed asked, slapping me on the back. "Four months and still wearing the same shirt, same pants, and same pair of boots, I see."

Suddenly self-conscious, I looked over my outfit and then at his. He too was wearing the same clothes, boots, and pack as he had in Yellowstone, but compared to what I wore, his gear still looked new. No stains or rips in the pants, and next to his almost pristine boots, mine looked done in. The shanks had split a few weeks earlier and the last of the rubber tread was worn flat. I was reminded of exactly how far I'd come.

It wasn't long before we were lost in conversation, trading high-lights from our summers as we shuffled through the dry, boot-top snow. Ed had made three trips to the Arctic since I'd last seen him, and for every bear story I related, he had one about barren ground caribou to match. We were so enthralled with each other's stories that neither of us kept track of where we were going.

"Woah! Wait a minute," I said when I realized what had happened. "I don't think we're on the right trail. We should be up there." I pointed to a rocky bench about a thousand feet above us, near the treeline.

Ed laughed then said: "I don't get it, Karsten. In Yellowstone you were still testing gear moments before embarking on an eighteen-month-long trip. And now you can't navigate along national park trails. Are you scraping through on blind luck?"

I smiled. "Just make sure you leave those parts out when it comes time to write up the story."

The hard work of climbing prevented us from talking much more that afternoon, and it wasn't until we struck camp in the alpine that Ed posed his first big question. Both of us were madly swinging our arms at the time, trying to get warm blood to cold hands after pitching our tents on the frozen ground.

"So, how has the trip met with your expectations so far?" Ed shouted. It was a question Justin and I had anticipated, and a few nights earlier we'd spent time going through my trail journal. I didn't hesitate.

"What I've walked through is more intact than I expected. The amount of grizzly bear sign is proof of that. On seventy-two of the eighty-six days that I've walked I've seen some sign – tracks, rub trees, or the animals themselves."

Ed made a mental note of what I said. "Eighty-five per cent is still wild enough to hold grizzlies?"

"It surprised me too," I admitted. "But what it says is that Y2Y isn't some pipe dream. It isn't some impossible scheme. It's mostly about keeping what still exists today."

"Mostly?"

"There are problem areas," I explained, citing Bozeman and the Crowsnest Pass as examples. "Areas where some restoration is needed."

"Restoration?"

"You know, deactivating logging roads, building wildlife over-passes across busy highways, using planning tools like zoning so that areas important for wildlife movement don't get choked off with development. . . ."

Ed interrupted. He wanted the numbers. "How many highways did you cross?"

"Eight paved roads. Five of them were two-lanes, the other three were four-lane freeways."

"That's only one paved road for every 250 kilometres! And to think it's only going to get even less developed as you continue north!"

"Yeah, and get this," I said. "Most of what I walked through is already protected. Sixty per cent of my days were in national parks or designated roadless and wilderness areas, 30 per cent were on unpro-tected public public land, and 10 per cent were on private property."

"Really?"

"Yeah, and much of that was already in conservation easements."

Ed shook his head in amazement as I threw a handful of rice and dried chicken in the pot and slid it onto the burner.

"What about personally? You've walked all this way. How do you feel? Do you feel like you've accomplished something significant?"

I thought for a minute. Jasper was a little more than halfway between Yellowstone National Park and the Yukon, but in terms of travelling, the worst was yet to come: remote, trail-less country, unbridged rivers, passes and ridges choked with snow. And I wasn't even midway through the number of presentations and interviews. With so much left to do, it was hard to consider it as an accomplishment just yet.

"When I look at a map, I'm amazed at how far I've come," I said. "But day by day, it doesn't seem a big deal. I think that's what excites me most."

Ed gave a quizzical look.

"It shows what's possible when one chips away at something," I explained.

Both of us were uncomfortably cold by the time we'd scooped the last of the rice and chicken into our mouths, and after rinsing our dishes with snow, we quickly hung up the food and crawled into our respective tents.

The temperature dropped to −15°C that night, and all the things that were wet when we went to bed – jackets, boots, gloves, and socks – were frozen solid the next morning. Even our tents were iced to the ground, and when we packed them up, each of us uncovered the outline of our sleeping body melted into the frost.

A fog rolled in soon after we rose. It was time to be moving. We skipped breakfast, and after I posed for a couple of cheesy photographs, Ed and I shook hands and set off in opposite directions – me to Jasper, he back to his car.

It had been a long time since I'd been on my own, and I welcomed the loneliness and stillness for how it brought the details into focus. The grey light brightened as I climbed up and over Shovel Pass, and as I approached the base of a rocky cleft called the Notch, the thinning clouds gave way to a dazzling dance of light. The fog had blanketed everything with hoar frost, and although the valleys were still hidden, my ridgetop route glinted in the sun. I sang as I set off across the shining backbone of mountains. Webster, who had to stop and chew the snow from his paws every few minutes, was holding his tail high.

There wasn't a wind to speak of, but it must have blown earlier in the week, for the snow had been scoured from the ridges and lay in deep drifts in the gullies to either side. It made for good travelling in exposed sections, but as I approached the last sheltered slope below the Notch, I began to worry. It was under these same conditions – bare ground one minute, deep drifts the next – that a group of high school students had died while trying to find an early-season ski run near Banff a year earlier. There had been so little snow that fall day that they had to carry their skis up the mountain, and yet the avalanche in the gully where rescuers finally found them had buried their bodies three metres deep.

I stuck to the bare rocks as I climbed, but thirty metres below the crest of the rocky pass, I was forced onto the snow. The only rocks left were the vertical cliffs that hemmed in a sheltered gully capped by a five-foot drift. I kicked at the snow and watched as a table-sized chunk broke free and careered down the slope. I kicked again and another sheet came loose, sliding into the rocks below in a puff of white dust. Two more hollow-sounding steps and I stopped.

"What do you think, Web?" I watched him wallow in my wake, panting as he swam through the loose, sugary snow my footfalls had exposed. I grabbed a handful of the crystals as I bent down to pat him and watched them run through my fingers like ball bearings. The Notch was only fifteen metres away – twenty, maybe thirty steps – and yet everything was telling me to turn around. If I did, it would add another ten kilometres on my final day into Jasper. I kicked at the slope once more, hoping that this time it would hold. No such luck:

another slab tore loose and exploded on the rocks in the most impressive slide yet.

OCTOBER 16 – *Valley of the Lakes, Jasper National Park, Alberta – After hiking 2,200 kilometres, a few extra don't seem to matter. I'm better off for having come down. A low-pressure system is blowing in and instead of freezing in the treeless alpine tonight, I'm sitting comfortably beside a small campfire, watching Orion and other winter constellations appear in the late-night sky.*

I had hiked down into the Athabasca Valley, the lowest, widest, and most fecund valley in Jasper National Park. But like Banff's Bow Valley, it was also the most developed. Two busy highways and a single railway ran along its length; a ski area, golf course, gondola lift, and numerous resorts sat scattered through its prime lowland habitat; and crowded along the streets of the town of 4,000 residents was a glut of candy shops, T-shirt emporiums, bars, restaurants, and souvenir stores stuffed with enough kitsch to supply the two million visitors that streamed through the park every year. It wasn't quite Banff, but it wasn't far behind.

It had started to snow when I got up the next morning, and by the time I reached the town of Jasper, enough had fallen to slow traffic to a crawl. Cars spun and skidded at intersections as I walked through, and people were out shovelling their sidewalks for the third or fourth time that day. Shortly after plunking my pack down on a friend's porch, news came that the highway had been closed. Wind, snow, and the avalanches that were beginning to slide down the mountains had made it too dangerous to drive through the valley, let alone walk.

My timing was perfect, and I started to wonder if something more than luck was at work. For months, catastrophe and danger had been either ahead of or behind me, but never close enough to throw off my schedule. Something, I felt, was watching over my journey. Fate, karma, destiny. Whatever it was, I just hoped it continued for the tough travelling that lay ahead.

7

"80,000 jobs to be lost due to Y2Y!" shrieked the front page of the Prince George newspaper. The northern town of pulp plants and sawmills was our last publicity stop before breaking for the winter, and would be the most challenging of any we'd made yet. The day before, British Columbia's Forest Alliance – a Vancouver-based, industry-funded lobby group – had launched a huge anti-Y2Y campaign. Across the country, dozens of newspapers ran the same story.

"Should be an interesting few days," Justin observed as we drove to our first stop, a local radio studio where I was a guest on the region's most popular talk show.

"How do you expect to push through an initiative that will cost $3.9 billion in personal income, $1.2 billion in provincial government revenues, and \$5.4 billion in provincial Gross Domestic Product annually?" asked the show's host as soon as I sat down. I quickly scanned the Forest Alliance's press release from which he'd read the alarming numbers. All of them were based on the assumption that Y2Y was a proposal for one huge 1.2 million-square-kilometre park, not a reserve network that would cover only a fraction of the region.

"There's been a mistake," I began, trying to find a persuasive argument while remaining diplomatic. "The Forest Alliance's assessment isn't accurate."

"A *mistake*?" yelled Justin incredulously once back in the van and on our way to the next interview. "*Isn't accurate*? You might as well have called it an honest blunder for all the impact you had! C'mon, Heuer, we're dealing with malicious intent here, not a fib. Next time try fearmongering! Fabrication! We have to confront this lying and call it what it is."

While Justin drove I leafed through the full fourteen-page report commissioned by the Forest Alliance. He was right. By reducing Y2Y to a simple "wildlife in, people out" issue, the Forest Alliance was attempting to undermine the Y2Y concept before it could gain any steam. It made sense when I learned whom the alliance represented: large multinational corporations which, for the past decade, had greatly profited from cutting more and more trees with fewer and fewer people, thanks to mechanization. It was a businessman's dream come true, especially as there were taxpayer-funded subsidies that went along with it. To protect its considerable interests, the Forest Alliance aggressively went after any people or groups that opposed their actions.

The Alliance had trumpeted its simple, fearmongering messages before: Jobs versus the Environment; Loggers versus Environmentalists; Southerners versus Northerners. Y2Y was nothing but a new name to insert into those same old lines, lines that, with the right distortions added, sent people already concerned about a faltering economy into a panic.

My anger at the Forest Alliance's deceptions mounted as Justin and I set up the slide projector for the public presentation that evening. A half-hour before the show was scheduled to start, someone discreetly dropped a box of the Alliance's reports at the entrance, and by the time we were ready to begin, every person in the room held one open on his or her lap.

"It's going to be a tough crowd," whispered Justin. Close to 200 people had come, and most of them sat scowling and cross-armed in their chairs. "Good luck," he whispered, giving me a slap on the back. "Come out fighting."

I followed his advice and denounced the report right off the start, struggling to remain calm. Then, eager to move on to more positive subjects, I used real-life stories, including Bill Kelly's, to explain how forestry and Y2Y corridors could both work in the region, how some logging in select corridors might even be possible. And through the case studies of Bozeman, the Crowsnest Pass, and the Bow Valley, I talked about the costly consequences of not having a decent plan. "For every important linkage that has been lost down south, opportunities still exist here," I insisted. "In northern British Columbia, there is still an opportunity to plan development in a way that will avoid expensive restoration later."

I paused and looked at Justin, who had been scanning the crowd to gauge their reaction. He nodded madly when we made eye contact, urging me to continue. I could hear the odd dissenting mutter at the back of the room, but the majority of scowls had disappeared. Fewer arms were folded. People were actually listening.

There is a fundamental satisfaction that comes from speaking the truth and setting the record straight. I had a hard time containing my smile when the lights went up. People in this hostile audience were actually nodding.

"Excellent show and very diplomatic, considering all the controversy," said a local mill manager before he left. "Good job."

Others came up afterwards too, some to say how inspired they felt and how something like Y2Y renewed their hope for the balance that seemed to be eluding the modern world. Finally, the journalist who'd been taking notes all night approached me and, after introducing himself, asked if I had time to answer a few more questions. I recognized his name. The front-page article he'd written about Y2Y two days earlier had been titled "Us versus Them."

"Thanks for setting the record straight," he said. "I learned a lot tonight."

Justin and I looked at each other. We knew we would never be able to repair all the damage inflicted by the Forest Alliance's smear campaign, but we were encouraged by the progress we'd made in just one day.

That first Prince George presentation marked the end of an intense five months for both Justin and me. I had walked 2,200 kilometres of the Big Wild, but in some ways Justin had had the more difficult summer. He had organized more than 60 presentations and 100 media interviews, had navigated an overloaded minivan over 30,000 kilometres of dirt roads and busy highways, had taken only five days off in 150, had slept all of his nights on floors or in forestry road ditches, and had been paid a fraction of what he deserved. Now, he could take a break at last. He would hitchhike north to visit a friend, while I would drive back south alone to Canmore, where I would plan, fund-raise, and ready the food for the final push to the Yukon. Unfortunately, Justin wouldn't rejoin the project when it was time to move north again. He needed a job with a decent salary, and he'd found a good, permanent position almost right away. While I skied and hiked the following year, Justin would be farming wind in southern Alberta.

The half-hour drive to Prince George's city limits didn't give me enough time to thank him for all he'd done, but I tried anyway. Ironically, it was the Forest Alliance that allowed us to part feeling better about our work than ever. "How was it," we asked ourselves as we wove through the pulp mills and lumber yards on the outskirts of town, "that two young activists on a shoestring budget could send billion-dollar multinational companies scrambling to respond?" Despite all the damage it was causing the Y2Y initiative, the Alliance's campaign had had one unexpected positive effect: the two of us believed, more strongly than ever, that it is possible to make a difference.

I hadn't minded hiking alone for extended sections between Yellowstone and Jasper, but to continue north the next year without the safety of a companion would be foolish, especially during the month-long ski traverse along the Continental Divide to Monkman Provincial Park. And so, months earlier, I'd put out the word to friends that I was in search of ski partners. Within weeks, Jay Honeyman and Leanne Allison – two friends I'd done week-long ski trips with before – had eagerly signed up.

I'd known Jay for five years, first as a fellow park ranger, then as a friend with whom I'd climbed, hiked, paddled, and skied. No matter what, Jay could be counted on for level-headed decisions, a handy skill for all the times he'd rescued injured climbers and skiers as a ranger, as well as for the expeditions he'd been on to in Peru, Alaska, and Canada's north. At heart Jay was an adventurer. For him, the prospect of being out on skis for a month, following a rugged route devoid of roads or people, was the opportunity of a lifetime.

Leanne's spirit of adventure was just as strong, a quality that had drawn us together when we had been in kindergarten together.

When we met again sixteen years later, we'd discovered that both of us were skiing, hiking, climbing, kayaking, and canoeing in the mountains at every opportunity. But while I'd dabbled on day trips from the city, Leanne had been in Mexico and Ecuador climbing high-altitude volcanoes, in Antarctica guiding scientists on glaciers, and on Mount Logan as part of the first all-women's team to climb the East Ridge of Canada's highest peak. It had been Leanne who took me on my first overnight ski trip, and it was Leanne on the other end of the rope when I'd first set foot on a glacier. With her and Jay, I couldn't have a stronger team for the journey ahead.

It was more than just the ski section that I was worried about doing alone. The area I would be crossing the following summer was very remote, and would include a month-and-a-half-long walk through the largest roadless area in all of British Columbia. I needed a companion, someone who was strong both physically and mentally and could be an equal in making decisions about routes and river crossings. Although tempted by the idea, Jay and the others I asked couldn't get the time off work that summer. Only Leanne took the invitation seriously.

"It'll be great," I said when I phoned her in Vancouver. "After the ski section is over, you can just stay on and we'll hike the final 1,000 kilometres to the Yukon. I've heard nothing but incredible stories about the wildlife up there," I continued, adding that biologists who had been there called it the Serengetti of North America.

"Well, uh . . ."

"Think about it," I encouraged after a few moments of silence, "and let me know in a few weeks."

Securing a leave of absence from where she worked at a Vancouver outdoor store had been the easy part, she later said. The bigger issue was the time she would be apart from Brian, the man she'd been living with for the past five years.

A few weeks later Leanne and Brian stopped by Canmore on a trip east. Leanne held his arm, her blue eyes dancing and smiling as the two of them stood in the doorway. She was coming to the Yukon.

"Have you looked at the route in detail yet?" Jay asked one December morning.

"I'm working on it," I assured him from somewhere amid the confusion of maps, computer hardware, dried food, and camping gear that filled the extra room where I was staying in his and his girl-friend's condominium. An old foamie stood against the wall, and each night I unrolled it into the six feet of floor space most easily cleared of pre-trip clutter. Then began an hour of lying awake and worrying. The fundraising wasn't going as smoothly as I had antici-pated; new press kits still had to be written; presentations needed to be scheduled; and months of food still had to be dried and cached along a route that lacked road access and was buried in snow.

Leanne returned for another visit, and together with Jay, we mapped our route north of Jasper, boldly drawing lines and arrows along ridges and across valleys that, to our knowledge, had never been skied before. We had all completed week-long traverses of other mountain ranges but never anything so long or remote. And travelling during the winter introduced a number of dangers that hadn't factored into earlier sections of the hike. Snow avalanches, unsafe lake and river ice, ski equipment failure, and constant sub-zero temperatures all increased the likelihood of a mishap. The length and remote nature of this ski trip would only accentuate those dangers. What if someone got injured? What if an animal ate one of the food caches on which our lives depended? There would be no way of calling for help should something go wrong. The entire route was out of cell-phone range and had no radio coverage, and our tight budget precluded a satellite phone. We were an experi-enced group, but still green when it came to a trip like this. We needed some advice.

I had met Don Gardner a year earlier, at the trailhead to a popular glacier ski circuit just west of Calgary. He was sorting through a milkcrate of faded and threadbare gear in the back of an old beat-up car.

"Where are you headed?" I asked him as a friend and I set off on skis from the parking lot.

"Oh, up the French Glacier, down the Haig, up the Palliser River and then eventually back over Burstall Pass," said the stocky man. His eyes twinkled as he spoke and his skin was dark from the sun. It was only the white hairs that poked out from his wool cap that gave a hint of his age.

"How many nights you going out for?" I asked, suspiciously eyeing his tiny pack. A few years earlier I'd backpacked a portion of the sixty-kilometre-long trip Gardner described, and it had taken me three full days.

"No, no, we're not heading out overnight," he assured me. "It's a day trip."

I learned a lot that morning. While my friend Alex and I laboured uphill with heavy metal-edged skis, climbing skins, and plastic boots, Don and his friend Neil Liskey, both of them twice my age, shot past us on thin, lightweight skis and low-cut leather boots from the 1970s. Using little more than ski wax to climb with, they had danced ahead of us, winding a sensuous route across small benches, ramps, and weaknesses, fairly floating up the mountain while Alex and I pushed a slow, arduous route right up the middle of the glacier. When we finally reached the top, the two men were specks in the distance.

"That trip I met you on last year, did you manage to do it all in one day?" I asked when I reached him on the phone.

"Oh sure," he answered matter-of-factly, and, after describing it in some detail, went on to say that it wasn't the destination that counted, but finding the melody of the mountains. "It's about rhythm, not about getting to the top, to the pass, or back to the car."

Gardner's trademark was travelling light. In 1992 he had stuffed a light nylon jacket, a down coat, a pair of extra socks, a sleeping bag, and some food into his pack and, after walking out the back door of his downtown Calgary house, had set out on skis along the shore ice of the Elbow River. Two days later he'd come to the first of twenty mountain passes he would cross over the next twenty-eight days, completing the first ski traverse of western Alberta and British Columbia on a whim. By sleeping in tree wells instead of in a tent, and by lighting small fires instead of a camp stove, Gardner had reduced the weight of his pack to less than thirty pounds for the 900-kilometre-long trip to the Pacific Ocean. Despite being alone, he'd averaged more than thirty kilometres per day. Jay, Leanne, and I, on the other hand, hoped to average only half that daily distance, even though there would be three of us to share the work of breaking trail.

"Now don't get any crazy ideas about how we're going to do our trip," warned Jay when I told him of my conversation with Don. "I'm not going anywhere with you and Leanne unless we have a tent. Crawling in holes under trees and sleeping in the soot of a campfire while the snow blows down my back isn't my idea of a good time. That's living like a rat!"

"Ah yes, living like a rat," sighed Gardner when I told him about Jay's comment a week later. "I like that."

I had taken him up on an offer to help me ski in one of the food caches, and he'd arrived in Canmore early, ready for the long drive to where we would begin skiing near McBride, British Columbia. "We'll do this the light way," he'd said. "No tent, no stove, no climbing skins." I'd managed to find a second-hand pair of old skinny skis for $25 the day before, and I showed them off proudly to Don before I slipped them beside his and closed the door to the van.

It took us six hours to drive to the small town of McBride, where we met Roy Howard, a local conservationist I'd met at a Y2Y meeting. After a short visit with Roy and his family, we left the van behind and borrowed his four-wheel-drive truck. It was dusk as we drove the narrow forestry road up the Morkill Valley, and by the time we reached the active clear-cuts at the end of it, our nerves were raw from a close call on a blind corner with a pickup full of loggers. Exhausted, I began fishing through my pack for some dinner and a sleeping bag.

"Eat? Sleep? C'mon, let's go!" Don said excitedly. It was dark, a time of day when most people would consider it too late to pitch camp, let alone start moving, but who was I to argue in the company of such experience? I stuffed my sleeping bag back into my pack, and after tying one of the two five-gallon metal pails that made up the food cache onto my pack, donned my skis and slid off after Don into the black forest.

The Morkill is one of a group of about twenty watersheds nestled between the Rocky and Cariboo mountains that, along with a wet strip in the main valley of the Fraser River, form Canada's largest inland rainforest, a magical place of giant cedar and hemlock trees and hanging lichens. There are smaller pockets of such antique forests elsewhere in the Y2Y region – in Idaho and near Revelstoke, British Columbia, for example – but none of them offers what the Fraser Headwaters still does: a place where the ancient paths of grizzlies, mountain caribou, and ocean-run salmon still cross in the shadows of thousand-year-old trees.

I thought of those salmon as the sound of the Morkill River drifted to where Don and I were making our way through the forest by headlamp. Every fall, they would arrive here, tired but determined after having made one of the world's longest salmon runs. Following pure instinct, they would turn off the slow-moving Fraser and into the cool, oxygen-rich tributaries of the Morkill, Goat, Raush, Holmes, Small, and other rivers in search of clean gravel to lay their eggs. Then they would die and feed the eagles, bears, wolves, ravens, coyotes, and countless other inland animals with rich ocean nutrients.

Until a few years earlier, the Morkill had been one of only three watersheds in the region that hadn't yet been developed. But the fifty-five-kilometre-long road Don and I had driven up had changed all that, and judging by the amount of flagging tape that fluttered from the trees as we skied upstream, it would soon be pushed farther up the hundred-kilometre-long valley. Of the other two still-wild drainages, the upper Goat was scheduled for cutting the following year, and the largest unprotected and undeveloped watershed left in all of southern British Columbia – the Raush – was scheduled for a road soon after that.

Don and I didn't get far that evening, and it took another half day of following the river and crashing through tangles of trees before we left the last of the flagging tape behind. I was struggling to keep up with Don who, despite moving fast, still had enough breath left over to talk without end. While I gasped behind him, he reeled off one story after another, snippets from a life of someone who's done everything from building trails and perfect replicas of native arte-facts to designing fetish wear for women. It wasn't until we were halfway up the river and forced to climb steeply around a canyon that the stories about birchbark canoes and Olympic ski courses eased and then stopped. While I negotiated slippery rock steps beside a water-fall and the tightly spaced trees of a regenerating burn, Don shot off ahead, leaving me rushing to catch up. After another half-hour, I found him poking at a hole under a giant spruce tree that was deep enough to swallow his ski pole.

"Well, it's not perfect but it'll have to do," Don announced, explaining that the tree well was a bit small and the branches a bit too thick to make an ideal camp. We packed the edges of the hole to make it a little wider, broke off a few dead branches, and started a small fire. We were too tired to do much more than stare at the flames and nibble at a few crackers. By eight o'clock, we were in our sleeping bags, asleep in the snow.

The next day, we threaded the last ten kilometres to where we dropped the food, working our way across one snow bridge after another, thankful that they didn't collapse under us into the bright blue water that churned below. By lunch, we were far enough up the Morkill that it was more of a creek than a river, and in the distance, we could see the Continental Divide – the line of white ridges that Leanne, Jay, and I would ski in another month.

"It looks incredible," said Don. "Nothing like the Cascades." Later that spring he would be returning to the Cascades in southern Washington State for the next leg of his latest project – a bid to ski from his door in Calgary to Disneyland California.

"Why Disneyland?" I asked, noticing old wolverine and pine marten tracks beside us as we hung forty pounds of food and fuel in a tree and flagged it. I hoped the metal pails would keep our food secure from all inquiring teeth and claws.

Don smiled. "You're heading to the Yukon. I'm off to Disneyland. Buddhists flock to the slopes of Mount Kilash in Tibet. We're all on pilgrimages of one kind or another." For him, Disneyland was the icon of North American culture. It embodied everything that our society worships: consumerism, materialism, commodifying animals and other parts of the natural world. He was going there to understand the madness from within.

Relieved of our loads, Don and I turned and raced down our broken trail. It was hard to stay with him, but I did my best, my legs and arms whirring and pumping to keep up. We hollered in delight as our skis shot over snowy boulders, past waterfalls and holes of green water roaring beneath two metres of late-winter snow.

"Oh Canada!" shouted Don, revelling in the flight of body and mind.

"Oh Canada!" I sang as the tracks of wolf, lynx, and wolverines appeared and fell away behind us.

"Oh Canada!" Don gasped, suddenly disappearing over a pillow of snow and a sheer drop hidden behind it. I crept to the edge and looked over the ten-foot cliff in time to see him shoot around the corner, still carrying speed after having somehow stuck the landing.

The next afternoon, figures obscured by smoke were burning slash piles when we emerged from the forest at the place where we'd left the truck. We stopped to chat to the friendly loggers, asking them about all the cables and pulleys strung up the mountainside did, while they asked us about the country where we'd been. But our conversation was soon lost in the roar of machinery as logs came skidding out of the forest. Dumping our skis and packs into the back of Roy's muddy truck, we knocked the last clumps of snow off our boots and clambered into the cab.

"Hang on, hang on!" barked Don as I turned over the engine and slid the gearshift into reverse. Leaping out, he grabbed a handful of snow and began to scrub at the back bumper. The dirt and mud fell away, revealing an old sticker. I honked the horn and a few of the loggers looked. "SAVE THE RAUSH" it read.

"Okay," said Don as he hoisted himself back into the seat. "We can go now."

I returned to the Fraser headwaters two weeks later to put in another cache at the head of the Holmes River, this time with the help of the truck's owner, Roy Howard. I arrived at his house to find him wrestling with the carburetor for one of the two old snowmobiles we would use to get partway along an unploughed logging road the next morning. I mentioned the cutting Don and I had seen up the Morkill.

"There's no doubt logging is central to everything around here," Roy said in his soft-spoken manner. "The problem isn't logging, though. It's the rate at which it's occurring."

Roy's life was based on the principle of sustainability. He had built his own log house from carefully selected trees, put up solar panels and a windmill, and installed a high-efficiency wood heater, a well-insulated refrigerator, and a composting toilet. They had all been costly undertakings, but by making a plan and sticking to it for twenty-five years, he and his family were finally at a point where they lived with minimal impact. Meanwhile, the provincial government continued to set forest harvest targets that, by its own admission, exceeded sustainable levels by 70 per cent.

"It's crazy," Roy said, looking up from the carburetor. "It's like eating the food for a year-long expedition in the first four months!"

It turned out that Roy had done a fair bit of logging and timber cruising over the past twenty-five years, along with just about every other trade in the valley. A handy guy to have along on the trip, I thought as he dug out the snowmobile I would use from three feet of snow. Three hours later he had the old rusted machine running and, by the light of a flashlight, he fastened a pair of heavy old downhill skis to the bottom of a makeshift plywood sled.

Despite all the late-night preparations, we didn't get going until 11 o'clock the next morning. I looked at my watch and sized up the two old machines and rickety sled with trepidation. To drop the cache at Bess Pass and get back, we would have to ride more than sixty kilometres, break trail on skis for another five, and climb 700 metres. Roy waved off my doubts with a quiet, patient shrug. "Sure, it's late, but we're ready to go so we might as well give it a try."

At more than six feet and 250 pounds, Roy spilled over his snowmobile as he rode ahead of me. The screwdrivers and vice grips he'd used for the last-minute carb adjustments still poked out of the pockets of his heavy wool pants. A home-painted hard hat, robbed of a snug fit by his woollen cap, towered off his head.

"Everything okay?" he shouted over his shoulder. I nodded, straining to see his eyes through the scratched lenses of the woodworking glasses he was using as ski goggles. Next to Roy's outfit, the expensive Gore-Tex jacket, ski pants, and gloves that I wore were embarrassing.

Two hours later, we stopped at the foot of the rocky peaks that cradled Bess Pass and listened to the last echoes of the cut engines.

The logging road continued up a side drainage where more clear-cuts were visible in the distance.

"It's pretty trashed," said Roy, adding that about half of the sixty-kilometre-long valley we had just ridden through had been cut in two operations over the last thirty years. "But not a complete write-off." I remembered the map he had shown me the night before, and his dream that, along with the unroaded Raush Valley, the Holmes would someday form a recognized wildlife connection between the protected areas on either side of the upper Fraser Valley. He was talking about Jasper, Kakwa, Mount Robson Provincial Park, and the Willmore Wilderness on the Rockies side; and Wells Grey, Bowron Lakes, and Cariboo Provincial Park in the Columbia Mountains. Despite all the logging in the Holmes, there was still reason to hope for such a corridor – at least for carnivores. Already we had seen the fresh tracks of a wolf pack in the upper reaches of the valley and, higher up, near the cache, I would spot the spoor of lynx and wolverine.

"We tried to promote the connection, as well as one that followed the Goat and Morkill rivers farther to the north," Roy said as he began unloading some of the food cache off the sled and into his pack. He was referring to the Land Resources Management Process (LRMP), a government-sponsored, round-table planning exercise whose success in balancing wildlife protection with human use had been widely applauded by the conservation community farther north in areas like Fort Nelson, British Columbia. But the process had failed miserably in the Fraser Headwaters. "It was like wildlife science and conservation weren't even at the table," Roy lamented. "There wasn't even a compromise. Forestry got everything they wanted."

Part of the problem, he explained, was the 12 per cent target for land protection set by the United Nations World Commission on the Environment in 1987. Back then, the consensus of experts was that protecting 12 per cent of the world's habitat would be sufficient to stave off most species extinctions, provided their other needs – things like clean air and clean water – were also met. It had seemed a good thing at the time: one by one, countries and provinces had committed to the target and, over the years, had started to protect a little of their lands. But expert consensus had changed a lot in ten years. New knowledge on genetics, the effects of large-scale disturbances, and wildlife movements had resulted in new targets. The most recent thinking was that between 25 and 75 per cent of any landscape would have to be somehow conserved if it were to support its native plants and animals. Meanwhile, government goals hadn't changed, nor had they yet given up the idea of individual parks in favour of protected networks.

The situation was especially bad in the Fraser Headwaters. By including Mount Robson, Kakwa, Bowron Lakes, and Wells Grey Provincial Parks in their calculations, officials with the local Forest District had concluded that 20 per cent of the area had already been protected. No matter that much of the protected area was rock and ice. The 12 per cent goal had been exceeded, and from their standpoint, there was no need to protect more or even to create connections.

Nightfall was only two hours away when Roy and I shouldered our heavy loads and climbed towards the pass, gingerly breaking a route across avalanche slide paths and into the cleft of a steep creek. My metal-edged skis bit into the slope but Roy was struggling on his snowshoes. After half an hour, he passed me the pail he'd been carrying and headed back to the snowmobiles.

The creek became steeper until I found myself weaving a tight, almost vertical path through huge, snow-covered boulders. I tried to memorize where the leg-breaking logs and rocks were for what promised to be a wild run down. Finally, near the top, I kicked steps up beside a frozen waterfall, then broke onto a flat bench with trees that were perfect for stowing the cache. I looked back and saw Roy as a spot, working his way down the jumble of snowy blocks far below.

By the time I had all three pails hung and the trees marked, the last of the sunshine had faded off the peaks and I was bathed in the glow of winter twilight. I shuffled to the edge of the bench, looked down the mountainside, took a deep breath, then pushed off with my poles.

It was something more than memory that led me down that creek bed safely. Back and forth I swung, dropping down a ladder of boulders, my skis flowing through the gaps and crevices like water running off a mountain. When I arrived at the cut-block where Roy had the snowmobiles ready, I was shaking with adrenaline.

"Yeah, it's getting cold and late," he said, not realizing why I was shivering. "We'd better get moving." The last light of day faded in the first few kilometres, and the world was soon nothing more than what the weak snowmobile lights illuminated – a wedge of trees, a flash of rock, glimpses of colour dancing past into the blackness behind.

Halfway down the valley, a moose staggered towards us, mesmerized by the lights. Checking the engines, we sat in the darkness, shouting until it moved off towards the river.

"You sure are lucky living around here," I said quietly. I was thinking of the moose, the wolves, the lynx, and the wolverine that roamed the dark spaces around us.

But Roy didn't answer. He just sat in the dark somewhere beside me, listening.

My persistence was finally starting to pay off, I realized when I got back to Canmore. It was mid-February and, after a frustrating few months of sending off unanswered queries, my fundraising efforts were getting results. Three of our previous five sponsors had renewed their support, and a week later, I received more good news from two new funders.

With financing in place, I could finally concentrate on other business. Eager to get involved again, Erica quit her job and assumed Justin's old role as publicist. Together we rewrote the press kits and scheduled presentations for the fall. Then, two weeks before leaving, I focused on getting the last two food caches in for the ski section. At Roy's suggestion I called the Park Ranger office in Prince George. As luck would have it, they were scheduled to snowmobile into one of their patrol cabins at Kakwa Lake in the next two weeks and, given the purpose of our trip, were happy to take a cache in for us.

"We'll leave it in the cabin," the ranger said. "You won't need to worry about wolverines getting at it in there, but you should be concerned about snowmobilers. On some spring weekends, hundreds of them ride in from the Alberta side." Before shipping the pails to him, I grabbed a large felt pen and printed our names and address on them in big block letters and the message, "PLEASE DO NOT TAMPER WITH CONTENTS. THEY ARE CRITICAL TO SKIERS' SURVIVAL."

Getting in the final food cache was the most problematic. The location, near the head of Wapiti River, was not accessible from the west, and to access it from the east, I would have to drive eight hours to the beginning of the Alaska Highway and ski in for four days. With only a week left before we were scheduled to leave, I was running out of time.

"You might want to try a friend of mine named Bryan," said Wayne Sawchuk, a trapper and conservationist in northern British Columbia whom I'd met at a Y2Y meeting the winter before. "He loves sledding and has explored a lot of the country up around there. If there's anyone you can trust to get your cache in, it'll be him." I was reluctant to have anyone put in a food cache on our behalf, but with only a week left, I had no choice.

"Oh yeah, one more thing," said Wayne as I jotted down Bryan's number. "He's a forester, and although he generally supports the Y2Y concept, I think he figures the area of interest up here shouldn't stretch quite so far east into all the merchantable timber."

I managed to reach Bryan by phone a day later.

"Yeah, Wayne told me about you yesterday. I understand you need some help."

"Yes, but I need to be up front with you about our purpose," I began.

"I've heard all about it," he interrupted. "Wayne has filled me in on Y2Y, so I know a little more than what the Forest Alliance would like people to believe." I relaxed. After chatting a little while longer, I explained our predicament. "Well, which way do you intend to go?" he asked.

I reeled off the names of passes and peaks.

"That might work," Bryan said, "or you might want to think about the next drainage north. Fewer willows." His intimate knowledge of the area was obvious.

"You're no ordinary sledder, are you?"

"No, I guess not," he chuckled. "My friends and I aren't interested in the high-marking and shredding through the alpine that motivates most other snowmobilers. We're pretty much driven by the same sorts of things as folks like you are. We like to poke our noses into unknown valleys and corners of the country to see if they're as beautiful as we imagine from the maps." He went on to describe a 400-kilometre-long trip he and two friends had done the year before just south of the Yukon border.

"You must know your machines pretty well," I commented, thinking about the danger of mechanical failure far from any help.

"Yeah, each of us has simplified our machines significantly," he said. "It makes 'em easier to pack around."

"Pack around?"

"Yeah, you know, like portaging a canoe." He laughed at my surprise. On a number of trips, they had taken their machines apart and carried them, in pieces, over ridges and through broken cliffs, he explained. One year, they'd gone so far as to winch them up a frozen waterfall.

"I hope that getting our cache in will be a little more straightforward," I said.

"Yeah, no problem. And I'll be sure to flag it well. I'll mark the spot and fax you a map."

"Listen, I really appreciate your help," I said at the end of the conversation. "I don't have much money, but at the bare minimum, I want to reimburse you for your time and gas."

"Don't worry about it. I'm glad to help out. Anyone putting in so much effort to see the country deserves the support."

I hung up the phone and sat back smiling. With the last food cache arranged, we were ready to go. In five days, we would set out from Jasper on skis.

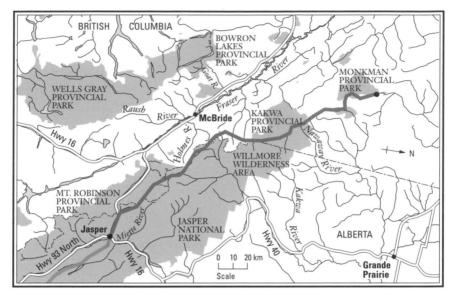

Jasper, Alberta, to Kinuseo Falls, British Columbia – 450 kilometres

8

The trip's character was about to change. There would be no bridged river crossings or signed trail junctions the rest of the way to the Yukon, no nearby park rangers or wardens should something go wrong.

"Compass, maps, headlamp?"

"Check."

"Probe, shovel, avalanche beacon?"

"Yes."

"Binding repair kit?"

"Got it."

"Ski wax? Down jacket?"

Jay and Leanne rolled their eyes in exasperation. We'd been through everything umpteen times. After a few last-minute adjustments, they shouldered their packs and poled off. I stayed behind a few minutes to say goodbye properly to Webster and my sister before they returned to Canmore.

It was always difficult to leave Webster behind. He had watched us pack and repack over the last few days, all the while guarding the door of Jay's condo so he couldn't be forgotten. But the snow would be too deep, the weather too cold, and even if he was swimming up to his head while we floated on top of the snow on skis, I knew he would kill himself before giving up. He had joined me while I skied the twenty-five kilometres between Jasper and our trailhead the day before, but it had been little consolation for a dog that yearned to come on the entire trip.

"No," I told him, while giving a few last pats to his head. "You have to stay."

The way he glared at me said that he knew full well what "stay" and "can't" meant. He slumped on the seat in disappointment. I gave him one last hug and headed off to catch up with Leanne and Jay.

The rumble of the highway and railway softened with each step, and after fifteen minutes things were quiet enough to hear the breaking of branches as a cow moose lumbered out of the willows and onto the trail ahead of us. We followed her heart-shaped tracks for a few hundred metres along the river, then began the slow, two-day climb to Miette Pass. Soon all we could hear was the sound of skis scraping across the snow.

It felt good to have a pack on again, to be moving, but it wasn't long before I felt the effects of a winter off. I'd gained weight, lost strength, and was stiff from too much sitting. I fiddled with my pack's shoulder straps and hip belt, trying to ease the strain of the seventy-pound load, but it was no use. There was no shortcut past all the pain of starting out again. The dues I'd paid back in the Gallatin Mountains almost a year earlier would have to be paid again.

Of the three of us, Jay seemed the most fit. Working as a park ranger, he'd been skiing almost every day that winter, patrolling trails and digging snow pits to assess avalanche danger. Maybe he'd been doing too much, though; he was tired and run down. Leanne, on the other hand, had been working a desk job in Vancouver, and city life had made her a little soft. When we broke out of the forest two days later and made our way to the warden cabin buried in drifts below Miette Pass, she was struggling. Like me, her muscles ached, but her boots were giving her problems as well. When she pulled off her socks in the cabin that night, her heels and toes were red with blisters.

"Twenty-five kilometres down, 425 to go," she said grimly. Jay dozed on one of the plywood bunks behind the wood stove while I absent-mindedly massaged my hips, listening to the wind squeeze through the cracks in the cabin's log walls. The skies had been grey and dark since leaving Jasper, and the storm that continued to blow outside only heightened our gloom.

The cloud lifted a little the next morning, which helped, but it was the wolverine tracks near the summit of the pass that really lifted our spirits. We'd seen plenty of signs of hares, martens, grouse, and ptarmigans on our way up the Miette Valley, but the saucer-sized prints left behind by the king of the weasel family – paired in a characteristic two-by-two, bounding pattern – sent a bolt of wildness through our hearts. I couldn't have drawn a more aesthetic line than the one it had etched across the snowy landscape. Every roll, bench, ramp, and weakness in the terrain had been used to its advantage.

"And you thought our route up was a good one," said Jay when we reached the sunny crest of the pass and looked back from where we'd come. Inspired by Don, we tried to make our route as musical as possible. But next to the hymn-like rhythm and cadence left by the wolverine, our own zigzag looked like the score of some heavy-metal number. The contrast was embarrassing, and when we pushed down the other side of Miette Pass into Colonel Creek, we stuck close to the wolverine's tracks. The beginnings of a notion that we could learn from such a seasoned wanderer had been planted in our heads.

Beauty isn't the first thing that comes to mind when people think of the wolverine. The thirty- to forty-pound animal is renowned for its ability to rob traps and ransack cabins, for its voracious appetite, for its ability to chew through steel and three-foot-thick logs, and for its fierceness when cornered. Glutton, caracajou, devil bear, trap robber – there are as many nicknames for the wolverine as there are stories of its mythical strength and raw determination, but because it inhabits such remote areas, and because it is so elusive, little of what has been written about it is fact. What scientific studies have discovered about the animal, however, only heightens its mystique, especially when it comes to its ability to travel. One radio-collared individual, for example, averaged more than thirty kilometres a day through rough terrain and deep snow for seven days straight – a feat that the most conditioned and well-outfitted skier would have trouble matching. Indeed, as we followed the tracks over the next two days, over Miette and Colonel passes and down into Mount Robson Provincial Park and the Moose River, it became apparent that we moved more slowly than the tireless animal that loped ahead. The five-toed prints aged as we moved north, getting a little more blown in and a little less crisp from the warm sun and blowing wind.

Despite two days of marvelling at the wolverine's endurance and choice of line, we remained attached to our plans, never wandering far from the route we'd pencilled onto the maps months before. And so when the wolverine tracks abruptly left that path and climbed off the river ice into the steep trees, we attributed the change in direction to a whim and blundered blithely on up the river.

A kilometre or so after the tracks had clambered up into the trees, the highway of ice narrowed and the steep riverbanks became cliffs. A deep twisting canyon lay before us, and short of turning back, our only choice was to work through the labyrinth of frozen waterfalls and shelves of ice that hung over the dark pools of water ahead.

"How does it look?" Jay shouted as I balanced across two iced-over logs.

"Pretty good. A couple more tricky moves and we might be home free."

"Might?" He and Leanne traded skeptical glances from where they stood fifteen metres back.

"Well, I can't quite see around the corner," I admitted.

While they followed, I continued edging my way around more open pools on tiny nubbins and ledges of rock. It was tough work, and I took off my poles and gloves to better grip the cold, slick sides of the water-worn canyon. With seventy pounds on my back and wearing heavy winter clothing and ski boots, it was some of the most demanding rock-climbing I had ever attempted.

There was a three-metre-high waterfall around the corner, and after kicking steps up an adjacent curtain of snow and ice, I put my skis back on and shuffled up the canyon to see what lay ahead. It was worse: another waterfall three times as high, guarded by a deep plunge-pool that crackled with chunks of ice. I looked back to where Jay and Leanne were still climbing up the last drop and grappled with my apprehension. The only way forward was along an airy system of snow and rock shelves that skirted the drop about halfway up the fifteen-metre-high canyon walls. After taking off my skis again, I kicked steps up a narrow snow gully that brought me to the first metre-wide snow ledge. Was it one that clung to the wall unsupported, or one that sat on top of a rock ledge? I struggled to recall what I'd seen from below, but in the end, stepped onto the narrow platform not knowing if it would hold fast or tumble into the water seven metres below.

It held. Still, crawling seemed the best way to move along the ledge system, spreading my weight over four limbs instead of two, hoping against hope that whatever held the snowy ledges in place – rock, ice, or air – was strong enough to hold me as well. I squeezed against the side of the canyon and slithered along, carefully looking ahead, not down. Images of catastrophe, of falling into the water and drowning as the slow current pulled me under the ice, flashed through my head. Focus, I told myself. Time slowed to an eternity as I crawled along until finally I hit solid ice. I had reached the top of the water-fall. The route had held.

"It goes!" I screamed down to Jay and Leanne. Ahead, I could clearly see the rest of the canyon and a straightforward route out. But they were still in danger. I watched, horrified, as they made their way up the gully and stepped onto what I'd assumed was snow-covered rock. In truth, whole sections of the route were supported by nothing but metres of air. It was a skywalk held together by the friction of snow on vertical rock.

"Spread out," I shouted, trying not to sound concerned. If something went wrong, if either of them died or got injured, I would be to blame. It was a risky and irresponsible route. I held my breath as they made their way across, half of me wanting to shout encouragement, the other wanting them to turn back. In the end, I didn't say anything, just stood there. They moved across in slow motion until, finally, they were beside me on firm ground.

"That," said Leanne looking back after I gave her and Jay a relief-filled hug, "was a miracle of stupidity."

Not long after we'd climbed clear of the cliffs and continued upstream, the wolverine tracks re-emerged from the trees.

"Well, whad'ya know," said Jay with heavy sarcasm, "there was another way around." All of us knew then that it had been a mistake to ignore the animal's wisdom, and we vowed to be more open to what wolverines might teach us in the coming weeks.

There were more wolverine tracks over the next few days, not all left by the same animal, and not all travelling in the same direction, but always offering another lesson about moving with grace through the mountains. Across flood plains they sought out the best ice, in the forests they gravitated to the consolidated snow, and as we learned along the Smokey River two days later, they consistently avoided canyons. We didn't hesitate to follow the tracks that time, readily abandoning the easy travelling we'd had along the river for a snarl of thick, clothes-tugging timber.

Bushwhacking is a whole lot easier for a half-metre-high wolverine than for a person on two-metre-long skis. After a half-hour of rattling through tight trees and bringing down a rain of snow, we couldn't help but question if we'd done the right thing. But the view from the canyon rim a few minutes later told us that the discomfort of cold necks and wet backs was worth it. We'd avoided another treacherous maze of rock and open water that, this time, ended in an impassable ring of bluffs and vertical blue ice.

In following their tracks, we caught a rare glimpse of the wolverines' wild and desperate lives. Behind Mount Robson, for example, we came across a deep trench excavated by one that had smelled a few frozen bones from an old kill through two metres of snow. And along the Smokey River, we stumbled upon the tattered hide of one that had met an untimely death. It was difficult to tell what had happened. The tracks from the skirmish had been trampled over by the steady procession of ravens and coyotes that had flocked to the site since. Not a scrap of meat, not a bone, not even the skull remained; everything but blood stains and its hide had been carried away.

More scavenger than predator, the wolverine is frequently at odds with other, much larger carnivores. Stories abound about its ferocious ability to push grizzly bears, wolves, and others off their kills, but new research – some of the first done on the elusive animals – sheds new light on the old tales. During a four-year study of nineteen animals in central Idaho in the 1990s, for example, almost half had died, either killed by cougars or from other, unknown causes. If this mortality rate were typical, then, given their low birth rates (females produce an average of less than one kit per year), it is easy to understand why wolverines – like grizzlies, wolves, cougars, and lynx – are threatened by extinction. Even in wild and undisturbed areas, there just aren't many of the animals around.

Wolverines have disappeared from roughly 40 per cent of their historic range in North America, the greatest loss having occurred in the southern United States. All that remains lies in relatively undeveloped mountains, which suggests a low tolerance for human activity. Indeed, recent research has shown that something as benign as a backcountry skier shuffling within a few hundred metres of where a wolverine mother is nursing her kits might cause her to abandon the den.

Wolverines are believed to still range across much of the Y2Y region, but not in great numbers: the status of pocket populations in Montana, Wyoming, and Idaho is uncertain, and their numbers in southern Alberta and British Columbia appear to be declining.

It's the same old problem. Like other wide-travelling animals, wolverines need thousands of square kilometres of space to survive. One male radio-collared in the mountains of northeastern British Columbia covered 7,500 square kilometres in a single year – an area larger than Banff National Park. The tracks we were finding in every valley and pass since leaving the Yellowhead Highway a week earlier had, in all likelihood, been left by only two or three animals.

Compared to their weight seven days earlier, our packs felt empty as we turned off the Smokey River and skied up Chown Creek in the northwest corner of Jasper National Park. Although it meant heavy loads of food and stove fuel to pack the next morning, we were all happy to find the cache that I'd stashed with Roy at Bess Pass hanging undisturbed in the tree. Without wasting time, we opened the three airtight metal tins and began what became a tradition at every food cache of the trip: we spread our new riches on the snow in front of us and celebrated the bounty with the bottle of whisky inside. It wasn't long before we were all a little drunk.

"Honeyman, you sure could have used a set of wolverine tracks to follow this afternoon," quipped Leanne as she passed Jay the bottle. He had lost his bearings in the thick trees and convoluted hillocks of Chown Creek and had led us in a kilometre-wide circle. All three of us had been surprised to find fresh ski tracks in the remote valley and had laughed ourselves silly when we'd realized they were our own. As Leanne ribbed him, Jay was embarrassed all over again, his stubbled face blushing.

"All right, all right," he said good-naturedly when she stopped. "We still have three weeks to go. We'll see if no one else makes the same mistake."

We should have set up camp before drinking the whisky. The patch we finally managed to stamp into the snow was less than flat, but with all of us enjoying a buzz, it didn't seem to matter. Within moments of pitching the tent and climbing into our sleeping bags, we passed out.

The next morning dawned clear, and we were out of the tent at first light to pack quickly and get moving. The sun, which was creeping down the flanks of the highest peaks, was the reason for our haste. Soon it would heat the start zones of every avalanche path we needed to cross that day. If our map reading and interpretation of aerial photographs were right, there was a route around the shoulder of Mount Bess that, if it worked, would save us a 600-metre climb out of the Holmes River Valley. The risk in the whole plan was the exposure. If an avalanche did come down, there would be little hope of any of us surviving the long ride.

MARCH 23 – *Bess Mountain, British Columbia – I wish we could have a bird's-eye view of where we are in this maze of cliffs and steep couloirs. I feel small on these slopes, looking up, always looking up, waiting for the world to come crashing down. All around us are reminders of the dangers we court, places where the debris from past avalanches lies in jumbles of broken trees and chunks of ice and snow. It's impossible to get across such devastation on skis, and so we crawl over them on all fours, hurrying as fast as we can. This is a deadly game we're playing, trying to crack the vertical code of a mountain while racing the sun. If I did have a bird's-eye view, it would be of three dots of colour in a tilted world of black shadow and white light.*

There were oases amid the danger – prows of protruding rock and islands of mature trees that had survived the surrounding slides for decades – and it was in those safe folds and wedges of timber and rock that we found the tracks of caribou and goats. Finally, after two hours of stressful exposure, we dropped into a chute and schussed onto a treed bench that led to solid ground beyond.

When it was safe, we looked back at the line we'd scratched across the mountain, and in the distance we heard the first rumbles. Somewhere in the sea of slopes behind us, the mountains were beginning to wake up. Rocks and ice that had been loosened by the night's frost were being freed by the morning's heat, and the debris falling off the cliffs was setting off the day's first snow slides in a chorus of thunder.

At Mount Bess, the landscape changed dramatically. The rugged peaks that had forced us over high passes and to follow long valleys in Jasper and Mount Robson parks suddenly became rolling ridges gentle enough to accommodate a traveller right on the crest of the Continental Divide. However, the surrounding peaks weren't nearly as subdued as the divide itself. There were deep-cut valleys and ragged summits on all sides, making our high path an anomaly, like some long-forgotten trade route through the chaos of mountains. For the next four days we skied along its gentle undulations, some-times travelling tightly together, sometimes far apart, with wolverine tracks and without, humming through snow squalls and sunshine in the crisp wind.

"I feel I could go on forever," I said when we were sitting around the fire at the head of Spider Creek three nights later. Jay and Leanne nodded as they stared into the flames, slowly waving one foot and then the other in the heat, watching the steam rise from their socks.

"I don't think I've ever been so comfortable travelling in winter," said Leanne. Our pattern of staying high all day and dropping down to the subalpine at night gave us the best of both worlds: skiing in stunning alpine scenery, and camping among trees with plenty of wood for a warming fire.

We were two weeks into the ski section – about halfway – and all the aches, blisters, and tiredness that had dogged us back in the Miette Valley were far in the past. I felt unstoppable as we skied the western edge of the Willmore Wilderness Area, striding with one ski in Alberta and the other in British Columbia. It wasn't our destination that motivated us any longer, it was simply the unfolding of the next view. Our travel had matured to a meditative rhythm of anticipation and awe, and we lost track of how far we'd come and how far we had left to go.

But then, three days later everything changed and the trip almost ended in disaster. It happened just shy of our second food cache, near the top of a 1,000-metre run from where we were still on the divide down to the beginnings of the Morkill River. Ahead lay an open inviting slope.

"See you slowpokes at the bottom," I said and pushed off.

The snow was perfect – light and soft, untouched by the hardening winds, and I was so enthralled with the feeling of weightlessness – of floating up and down from one turn to the next – that I not only forgot the heavy pack on my back, but also everything that can go wrong in the mountains. Back and forth I carved, dropping farther down the yawning slope until, suddenly, the world dropped away.

MARCH 27 – *Morkill River, British Columbia – Everything moves at first, all surfaces crack open, angles growing and running in all directions. I try to comprehend all the motion as I fall over, struggle to know which way is up as the snow slabs pull loose and run down the mountain. It's only when I reach out to anchor myself that I realize I'm not in it, I'm not part of the avalanche I just triggered. Clinging to the crown of a slope, I watch, thankfully, as the avalanche hisses below me, then breaks into a turbulent cloud of snow and air.*

It hadn't been a large slide – maybe enough to bury us to our waists – but it warned of a hidden and dangerous layer that had escaped our notice. Inspecting a few of the larger blocks, Leanne now found the cause of the avalanche: surface hoar. Large, plate-like crystals, virtually invisible to the naked eye, lay buried in a tiny but uniform layer. My weight had made a few of these unstable crystals shift, setting off a chain reaction.

Shaken by the close call, we moved tentatively through the debris, amazed at how the light, ski-able powder of minutes before was already hardening into solid, rock-hard blocks.

"Could one of us have ridden that one out?" I wondered aloud. Jay poked at one of the snow boulders with a ski pole and was about to answer when a flash of feathers exploded from beneath his feet.

"Ptarmigan!" he shouted, pointing to where something had landed near Leanne. The pure white pigeon-sized bird, known to dig itself into the snow for insulation in the high mountains, had been caught in the avalanche. Still stunned by the ordeal, it ignored us as we filed past; it gave a few flustered clucks, then took flight and melted into the white landscape ahead. A good omen, we figured, then carefully moved on.

Something about the mountains seems to know when you let your guard down, something that's always ready to remind those who take the risks too lightly. And so it was for us. No sooner had we started to forget the avalanche than another near-disaster struck two days later.

I got my first hint of danger when I crested the ridge above Featherstonaugh Pass. According to the map we'd studied the night before, the ridge should have dropped away into a steep but ski-able bowl. But there was no bowl to be seen, just a wide swath of snow that stretched out to a sharp horizon ten metres away.

There had been many cornices along the route so far, but none this huge, none that barred access to the slope below. The risk wasn't in the cornice itself, but in its potential to collapse without warning. Hundreds of skiers and climbers had died venturing out on similar ridge-top drifts, victims to the long falls and catastrophic avalanches that resulted when the whole thing broke off. I resisted the temptation to go look over the edge and opted, instead, to make my way to a rock promontory a few hundred metres away. Careful not to wander more than a metre from the line of rocks that guaranteed solid ground underfoot, I started along the cornice.

A metre was still too far. Without warning, the thin veneer of wind-blown snow suddenly became a gaping crack of hollow blue light. I fell.

My pack was what caught on solid snow, leaving me hanging from the shoulder and hip straps while my skis circled in the air below. I glanced down at the eerie, cavernous space that had opened up beneath me, then splayed out my arms and poles, grabbing for anything that would stop me falling the rest of the way through the mountain.

"Roll and grab for the rocks," shouted Jay. He was skiing as fast as he could to come help but it was going to take too long. The fragile balance of friction that held me on the surface was gradually melting with the heat of my body. "Try to roll out!" I heard him shout again, this time with urgent concern.

I traced a few circles with my feet, hoping that a ski would hit a step of solid snow that would allow me to work my way out. Nothing. Slowly, moving as gingerly as possible, I wriggled far enough out of one shoulder strap that I could reach the closest rock with my right arm. "Please hold," I said as I gave it a good, sharp tug. It did. In one heave, I managed to pull myself – and the pack – out of the crack, kicking and scratching as I did. I rolled onto the bed of rocks and lay there for a few minutes trying to catch my breath. It wasn't comfortable, but it was safe, and I much preferred the sharp rocks pressing into my ribs than the sickening wrap of empty air.

"Are you all right?" Both Jay and Leanne had taken off their skis to clamber to my rescue, and as I looked up to see them running towards me, I could hardly believe what I saw. Slightly windblown and melted out, a whole line of wolverine tracks led right past the danger, and followed a much safer route to Featherstonaugh Pass.

"You guys skied from where in how many days?" The leather-clad snowmobiler was incredulous. After climbing through a series of high passes that stretched north of Featherstonaugh for another two days, we'd dropped down to Kakwa Lake and the patrol cabin where our third food cache was stored. I remembered the park ranger's words about snowmobilers, but after twenty days of seeing no one, nothing could have prepared us for the spectacle of the hundred-odd machines that were in the area for the Easter long weekend.

"Now let me get this straight," continued the man as he peeled off his jacket, revealing a Harley-Davidson T-shirt and a pair of bright red suspenders. "You guys *skied* from Jasper?" He was trying to be polite and talk to all of us but his gaze kept returning to Leanne. He was having a hard time believing our story, and the fact that a woman had undertaken the trip appeared to completely bewilder him. "Whip's my name," he said shaking his head and extending a hand. "Whip Funk."

Our first reaction to all the people and machines had been to cringe. The high-pitched whine of engines had floated down from every valley as we approached, and when we emerged near the cabin, the haze of blue smoke that lingered from all the snow-mobiles made the clearing seem like a parking lot. But soon our hard-line stance softened. Whip and his friends invited us into the cabin and began shoving moose steaks, bacon sandwiches, and beer in front of us.

"I've been sleddin' in these parts for more than thirty years and I've never seen a skier before," said Bob, the oldest member of the group, sipping a glass of whisky after dinner. Whip walked around dropping cubes of glacial ice into everyone's drink while Bob continued. "And I guess when it comes right down to it, we're all out here for the same reasons – gettin' away from the clatter of everyday life, exploring and seeing what's around the next corner." He paused for a few seconds, throwing us a quick wink before delivering the punch line. "The only difference is that some of us just like to burn a little more gas while we're doing it!" The cabin erupted with laughter.

All joking aside, Bob had a point. Everyone in that cabin had a connection to the outdoors – it was why they were there, and for many of them, was why they had jobs that kept them out of an office. That evening we shared conversation with oil-rig roughnecks, well-head operators, and logging-truck drivers, and found none of them to be the uncaring, shallow characters that we'd supposed them to be. And they were probably just as surprised to find that we weren't the dope-smoking, granola-eating, misguided urbanites they supposed conservationists to be either. Crammed into that backcountry cabin, age-old adversaries were listening to what each other said.

"You know, we're already doing road closures like them ones you were talking about last night," said Whip while getting his snowmobile ready the next morning. "Like in the spring – when the woodland caribou calve. But I'm not sure anyone's thinking about doing the same thing just so those critters can move between summer and winter range."

Despite numerous offers to join the group for a ride, Leanne, Jay, and I stayed back at the cabin that day to clean up. After three weeks without a shower, things were getting so bad we could recognize one another solely by the smell.

"I feel so clean," said Leanne as she emerged from the cabin an hour later with what looked like a new head of curls. Taking her hint, I went in and heated up my own pot of water for a thorough wash.

It was a warm spring day, but not warm enough for the clothes we'd hand-washed to dry before the snowmobilers returned, which made for numerous jokes that evening as everyone stooped and weaved through the maze of still-damp socks and underwear that hung from the rafters.

"Would you like ice with that bra, I mean beer," Whip joked as he attended to everyone's drinks. "Wine with your knickers and panties, I mean crackers and paté?"

It was another evening of laughs and conversation, but when it came time to go to sleep, the cabin was too full and cramped. So while Jay stayed behind in the only spare bunk, Leanne and I grabbed our bags and made our way to the tool shed. We stumbled up the hill through the shadows of a full moon, and by the light of a headlamp, rearranged the frost-covered wheelbarrows, trail axes, and chainsaws to make room on the floor for a comfortable bed. Clean and drunk, we nestled closely, and I felt an inkling of regret for not having made our brief romance work six years earlier.

We rose early the next morning, packed up, and made our way back down to the cabin in time for breakfast. "Heart attack on a plate" was what one of the snowmobilers called it, but for Leanne, Jay, and I, the greasy mixture of eggs, bacon, sausages, and pancakes – all of it cooked with a liberal spoonful of lard – was a hit of energy we would need for the final 150-kilometre push to Kinuseo Falls in Monkman Provincial Park.

"I know a lot of easier ways to get to them falls," Whip remarked as he followed us out the door and watched us put on our skis. He was pointing at his snowmobile as he talked. "I could have you there in less than eight hours."

There would be many times over the next week and a half when we would think back wistfully to Whip's offer, but standing there in the warm sunshine, with nothing but the promise of blue skies and good spring travelling in the days ahead, we were happy just to play out the joke.

"Eight hours?" Jay said with a smile. "That sounds pretty good compared to the nine or ten days it's going to take us!"

The hard work began after we'd travelled for two of those ten days, across Jarvis Lakes and up and over Moonias Pass. Unlike the rolling ridgeline south of Kakwa, the divide that stretched north was a haphazard jumble of glaciated peaks and impassable cliffs, forcing us eastward and into a grinding rhythm of climbing to high passes then descending into low valleys. The Narraway River, Herrick and Framstead creeks, Warner and Wapiti lakes – each valley greeted us with its own grim combination of fallen logs, deep tree wells, problematic canyons, and vertical mats of thick vegetation. And to make matters worse, the temperature was climbing. The snow had grown heavy and sticky, and many of the waterways – natural paths when frozen – were melting, forcing us into the bush. At times, we searched for kilometres before finding a still-intact bridge of snow or ice.

"Christ, I could have crawled as far as I skied today and probably used less energy," said Jay the night we reached our final food cache at Warner Lake. He wasn't exaggerating. We'd spent all day negotiating a seemingly endless maze of rock, wood, water, and rotten snow. It was an obstacle course that demanded the strength and balance of an Olympian.

There were still animal tracks north of Kakwa but they weren't as plentiful as they'd been in Jasper or the Willmore Wilderness, nor did following them lead to much easier ground. Moose tracks circled in the willow meadows, and the no-nonsense wolverines seemed to have switched to more haphazard methods of negotiating the terrain. It was as if everything struggled to move in those valleys. There were no patterns, only complexities, and so we wandered on, growing more exhausted and frustrated with each passing day.

It got worse before it got better. A series of warm storms engulfed us just north of Warner Lake, covering everything in a thick, wet layer of snow that soaked through our packs, clothes, and the tent. The snow continued for three days, accumulating into a heavy, fifty-centimetre-thick trail-breaking nightmare that slowed our pace to a crawl and left us without a fire for two cold, wet nights. Thick mists rolled in over the passes, leaving us unsure of whether we skied on snow or on cloud, and on two separate occasions, Leanne and I each led the group in a slow, unintentional circle while searching for landmarks. Despite what had happened before, there was no good-humoured ribbing from Jay. We were all too tired.

"So how far did we get?" I asked Leanne as she pored over the map in the soggy tent at the end of a thirteen-hour slog to Wapiti Lake. Jay sat in one corner massaging the shin splints he'd developed from the heavy trail-breaking, while I lay in the other, shivering in my wet sleeping bag.

"You don't want to know."

"C'mon, how far today?"

She double-checked the distance before delivering the disheartening news: a meagre four kilometres.

Leanne was tired too, but of the three of us she seemed to be faring the best, even though one of her ski bindings had broken the day before. We'd cobbled together some wire, hose clamps, and rope, but it was a sloppy, insecure arrangement. She forged ahead, though, cranking turns down the descents, breaking trail, and carrying her share of the weight.

When we finally broke free of the vegetation and storms, and climbed into the high, open expanse of Limestone Lakes, we were too weary to appreciate that we were amid the most spectacular scenery of the entire ski trip. Huge cliffs dropped out of the clouds, their pale, grey faces stitched with frozen waterfalls and rivers of glacier ice. Even when the sun emerged and the clouds lifted, we complained instead of seeing the beauty. Now the snow stuck to the bottoms of our skis, forcing us to push even down the hills.

APRIL 10 – *Limestone Lakes, British Columbia – Twenty-six continuous days of skiing and winter camping and the unanimous feeling is that it's been too long. All the happiness and anticipation on the high ridges before Kakwa is just a memory now. There is no curiosity to see new vistas. Even the fascination for wolverines seems to have dulled. One came within ten metres of our tent last night and yet we hardly even commented on the furrow of fresh tracks while packing up this morning. It's as though we've been defeated by the trying conditions. Our spirits have wilted. All we look forward to now is a warm hotel room, a hot shower, and crisp sheets in a soft, dry bed.*

We arrived the next day at the logging road that would lead us to all those comforts. A wide road with freshly cut ditches and bright red mile markers, it had been pushed up the Murray River just the year before. It hadn't seen a plough all winter though; the only sign of recent human activity was a set of melted-out snowmobile tracks that we followed for forty kilometres to Kinuseo Falls.

I felt quite differently about this logging road than the last one I'd been on more than 750 kilometres south, just outside the Height of the Rockies Wilderness Area and Banff National Park. I had been frustrated with all the development in the Crowsnest Pass back then, and would have been happy if I never saw another road for as long as I lived. Now, after a month out on skis, I welcomed everything that a road represented; a direct path that avoided open rivers, cliffs, and thick swales of bush, a guaranteed route past all the difficulties.

"Y2Y trekkers rejoice at sight of logging road in BC wilderness," Jay shouted out in a mock headline. Even his tired spirits had been lifted by the certainty of the route that lay ahead.

The attractiveness of the road wore thin over the next forty kilometres, however. Letting the mind drift for a few hours was one thing, but two days was too much. Without difficulties to keep us busy, we focused on the next important thing: our discomfort. Our feet were perpetually wet, and despite almost a month to get used to them, our packs still cut into our shoulders and stressed our backs. Every kilometre was a trudge.

Kinuseo Falls were a reprieve from all the monotony, a sixty-metre-high veil of electric blue ice wreathed in mist. While I took pictures, Jay and Leanne craned for a glimpse of the bottom of the frozen drop. It was there, in the huge plunge-pool that had been carved by water for thousands of years, that Leanne and I planned to launch a canoe in another two months. A five-day paddle down the Murray and East Pine rivers would be the kickoff for the final two-and-a-half-month push to the Yukon. It was impossible to scout for an appropriate boat launch now, though; a huge cone of ice arched from one shore to the other, and the water that would soon pound over the drop was still frozen. We would have to wait until we returned in late spring.

An hour later and five kilometres down the snowed-over logging road from the falls, we heard snowmobile engines. Two local coal miners, out for a day of ice-fishing, roared out of the trees and, after we'd waved them down, stopped long enough to throw out a couple of ropes for a tow.

"Grab on!" they shouted and roared off with us schussing along behind. In twenty-five minutes, we covered the final fifteen kilometres to where their trucks were parked at the end of the ploughed road.

Unlike Whip and his friends back at Kakwa, Barry and Von weren't curious about the trip we'd just made, which was fine by us; we were more interested in hearing what had gone on in the world over the last month. But despite our probing questions, neither of the soft-spoken men wanted to talk about global events either. We were visitors, after all, and what they wanted was to show off the country and wildlife they loved.

"Great moose hunting up that valley," said Barry, pointing up a wide creek lined with willows as we drove east out of the mountains, towards the town of Tumbler Ridge. After a few more twists and turns, he gestured up another stream. "See those boulders and little drop-offs? Caught a real nice bull trout in there just last summer." He drove with his knee for a few seconds so that he could frame the length of the fish with both hands. "A real trophy."

Barry grabbed the steering wheel again, and just in time. Coming around the next corner he slammed on the brakes with such force that I had to grab the dash.

"Holy! You see it? There! Right there! Grizzly bear! You see it? What a beauty!"

Before I could answer, Barry was out of the truck, tromping through the bush to where the animal had disappeared in a shower of snow. After waiting a few minutes, I followed.

"What the . . .?"

"Buried gas pipeline," said Barry as I stared at where the bear had fed: a perfectly straight line of green grass that cut through the snowy forest. "Heats the earth and gets green-up going a few weeks ahead of everywhere else. The compressor station's just over there," he said pointing in the direction of a low, steady hum.

We passed more compressor stations, more gas lines, and more forestry roads as we drove out of the Front Ranges and into the foothills. It was the same pattern of industrial activity I'd witnessed in the East Slopes of Alberta and Montana's Rocky Mountain Front. The only difference here, in northeastern British Columbia, was the shocking crescendo of development we rolled through twenty kilometres later. We drove under transfer belts and pipelines, over railway tracks, through tunnels, and finally arrived at the heart of a huge open-pit coal mine. Oversized trucks and bulldozers ground away at the earth while a processing plant belched smoke.

"Head office," Barry chuckled as we drove past a small high-rise. The four-storey building of shiny windows and mirrored glass was like a mirage amid all the dust and machinery. "Won't be long now before that closes down too."

More than $2.6 billion had been pumped into the Tumbler Ridge area in the early 1980s, part of a B.C. government megaproject to develop the large coal deposits found in the northeast corner of the province. The heavily subsidized project had been a development of remarkable proportions. A $500-million rail line, complete with two tunnels, had been built across the Continental Divide, and a town for more than 3,000 people had been carved out of the wilderness almost overnight, including a new town hall, school, shopping mall, recreation centre, and bank. But only two decades later, low coal prices were making both the Quintette and Bull Moose mines unprofitable. Five hundred jobs had recently been lost and the rest were soon to follow. The mines, and the town that had been built to support them, were closing down.

"Yeah, kind of a shame," Barry said as we drove through the outskirts of what appeared to be a new but almost abandoned community. Paved streets that weren't even old enough to have sprouted cracks were empty, and the windows and doorways of modern houses and apartment buildings were boarded up.

"It's all part of the business," he explained. "We've done this before – moved from one mine to the next. First it was Newfoundland, then it was northern Quebec. But leaving this place, moving the family from a spot we've really grown to love. . . . It's going to be harder than ever this time around."

While Barry talked, I crunched a few numbers in my head: $2.6 billion for 2,000 jobs over twenty years. That worked out to a government subsidy of roughly $65,000 per person per year. I couldn't help but think how that sum could be used on small projects to support Y2Y. It could be spent on setting up a number of community-run, small-scale forestry operations; on wind energy farms and small-scale hydroelectric programs; on training workers in small mills and manufacturing plants to make furniture and other products from locally grown wood; on developing the local tourism market. In short, it could help build a diverse, local economy that not only maximized jobs, but also made a community like Tumbler Ridge sustainable over the long term. Instead, the money had been spent plundering an area for what it was worth before packing up and moving on. The greatest tragedy in it all was that most people believed such a boom-bust cycle was the only way business could work.

By the time we pulled into the parking lot of the only motel in Tumbler Ridge, we'd had a full tour of the half-abandoned town. After thanking Barry and Von, we jumped from the trucks but nearly crumpled when our feet hit the ground. It was the first time in a month that we'd had anything more solid underfoot than snow. The pavement sent shock waves through our bodies with each step. Giggling and hobbling, we made it across the parking lot and set about booking a room.

Once inside the heated motel office, we could smell ourselves – a sour scent of wood smoke and dried sweat so strong that we apologized to the clerk as she handed over the key. Jay made his way to the room for a shower, Leanne went to buy some fresh underwear, and I set off to buy cold beer. Ten minutes later I returned with a six-pack under my arm and opened the door. Still steaming from the shower, Jay stood before a mirror with a towel around his waist, whimpering at his reflection: rounded shoulders; sunken chest; ribs poking through a thin layer of skin. We had all lost weight, but Jay looked like he'd been squeezed through a pipe. He was teeth and hair, not much else, and after one beer, was drunk enough to stumble around the room and natter on endlessly about how great it was to walk barefoot on a warm floor.

We were all a little tipsy by the time we wandered over to the only restaurant in town, a small Chinese eatery. Like kids in a candy store, we sat down and ordered dish after mouth-watering dish on the four-page menu.

"We've been skiing and camping in the mountains for a month," Jay explained to the waitress whose eyes widened at our huge order.

He pointed at his ski boots and then west towards the mountains, but she still looked shocked as she hurried into the kitchen. Within seconds, the entire family piled through the swinging doors to gawk at the three red-faced and wild-haired skiers who kept them cooking for the next hour. Soon after the food arrived, however, we realized our eyes had been larger than our shrunken stomachs. We ate what we could, then asked for the remainder to be bagged. Our metabolisms were still racing, though, and after an hour back in the motel room, we were eating once again.

Leanne and I both woke early the next morning, and left Jay to sleep while we went to the café to chat over a breakfast of toast and eggs. It was a debriefing of sorts. The final few days of trudging down the logging road had given me ample time to sort through my thoughts, and I'd decided to be honest about how I felt.

"Since that night at Kakwa I've been thinking," I said.

"Thinking about what?" Leanne put her toast down. Underneath the table, my palms began to sweat.

"About us." I told her how things had changed, how I couldn't just be a good friend to her and, in my heart, wanted more. It changed things, and I offered her the option of backing out of her promise to join me for the next stretch of the hike to the Yukon.

A few days later we hugged goodbye. She was heading back to Vancouver and I to Canmore for the month and a half it would take for the last of the snow to melt and the river ice to break up. There was confusion in her eyes when we parted, and I wondered if I'd done the right thing. What if she decided not to complete the rest of the trip at all?

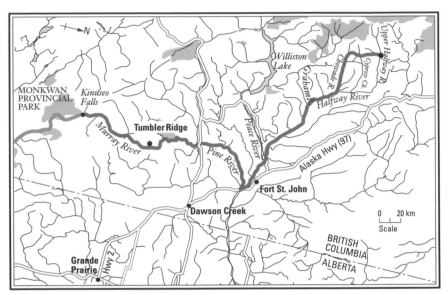

Kinuseo Falls to Upper Halfway River, British Columbia – 590 kilometres

9

A lot had changed by the time Leanne and I reunited just outside Tumbler Ridge. Leaves and blooms covered what had been bare limbs and frozen ground six weeks before. Fresh clumps of bear dung littered the margins of a road that had been blanketed in snow. And, after a tumultuous few weeks in Vancouver, Leanne had returned single.

We were awkward with each other at first, a feeling that was only heightened by Leanne's lingering sorrow. Five years had been a long time for her to be with someone only to have it end so abruptly.

"There are no expectations," I told her, "and no pressure to do this trip as more than friends. We're two adventuresome spirits heading off into the wilderness together." She smiled but said nothing more.

We began to relax a little as we drove into the mountains towards Kinuseo Falls, marvelling at how the landscape was so different without the snow. Driving into the parking lot above the falls, we passed families picnicking at tables that we'd unknowingly skied over in April, and a cataract thundered where the towering ice columns had stood silent and frozen before. We watched, awe-struck, as entire trees plunged over the precipice and churned in the muddy pool below. The Murray River was in full spring flood.

It was with some trepidation that we launched our small canoe into the pool at the base of the falls. Leanne steered from the back while I pulled with my paddle at the roiling current, trying to avoid the logs. Webster lay on the mound of camping gear lashed into the boat, rigid with the tension that gripped all three of us. Leanne aimed the boat into the main channel and I leaned right, bracing with my paddle in the water as the current snapped us into a turn and sent us racing downstream.

Not until we were out of earshot of the thundering cascade did our nerves settle to the point that we actually began to enjoy the river. Old, familiar strokes provided comfort, and two bends later, we slipped confidently into the first in a series of gentle rapids that would characterize our journey for the next five days: enough white-water to be interesting, but nothing too hazardous.

My own foolhardiness led us into the greatest danger of the canoe trip. Excited to be so far north, and eager to celebrate the summer sol-stice in a novel way, I got it into my head that we should paddle through the shortest night of the year. After a late dinner and with the sun still lingering above the horizon, we pushed off at 11 p.m.

We weren't far enough north for the sunlight to last, though. By 1:00 a.m., the day's light waned from the sky, leaving us adrift on a ribbon of moonlight. A great horned owl fell quiet as we slipped past its tree; a beaver slapped its tail and dived into the inky shadows. Like a floating leaf, we drifted through the star-filled night.

At 1:30 a.m., a cloudbank rolled in. The moon disappeared, and we suddenly found ourselves blinded with only sounds to guide us.

"What's that?" I whispered. It sounded like rapids, but could have been a strainer – a tree that leans into the river and combs all objects from the current. I had been caught in one of those once and had it not been for the quick action of a friend, I would have been pulled under and drowned. We backed away from the sound and pushed our paddles down into the water, trying to gauge how close we were to shore. Neither of us hit bottom, and I felt a twinge of panic. Without being able to see what lay ahead, our solstice folly had suddenly turned dangerous. As casually as possible, I suggested we go ashore.

Leanne steered the canoe towards the right bank, but the sound of another strainer soon had us back-paddling. We waited a few moments before trying again, but found ourselves paddling madly upstream to avoid being swept into a log jam. Rattled, we turned and made for the opposite bank, both of us stroking into the blackness until we heard the slip of water on land. We edged forward, peering with our headlamps into the darkness, trying to tell if what lay ahead was a cliff or beach. Silently we drifted, alert for the sound of more strainers, seeing nothing but featureless night. After long minutes of creeping closer, we heard the welcome sound of mud under the hull and jumped ashore.

We didn't realize how cold we were until we hobbled into the trees, joints stiff and aching from hours on the water. I kneeled on the ground and touched my lighter to a carpet of dry leaves, fanning the flames as I groped around for sticks, logs, anything within reach, to feed the hungry fire. Within minutes we had a roaring blaze. Above, the morning's first light was already brightening the sky. I looked at my watch: it was 2:15 a.m. We were north, but not far enough for an all-night paddle down an unknown river. Settling beside the fire, we lay down and slept away half of summer's longest day.

Late the next afternoon, after working our way through a maze of braided channels and gravel islands, we paddled into the clear waters of the Peace and pulled across its 500-metre width. We fantasized about yielding to the current, of letting it pull us east to Great Slave Lake, north into the Mackenzie River, and, 4,200 kilometres later, past the town of Inuvik and into the Arctic Ocean. But instead, we paddled across the current, pulled out, and waited for the pickup we'd arranged to take the canoe and paddling gear away. For the next six weeks we would be walking north.

We hadn't seen much in the way of development while canoeing the Murray and the East Pine rivers – a few houses, the odd gravel road, a railway and highway bridge – nothing compared to what greeted us along the Peace. Ranches lined the banks of the mighty river, oil refineries smoked on the horizon, and the resource towns of Taylor and Fort St. John hummed in the distance. Over the past five days, we had slowly paddled east as well as north, and in doing so, had floated out of the mountains into the developed foothills.

It was a big detour from a route that had otherwise gone northwest, but there had been no option. Had we continued on foot along the mountains from Kinuseo Falls, we would have found ourselves stranded on the shore of a massive reservoir within a few days.

Covering 1,800 square kilometres, Williston Lake was the largest body of water in the Y2Y region, and the tenth-largest man-made lake in the entire world. The result was electricity for much of two Canadian provinces, but at an environmental cost that, thirty-one years later, was still being measured. Not only had wildlife habitat been flooded when the reservoir was first filled in 1967, but fish movements had been disrupted as well. The huge earthen dams had split river systems into isolated fragments and had made free-swimming river fish into captives of a still lake. Non-native fish had been introduced in the meantime, and the stalwarts of the mountain streams – grayling, mountain whitefish, and others – were slowly dying out.

These were not the only problems. Downstream of the dams, important trout-spawning channels were becoming silted, and, 1,200 kilometres away, the Peace-Athabasca Delta was drying up. Waterfowl were abandoning once-important nesting sites and staging areas, and by altering downstream vegetation, the dam had even affected bison and wolves in far-off Wood Buffalo National Park. And the range of animals that had remained after the reservoir was filled was also altered. The fifteen-kilometre-wide lake cut right across the Main Ranges of the Rockies and spread up three major valleys in 300-kilometre-long arms. Williston was more like an inland sea than a lake, and boater warnings were regularly issued for the high waves that swept across its surface. In the wider spots, it was nearly impossible for an animal to swim across, and it would take days, if not weeks, of rough travel to walk around. Williston had forced us down the Murray River and out of the mountains. Now, safely across the Peace River, the question was how to get back.

"That'll all be water in there," Brian Churchill said, pointing to a dark spot on the map. "You'll want to cut across this land and find the old RCMP trail along the Halfway River."

We'd tracked down the veteran wildlife biologist on the advice of a friend and, after walking into the town of Taylor and hitching a ride into Fort St. John, had arranged to meet him and his son at a local restaurant. He arrived with a roll of giant aerial photographs under his arm, but after spreading them across the table, realized some key ones were missing.

"Go get copies of 94A2, 94A7, and 94B8 printed up," he barked out, reeling off the numbers from memory while he stuffed a fistful of twenty-dollar bills into his son's hand. While the boy was gone, Brian told a few stories from the three decades he'd spent studying deer, elk, moose, and other animals in the area. Every local river valley, meadow, and hillside, it seemed, had left its imprint on him.

"Here, this is where you need to go," he said, tracing a line along one of the freshly printed copies when his son returned fifteen minutes later. "The saskatoons will be in bloom here above the Halfway River. It'll be beautiful." The smell of still-wet blueprint ink wafted up from the paper, but Brian was oblivious to the dark smudges that rubbed onto his hands. He was lost in memories. "There's an old RCMP trail in here," he said pointing at a faint line. "It's a little wet and a little grown over, but the canyon it skirts is beautiful." He paused for a few seconds, his smile fading as he better remembered what it really was like. "It's your best option, but it is a little swampy."

It was swampy. And buggy. Swarms of mosquitoes, blackflies, deerflies, and horseflies forced us to don headnets, long pants and thick-sleeved shirts. It was too warm for so many clothes, but Leanne and I wanted to avoid using chemical insect repellent if we could. And so we sweated as we walked, swiping at the insects that crawled inside our shirt and pantcuffs, slapping at our own heads when something squeezed far enough through the mesh to draw blood. The only respite came when we moved quickly or stayed inside the tent.

> JULY 5 – *Lower Halfway River, British Columbia – Red streaks and insect carcasses decorate every panel of the tent walls and roof. It's a wonder that Leanne and I still have any blood. This evening I lie on my back cheering as a wasp on the nylon roof stuffs mosquito after mosquito into its tiny mouth. It makes me so happy I can't help but wonder if I'm already going a little crazy. Will it be this bad with bugs the rest of the way to the Yukon?*

The incessant bugs were a hassle for Leanne and me, but they were far worse for Webster. A haze of airborne pests followed him everywhere he went, probing his thick coat as he trotted through the forest, and biting his exposed muzzle. He stopped periodically to paw at his bleeding snout, but his tail was still upright and wagging despite the trail of red splashes he left on the rocks. His obvious happiness did wonders for our own spirits and helped to put what was a minor amount of suffering into perspective.

With the rituals of setting up and breaking camp marking the start and end of each day, Leanne and I soon fell into a rhythm that made the miles pass underfoot quickly. We had missed the simple and healthy lifestyle of the trail since finishing the ski trip, and, despite the swamps and mosquitoes, were happy to be moving, even if it was through rolling ranchlands instead of untamed mountains.

The landscape still held its share of wild surprises. Tucked between pastures and old clear-cuts, we found sheltered patches of spruce and aspen trees that still harboured red foxes, eagles, and, in one, a black bear feeding on the lush plants growing beside a cool stream. On the open slopes, white and purple wild roses hung from thorny stems, and, in one meadow, we found Brian's beloved saskatoon bushes, every branch bent over with the weight of unripe berries. The wildness wasn't continuous, but it was still there, and it brought a calm to our days that made it easy for Leanne and me to grow closer.

The number of ranches began to drop off as we approached the mountains, but in their place came roads, seismic lines, pipelines, and drilling pads in ever-increasing numbers. By the end of the next day we were completely overwhelmed. It was the most intensive amount of oil and gas activity I had seen yet, and nowhere in its midst could I find signs of the grizzly. The last hint we had seen was a track on the lower stretches of the Murray River a week before.

"Haven't seen a grizz around here in years," said two ranchers we ran into driving along a well-used road. In contrast to many of their counterparts back in Montana, they seemed happy to see us crossing their land, and even detoured over to visit, rolling down their windows as they drove up, asking us where we were headed. "You'll find them up in the hills," said one young man, still talking about the bears. "That's their last stronghold."

Top: "It ain't the grizzlies that you gotta look out for, it's the black bears." George (far left) and fishing buddies on quads along the Chowadee River, B.C.

Right: Game trail littered with antlers, Cypress Creek, B.C.

Top left: Leanne studying the valley bottom, Sikanni Chief River, B.C.

Top right: Leanne swimming across the upper Akie River, B.C.

Opposite: Yellow cinquefoil growing along the Sikanni Chief River.

Top left: Leanne and Webster gaze at
the high mountain mist shrouding the
headwaters of the Kwadacha River, B.C.

Top right: A curious caribou approaches
Leanne near the headwaters of the
Kwadacha River.

Opposite: A tributary at the headwaters
of the Tuchodi River, B.C.

Top: Ivan (left), Stu, and Leanne near the upper north fork of the Gataga River, B.C.

Left: Easier than bushwhacking: Leanne wades in the upper Gataga River rather than dealing with all the blowdown on land.

Top: Rendezvous at Wayne's cabin
before canoeing down the Gataga.
Left to right: Wayne Sawchuk,
Jim Kievet, John Dupuis, Heather
Swystun, Karsten, Leanne,
Dave Ford.

Right: Sunrise, Kechika River, B.C.

Top: Webster and Karsten
walking the final leg of
the hike along the
Alaska Highway, B.C.

Right: Last camp, on the
Liard River, B.C.

There had been sightings of grizzlies in the area in previous decades, though, the most dramatic of which had made national headlines in the late 1960s. A large boar grizzly with an abscessed tooth had stumbled out of its winter den and into the nearby town of Fort St. John on a cold February day. A local hunter, Harvey Cardinal, had tracked it, but in a chilling display of the bear's intelligence, had been outwitted and killed by the very animal he hunted. The bear had subsequently been shot dead after being chased with a helicopter.

The Fort St. John area had changed a lot since then. Fuelled by a boom in oil and gas exploration, what had been a small town ringed by a few farms and ranches where grizzlies still roamed had grown three-fold into a sprawling industrial centre that serviced hundreds of gas wells and oil rigs, as well as petroleum exploration in the surrounding country. Bruce Simpson, the rancher who lived on the last chunk of private land we crossed before finally heading back into the mountains, was reeling at the pace by which the hills around his property were being roaded, logged, and drilled.

"Doesn't make much sense how much traffic is out here now," he commented as we chatted on the porch of his mobile home. A steady stream of pickups, logging trucks, and heavy equipment had rolled past us all afternoon.

"Wasn't more'n ten years ago we got a phone out here and at that time we were still at the end of the road," he recalled.

Simpson's ranch wasn't anywhere near the end of the road any more. In the last ten kilometres we had passed five new road junctions, each bristling with signs pointing to numerous oil and gas wells. But despite his disdain for what was happening, it looked as though Bruce – like many of the other ranchers in the valley – had been forced to join the problem. Parked among the rusting farm machinery and derelict outbuildings in the old farmyard sat a well-used bulldozer and a number of newer pieces of heavy equipment.

With a downturn in cattle prices and a rise in the cost of farming, Bruce had switched to building roads and clearing seismic line.

I wanted to tell Bruce about the Hilgers, Siebens, and others I'd met farther south who'd worked with conservation groups to battle the cash squeeze. But the poverty I witnessed kept me quiet. Within minutes of our arrival, the first in a long procession of sons, daughters, daughters-in-law, and grandchildren filed out of the small trailer. Despite the tax incentives, and despite the obvious benefits for wildlife, conservation easements were no solution for a man pre-occupied with the immediate survival of his family.

With the local citizenry struggling alongside the wildlife, there was only one party left with the power to change things: the oil companies themselves. Curious about their position on Y2Y, I had wandered into the downtown Calgary offices of the Canadian Association of Petroleum Producers (CAPP) during the winter.

Yes, CAPP was aware of Y2Y, one of the executives had said as we sat down in the boardroom. And yes, they supported the principles behind it. In fact, they had even gone so far as to start a Y2Y map of their own, he explained, unrolling a draft on the table before us. The map, which covered the same region that was of interest to Y2Y, was a work-in-progress, the beginnings of an exhaustive inventory of current and future oil and gas developments in the region. "When the Y2Y network map comes out, we'll be able to overlay ours and immediately identify any areas of conflict."

After all the fear mongering by the B.C. Forest Alliance, CAPP's response to Y2Y seemed remarkably constructive. But the true worth of the petroleum industry's interest in conservation would show in the years ahead, when those "areas of conflict" were identified and real profits hung in the balance. In the meantime, I worried that the industry had already imposed too much on the landscape in some areas, such as the Peace District.

"How are you guys going to get across the Chowadee River?" asked Bruce as he watched us stuff the last of the supplies that we'd sent ahead to his ranch into our packs. "With all this warm weather and snow still in the mountains, she's going to be pretty high."

She was pretty high – over our navels – and we half-walked, half-drifted as we fought the current a day later. It was our first major ford of the trip, and we congratulated each other as we wrung out our clothes on the other side. Little did we know how gentle a prelude it was to the many difficult river crossings we would tackle in the month ahead.

> JULY 9 – *Chowadee River – The breeze is stiff enough to keep the bugs at bay so this afternoon we bare all and dive into an inviting deep pool. Drying in the sun afterwards, I spot the green shapes of fish hovering off the silty bottom and, using a small fly and a few metres of fishing line, hook one. The whole pool erupts in flashes of silver as I reel it in. Within seconds, a whitefish emerges from the water and, after clubbing it with a stick, I roast it over a small fire. Leanne and I eat it like cavemen, squatting in bare feet, still half-naked, tearing off chunks of the fatty meat and savouring the hot grease that drips down our fingers. Ten minutes later, the fish that emerged alive is returned to the same lazy section of river, a white skeleton shining through the green shadows.*

The Chowadee was a waypost of sorts, a turning point where the trip's character shifted. An hour after our impromptu feast, we saw our first grizzly bear track in more than a week, followed by wolf prints heading both up and down an old seismic line. Farther along the clearing, we encountered three men travelling on quads, fishing the Chowadee on a day out from the nearby town of Dawson Creek.

"Where are you two headed?" asked the group's leader. He introduced himself as George, a retired pipeline worker.

"The Yukon," said Leanne.

"The Yukon! Either of you got a gun?" He leaned off his seat to examine our packs. "There's lots of bears where you're headed. Mean buggers too! And it ain't the grizzlies you gotta worry about. It's the black bears." He patted the rifle strapped to the side of his four-wheeler.

Leanne and I nodded politely. His wasn't the first unsolicited advice we'd received about how to deal with bears, and like the rest, we dismissed it as paranoia. Both of us had run into dozens of black bears over the years, none of which had ever been a problem. The two we'd spooked in the past week were a good example: one had disappeared into the bush like a dark rocket; the other had hauled itself up a tree.

I assured him that we'd be careful.

"Careful? You'd better be on guard!" said George, raising his voice. He started his engine and signalled for the others to do the same. "I wish both of you luck." He waved with one hand, hit the gas with the other, and in a roar of pistons, was gone. They were the last people we would see for more than a month.

It felt good to turn off the seismic line the next morning and bushwhack up a small drainage that would lead up and over a ridge to Cypress Creek. We found a good game trail that was littered with old bones and antlers, and still used by moose.

"How many was that?" I asked while writing in my notebook later that night.

"Let's see. Three bulls, a cow, and a calf," answered Leanne. The next morning, we saw two more.

After a week of monotonous walking along roads and seismic lines, the bush seemed alive with possibility, and we moved through it eager to see what lay around each corner. We felt strong, comfortable, and fearless and had even adjusted to the bugs.

And then the bear charged.

Webster first sounded the alarm, a rare bark that warned of an incoming animal. I was shocked at first, uncomprehending as the willows thrashed down towards us, followed by a blast of sharp huffs, and the sound of ground churning. When a blur of dark fur exploded from the bush and bore down on us, I suddenly remembered every one of George's sage words. "Bear!" I shouted out to Leanne. "Black bear! Coming in!"

The animal closed in fast, running at first, then slowing to a walk when it was within thirty metres. It hesitated for a moment, stopped to slap at the ground a few times, then started forward again, prowling more than walking, its head, shoulders and back bristling with anger. Webster lay rigid at my feet. Leanne edged closer. Every written account of black bear attacks that I'd read played through my head.

"Go on, get!" I shouted, waving my arms and jumping in the air. I screamed and cursed, hoping that a show of aggression would halt it, but all my harsh words failed. I thought of Kim and Otis's friend, how they'd found him dead with a bear chewing on his head, and my voice grew feverish. But still the bear closed in. Finally, less than ten metres away, it stopped and stood up on its hind legs.

I became focused in that moment. A calm washed over my panic. Everything slowed down. Details crowded into seconds: how the bear's shoulders flexed in the sunlight; the huff of its breath; the saliva spilling from its mouth. I was aware but unafraid in those moments, part of the standoff but also distant. Then, in what seemed to be slow motion, I reached for my bear banger and pulled back the trigger.

The boom sent the bear scattering for cover, but only temporarily. Within seconds it came back, this time growling. I quickly loaded a second banger while Leanne pulled out her canister of bear spray. Webster, quiet and shaking, pressed in closer against my legs.

It ignored the second cracker. There was only a slight flinch in its black eyes that fixed our every move with an uncompromising stare. Huffing and popping its jaws, the bear seemed more upset than ever. It came to within ten metres again and, after pawing at the ground a few more times, moved forward.

"We're getting out of here," I said in a low voice to Leanne. Fully expecting the bear to attack at any moment, I drew my knife. "Let's go!" I said, taking a few steps uphill. "We're leaving now!"

"It'll be faster to go downhill," said Leanne, already moving in that direction with Webster following behind. She was right, and I set off after her, looking over my shoulder as the bear followed us, step for step, down the slope.

"Easy. Whoa. It's okay, we're leaving now," I cooed. The shift in strategy – reducing the threat we posed rather than fighting back – seemed to be working. After another fifty metres, the bear stopped, watched us for a few minutes, then turned back towards whatever it had been guarding – perhaps a kill. Eager to put as much distance as possible between us and it, we kept on down the mountain for another hour. Finally, in the middle of an open meadow, with a good view in all directions, we set down our packs and hugged.

"Oh my God, did that really happen?" Leanne's voice was still shaky.

"I think so."

Chickadees and kinglets flew over the clearing and filled the surrounding forest with song. It was hard to believe that the anger and aggression we'd witnessed an hour earlier existed in the same world. We collapsed onto the ground and told each other the experience from our different perspectives. I had seen aggressive bears before, but had never been so terrified. For Leanne, it was the closest she'd ever been to any bear, let alone one that seemed intent on attacking.

"And I thought the scariest things out here were the bugs," she said. Still giddy with adrenaline, I burst out laughing.

JULY 12 – *Between Cypress Creek and Upper Halfway River, British Columbia – It's as though the bear charge was needed so that our arrogance stayed in check. Like the oil companies we've cursed over the last week, our approach to the land had grown*

too self-centred. Not any more. If fact, the bear might have
pushed the balance too far the other way. We jump at every rock
and dark stump lurking in the forest, and shout out until our
voices are hoarse. The once-dull edge between feeling comfort-
able and respectful in the wild has been sharpened to a thin
blade of fear.

Walking was what eventually gave us some perspective. The
slow meditation of miles gradually sent the dangers to their rightful
place – somewhere in the midst, rather than the forefronts, of our
minds. But it wasn't until two days later, while packing up our camp
at the head of Fiddes Creek in a steady drizzle, that our feelings
about the wilderness shifted once again.

It started with another deep bark from Webster, the same husky
bellow that had preceded the encounter with the bear, and hearing it
again threw my heart into spasms. There was no bear this time
though, only three rain-soaked wolves watching us like ghosts about
fifty metres away. Webster went quiet as soon as he knew we'd seen
them, and for the next minute, the six of us were silent, staring at one
another across the meadow. Webster whimpered, and one of the
wolves took a few curious steps forward. After a few seconds it turned
and followed the other two animals as they trotted off towards
Cypress Creek.

We walked over to where they'd been, and, after inspecting their
saucer-sized tracks, headed into the forest on the same game trail
they had used. It was a good path, and we followed it north for most
of the day, cutting high above the canyons that squeezed the lower
reaches of Fiddes Creek, and then dropped quickly to the meadows
that fringed the Halfway River. It rained steadily all day, just as it had
all week. The only time we pulled back the hoods of our rain suits
was in the middle of the morning when a chorus of wolf howls
drifted up from the south.

"Sounds like more than the three of them calling," Leanne remarked. It did, but I wasn't sure. I had once watched five wolves throw back their heads and howl in Banff National Park and had been surprised that they sounded like a pack of twenty. Inspired by the mournful sounds, we pushed ahead, and, after a few more kilometres, began to see old saw and axe marks where someone – presumably a hunter or a guide-outfitter – had cleared a trail many years before. It made for easier travel, and we covered the last ten kilometres down to the Halfway River in less than two hours.

By now, we had set up camp so many times that we fell into the tasks with ease. There was no pattern, no individual tasks that one person routinely did. Instead, one of us simply started one thing, and the other began another until, an hour later, the long list of jobs was done. Pitch the tent, fetch water, set up the rope to hang the food, collect wood, start a fire and, if it was raining, string up the tarp.

I helped Leanne change into dry clothes once we'd pitched camp, and left her under the tarp beside the fire while I set off to scout a good place for us to cross the river the next morning. Lured by a path, I soon found myself upstream at the edge of grassy green meadows. I stopped there, not quite able to comprehend what I was seeing. Trails, hammered deep into the earth, converged and radiated out from a number of huge, muddy wallows, bleached bones and handfuls of woolly brown hair lay scattered everywhere. The rain stopped and shafts of sunlight poured down, leaving me mesmerized, feeling as though I'd entered some long-forgotten world.

"Bison!" I knelt down to inspect a huge pile of scat and a number of the large, round prints. The last time I'd seen such tracks had been in Yellowstone, 2,500 kilometres south. I hadn't expected to see signs of the massive, lumbering animals for the rest of the hike.

The Halfway River was part of the historic range of 168,000 wood bison, which, like the millions of plains bison to which they were related, had been overhunted in the 1890s. In 1906, the last known animal from the original herd was shot about a hundred kilometres away, just outside the town of Fort St. John. The animals that had left the tracks I was seeing were the progeny of forty-eight yearlings introduced illegally by local guide-outfitter Lynn Ross in the early 1970s.

It was probably Ross, or one of his employees, who had cut out the trail we had followed down Fiddes Creek, and it was probably he who had set fire to the cabin whose charred remains Leanne and I had noticed along Fiddes Creek. Ross had allegedly torched all the outpost cabins in his 3,600-square-kilometre guiding territory in a last act of defiance before the B.C. government had revoked his guide-outfitting licence a few years before.

Despite his rogue reputation, and overlooking the fact that he had introduced what many considered to be the wrong subspecies, Ross had unwittingly achieved something remarkable. While a number of government-led initiatives to reintroduce bison to other parts of the Y2Y region had stalled or failed, in three decades his bison had multiplied to approximately 1,500 animals. It had come to the point that a tightly controlled, limited-entry hunt had needed to be started, a business that, quite unexpectedly, had attracted sportsmen from all over the world to pay local First Nation guides thousands of dollars per week. Suddenly, there was local interest in protecting the wildlife of the area and there was talk about conserving movement routes so that the bison (and the hunt) could eventually expand to other valleys. The dream of reintroducing bison to every Front Range valley between Yellowstone and the Yukon seemed more possible than ever.

I daydreamed a little longer in the upper Halfway, imagining all the sparring, rolling, and grazing that must have gone on only a few days earlier. There were no bison to be seen now, though, and after surveying the surrounding meadows and slopes with pocket binoculars, I followed another of the well-worn trails back downstream along the river, scanning the current for a good crossing point.

Nothing seemed reasonable at first; the banks were steeply undercut and the deep river was more than fifty metres wide. Then, about one kilometre downstream, one of the many bison trails cut through the bank and dropped into a fast but narrow section of the river.

"What does it look like?" asked Leanne when I returned to camp an hour later. She looked warm and happy as she sat reading and stirring a pot of dinner that bubbled over the fire.

"Cold and fast," I told her, "and deep enough that we'll need to swim." But if a bunch of one-tonne bison could get across, so could we.

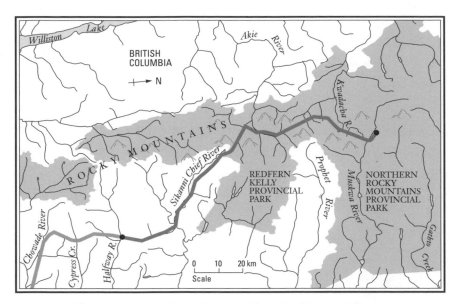

Halfway River to Muskwa River, British Columbia – 185 kilometres

10

H ow to cross the rivers we'd encounter in northern British Columbia had been a question ever since we'd started planning this section of trip, and one that had led us to a number of people and books for advice.

"You're gonna need horses for sure," most outfitters and trappers we'd talked to had suggested. I'd had enough experience as a backcountry park warden to know horses were a lot of work, and the thought of finding feed and cutting trail for a whole string of them wasn't attractive. I'd rather that it was only ourselves we had to worry about.

Although cold and a little dangerous, we figured getting ourselves across the rivers would be relatively straightforward – wade until it got too deep then swim like hell. How to get our gear across was the bigger concern. We'd consulted wilderness survival manuals, as well as swiftwater rescue experts before leaving, and the advice we'd gleaned was as diverse as the suggested equipment. Bicycle pumps, inner tubes, air mattresses, dental floss, waterwings, bows and arrows, chainsaws, lifejackets, ropes, pulleys, carabiners, and inflatable boats had all been recommended. Limited by the weight and bulk we were able to carry, we'd opted for 55 metres of rope, two lightweight sailing pulleys, a couple of heavy-duty garbage bags, and a 180-metre roll of mint-flavoured dental floss.

We didn't need the dental floss for the Halfway River. It was narrow enough that, with the weight of a tied-on rock, Leanne could throw an end of the rope across to me after I'd made the short, cold swim. Then she tied the remaining line around the packs, wrapping them with garbage bags and our sleeping pads, and floated the whole works in the water while I pulled from the other side.

We needed the floss two days later, though, when, after a wet bushwhack up and over another ridge, we arrived at the much wider Sikanni Chief River. After waterproofing our packs, I mustered the nerve to strip down to my shorts, shivering while Leanne tied one end of the floss around my waist.

The thin floss didn't create any drag as I swam across, and after thirty seconds of frantic stroking, I emerged on the opposite bank with Webster close behind. I did a few jumping jacks while he shook, and once I could feel my arms again, pulled the floss taut while Leanne tied her end to the rope that would eventually pull across our pack. But as soon as I started to bring the bigger line across, the whole system failed. Despite our efforts to hold it high, the rope drooped into the current and in a fraction of a second was swept downstream. The floss bit into my hand, then broke. Leanne reeled in the rope, then looked across at me, wondering what to do next.

"Try throwing it," I shouted, swatting at the mosquitoes that swarmed my bare chest, back, arms, and legs during a lull in the rain. But despite repeated attempts, Leanne could get the rope only about halfway across. Still frozen from my first swim, I plunged into the water and swam back to grab an end of the rope, with Webster loyally paddling behind.

I expected the rope to pull tight at any moment on that last swim, for it to catch and yank me back, but I made it to the opposite bank, and managed to wrap my arm around a muddy log just as it went taut. Webster followed again, and five minutes later, Leanne sent the packs across after him.

An electrical storm had been brewing all afternoon, and it hit just as she waded into the water. The green river turned black and a strong wind whipped it into a chaotic chop.

"C'mon," I shouted over the hail that exploded across the water like gunfire. I grabbed her hand as soon as it touched the bank and, running, pulled her into the trees.

JULY 17 – *Sikanni Chief River, British Columbia – Rain every day for the past two weeks. Every hole, depression, and gully is full of water and the rivers – already high from a late spring snowmelt – are still rising. I'm worried. Of all the people we talked to before leaving, no one even mentioned the Halfway or Sikanni. The rivers they said would be swims are those farther north – the Muskwa, Tuchodi, and Gataga. Will they be even bigger? And will there be others we hadn't expected? We pull out the maps and consider our route in a whole new light, counting tributaries, measuring drainage basins, and looking for glaciers. We begin to see in terms of watersheds, not mountains, and in doing so, identify the crossings we need to worry about. The next one is the Akie River, about fifty kilometres away.*

We caught a glimpse of the west branch of the Akie three days later, a ribbon of whitewater threading through a deep canyon 300 metres below us. It was bigger than we'd imagined, and our anxiety grew over the half-hour it took to climb down to its shore. It had shone an opaque blue from above, and when we reached its edge, I dipped in a hand to confirm what I'd suspected. It was glacier-fed and colder than anything we'd crossed so far.

It would also be more serious. There was only one place to cross the press of rapids before the water squeezed into the canyon, and it looked far from reasonable: a hundred-metre-long chute of haystack waves and fast-flowing water that drained into a stretch of jagged boulders. If we drifted into that mess, there wouldn't be much chance of our coming out the other side.

Leanne and I discussed strategy, yelling over the roar of the river, pointing out the waves and hydraulics that indicated rocks hidden deep under the racing water. I noted a car-sized boulder on the opposite shore, serving as a marker to signify trouble just down-stream. I shuddered as the river pounded past, partly from fear, and partly because of the cold rain. The prospect of stripping down to swim only made me shiver harder.

"What do you think?" asked Leanne as we began repacking everything into the garbage bags.

I shrugged my shoulders. "Do we have a choice?"

"Here." She handed me one of the only two candy bars we had left and opened the other for herself. We chewed the sweet snacks in silence, hoping the sugar would hit our blood in time for the upcoming swim.

"Ready?"

"Are you?"

While I stripped to my shorts and stuffed the rest of my clothes inside the garbage bag, she tied the end of our fishing line around my waist. We'd burned the useless dental floss in a campfire a few nights earlier.

"Okay," I nodded. The time had come.

It was like ice when I stepped in. Liquid winter. Pain followed by fear. I had expected the cold, but not the power of the current. It pushed my knees straight and set my feet raking across the shallows, and before I was a few steps in, my plan went wrong. There was no time for new strategies, no time to decide where to start swimming. My boots slid across the rocks, and the bottom dropped away.

I tried not to panic, but I was overwhelmed. Alive or dead, I was nothing to a river that had flowed for thousands of years. Elk, bears, and caribou had died along those banks; hundreds of moose calves had been lost in the turbulence. I fought for the other side, but my will was nothing against the forces that had carved canyons out of mountains.

I kicked and waved madly as the cold stabbed deep into my core. Fatigue spread from limbs towards my heart and as I looked for the car-sized boulder on the opposite shore, panic finally set in. I saw nothing. Waves and silt streamed into my eyes, blurring everything. Even the sound of my own gasps was drowned out by the roar of the water. I sucked in one last breath before another wave hit and I felt myself go under.

My hand hit something solid but I kept swimming. My numbed fingers scraped across the riverbed, but still I didn't stop. It was only when my stomach brushed the rocks and my knees bumped the hard bottom that I ceased kicking and staggered ashore, dizzy and disoriented. It seemed like I'd been swimming for hours. The rain had stopped; shafts of sunlight now dappled the ground.

Slowly, I remembered where I was and looked for Leanne, finding her only when I'd scanned far upstream. I had drifted 150 metres — much farther than I'd expected, and well past my marker rock. Another twenty-five metres and I might not have emerged at all. I gave Leanne a half-hearted thumbs-up, trying to hide my shock and fatigue. I had proven the crossing possible, but the tight-lipped smile she flashed back told me I had failed to mask its danger. It was only when she pointed at the spool in her hands that I remembered the fishing line. I groped for the knot on my shorts, and pulled it in.

While I anchored the rope around a large rock, Leanne tied the other end around the packs that were already bobbing in the water. Our life was in them – shelter, food, maps, and clothing – so she hung onto the flotilla until the last possible moment, double-checking the knots as the rope groaned with the force of the current. No sooner had she let go of the packs than they were plunged under by the force of the water, bobbing up again a few seconds later, still attached, swinging towards my shore.

We both cheered when they bumped into the rocks, but not for long, for as soon as I had plucked the packs from the water I heard Leanne cry out. I looked upstream to where she pointed and caught a glimpse of the black body just as it plunged into the water. After watching us struggle for two hours, Webster had decided it was his turn to come across.

Unlike Labradors or golden retrievers, border collies lack the large paws and buoyant bodies that are well suited for water. But what Webster lacked in physique, he made up for in cunning and strength. Where he had entered the river was good – far above the boulders – and he stroked so hard that the upper part of his chest lifted above the surface. Waves slapped sideways over his head and he lashed back, snapping his jaws as he battled for the shore.

"C'mon, Webster!" I shouted as he swept past. I raced down the bank to where his paws finally hit the falls. He'd swum twice the distance I had, and he pulled himself wearily onto the bank. Wet and dripping, he was just skin and bones. I called him but he was too tired to come, too exhausted to even wag his tail. I wrapped my arms around his trembling body and flooded him with praise.

Alone on the other side, Leanne was probing the water for a good entry point. She had stripped naked to cross the Halfway. On the Sikanni she'd swum in shorts. But on the Akie, she was getting ready to jump in wearing everything, as though the clothes and boots would somehow insulate her from the greater danger. Perched on the edge of a boulder, she spotted a seam in the waves and plunged forward, teeth clenched, hands splayed out ahead of her, already groping for the other side.

All I saw was her head and arms stroking wildly, and while she drifted towards the whirlpools and waves that boiled downstream, I stumbled along the bank. She was only halfway across by the time she passed my marker rock, and my anxiety mounted. It was my best friend in there – more than my best friend – and it was more than responsibility that twisted my heart. Finally, she broke free of the river's grasp and, after a few tired strokes across the back eddy, kicked bottom so hard that her whole body jumped from the water.

"That's it," she muttered as I hugged and kissed her. "That's my limit." The river streamed out of her hair, down her neck, and had drained all colour from her lips and face.

Getting ourselves and our gear across the Akie had taken more than four hours and we were exhausted. Nonetheless, after a short rest we continued to walk upstream, lured by the prospect of dry shelter and a wood stove in a hunting cabin we'd heard about from an outfitter we'd talked to months earlier.

"Tonight," croaked Leanne as we reluctantly left the fire we'd started after crossing the river, "I want to hang my coat on a goddamn nail!"

Not much had been easy for us the past few days, and following the faint and overgrown trail to the upper Akie was no different. Working our way through the head-high carpet of willow and birch bushes was a full-body workout; the branches were so enmeshed that we had to pry them apart with our hands. Like some endless alley of thieves, the shrubs clawed and ripped at our legs, pulling our binoculars, bear spray, and knives off our belts.

We didn't see many tracks – just a few grizzly and moose prints – but mixed in with them was the odd faint hoofprint and mouldy, disintegrating ball of half-digested oats. Hunters, and all the supplies to feed and house them, would have been flown into the remote camp that lay ahead, but the horses they used were strung in and out by the outfitters once a year. It wasn't enough use to keep the trail we followed clear of vegetation, and it faltered frequently, disappearing at every bog and patch of poorly drained ground.

This pattern had frustrated me before. But I had no energy to be irritated at this point, and in the calmness of fatigue, I realized that although trails are lost, they don't just disappear. Instead, they are ghost paths, small, imperceptible threads hiding until a ridge, a shoreline – any edge favoured by animals – appears again, and enough of them gather to re-form the fabric of a visible trail.

The trail did improve as we neared the camp. Old horse and fresh moose tracks merged in from side valleys until what we were walking along was a well-travelled trench worn deep into the mineral soil. Our legs were heavy by the time we came to a flower-filled meadow and spotted the weathered log structure at its far edge. The camp was empty – hunting season wouldn't start for another few weeks – but the flash of evening sunlight that reflected off the patched tin roof was more welcoming than any candle burning in a window. Weary and footsore, we dropped our packs in front of the dilapidated cabin and pushed open the door.

JULY 23 – *Upper Akie River, British Columbia – It looks like whoever was here last departed in a hurry. Tarps, propane hoses, and chewed horse halters are strewn across the ground outside while, inside, there is a half-full kettle of coffee on the kitchen counter. Cans of pie filling, boxes of macaroni, and bags of flour sit on dusty shelves beside a long table whose edges have been polished smooth by hundreds of sleeves and card-playing hands. A few foam mattresses are draped over the rafters, out of reach of the mice whose droppings cover the floor, and on the table are stacks of hunting and gun magazines. Scattered among them are a few blank big-game scoring forms, and above the table, carved into the log walls by some of the hunters are the animal horn and antler measurements of trophies past:*

Phil Roberts, State College, PA / 9" goat Sept 93 / Chased griz. Skip Waylett – Fort Mill, South Carolina, 1995 / 38" sheep / 7" goat / 8' grizzly.

Even though I knew trophy hunters help to get habitat protected, the words were hard to stomach. The mindset displayed on those walls was a world away from my own beliefs. The bear incident and the terrifying swim across the Akie had only made me feel insignificant, while the hunters' tallies were all about making the writer feel bigger. In a world where wildlife and wilderness were becoming increasingly rare, and tourists were willing to pay thousands for a glimpse of a wild grizzly or wolf, I wondered if all the same infrastructure – remote cabins, trail-hardened horses, good cooks, and guides who consistently got clients within view of elusive animals – couldn't service a wildlife-viewing industry instead. Not only would such a service feed a hungry market, but it would also do away with the pursuit of size and magnificence that, aside from killing hapless animals, only stroked a human ego.

"Why don't we take another rest day here?" Leanne suggested two mornings later. The idea was hugely appealing. The thick foamie we'd fetched from the cabin had transformed our little tent into a comfortable nest, and despite having logged more than twenty-five hours of sleep over the last two nights, I still felt weary. Even Webster hadn't moved except to eat and relieve himself for the past day and a half. The appeal of another lazy afternoon only increased with the sound of raindrops on the tent-roof.

"I'd better check." Feeling a little guilty, I pulled out my journal to look at the itinerary taped inside the back cover, then relaxed. There was plenty of time. After learning my lesson the summer before, I'd scheduled a number of days off, none of which we'd taken. And because it is so remote, there were no presentations and media interviews to do along this section of the trip. Instead there would be a month of publicity and travelling once the whole journey was over. There was only one appointment we needed to keep in the near future, a rendezvous with a bush plane carrying our next food cache and Ted Wood, a photographer on assignment with the prestigious *Smithsonian Magazine*. That was on the Muskwa River, sixty kilometres away, but even if we took another day off, we still had four days to get there.

I had talked to Ted more than a month earlier from a pay phone in Fort St. John, finalizing plans for this rendezvous. It had seemed ludicrous to set a date given all the unknowns. There would be no way for us to send word if we ran into problems, I had told him, adding that he'd better bring his own maps and food in case we didn't show up. Even now, even when we were so close, I worried that something we weren't anticipating lay ahead, another river crossing, an impassable creek, or a horrendous bushwhack that would prevent us from making it on time. Leanne, always the optimist, thought differently.

"Looks like we might make it a day early, eh?" She nudged me as we pored over the maps later that afternoon. It would be mostly alpine travel for the next few days – fast, bush-free walking.

"Maybe. Maybe not." I was looking over the final twenty kilometres in detail, scrutinizing the contour lines of a steep, narrow valley. "You just never know for sure," I said. I didn't want to dampen her optimism but the surprises that had already caught us off-guard were still fresh in my mind: the charging bear, the rivers we'd expected to be creeks, the trails that weren't really trails at all.

We ate a lot that day: a pancake breakfast, two lunches, a hefty dinner, and snacks of scones that Leanne baked using a bag of stale flour and a handful of rock-hard raisins she'd found. Between feedings, we focused on getting ourselves, and our clothes, clean. We filled every available pot with water from the creek and, heating them on the wood stove, shared a shallow bath in a galvanized tub we found outside. Then we did laundry. We washed everything – even what we wore – and so we sat around the warm stove naked that evening, waiting for the garments to dry.

The walking was almost effortless over the next two days, and we covered forty kilometres with ease. Alpine meadows stretched before us like the open prairie, and at the top of each pass and rise, we could see the hours of travel that lay ahead. As we came closer, brown dots slowly turned into caribou, rusty smudges became elk, and lines across old drifts formed into the fresh tracks of a lone wolverine. But soon the clouds and fog rolled in and the world went grey with more rain. It was too bad because, according to the map, we were in the midst of one of the most spectacular sections of the trip. Occasionally, we caught a glimpse of icebergs floating in turquoise lakes, a hint of the many glaciers that hung in the valleys above. I didn't mind that we couldn't see more. I loved the mystery of rainbows, waterfalls, and blue ice poking down from the sky. I loved the drama of a lone caribou emerging from a wall of mist and curiously approaching to within a few steps. Even if the clouds had been as low as my head, I would still have been laughing. The country was that beautiful, and the walking that easy.

Everything was different when we dropped into a tributary of the Kwadacha River. Where we expected to find a subalpine meadow of willow and birch there was a V-shaped valley of rocky bluffs and head-high alder. We searched for the beginnings of a game trail but couldn't find a track. It seemed that wildlife routinely avoided the valley.

It was B.C. bush at its worst. The moss-covered alder were so intertwined that there was no way through the mess of branches, only over. Each step was a balancing act over a scaffolding of springy stems and sharp rocks. It was a struggle to stay upright. I was looking for a route I'd heard about from an outfitter. Shoving a canister of bear spray into my shorts and giving a whistle, I headed off.

Webster was uncharacteristically reluctant to follow right from the start, and not more than a kilometre from camp that reluctance turned to refusal. We had entered a small canyon by then, and although it didn't look promising, I wanted to check just a little further upstream. The rendezvous with Ted that had seemed so sure the day before was suddenly cast in doubt.

Leanne and I tried to buoy each other's spirits, but it was Webster, plugging away tirelessly through the tangle, who became our model for resolve. The travelling was even tougher on him – his pack kept snagging and he repeatedly fell through the shrubbery. At one point he became so enmeshed it wasn't until he yelped that I found and extracted him. No sooner was he free than he was off again, backing up and looking for alternative routes whenever thwarted, letting out growls of determination as he charged ahead.

After an hour of tough going, we broke out of the alders onto a snow-covered avalanche path. Leanne groaned when she saw we hadn't even gone a kilometre down the bush-choked valley. We looked ahead hopefully, then looked at each other.

"What do you think? Which side of the creek?"

The avalanche had left a bridge of snow and ice across the creek, which was already carrying enough water to make wading a dangerous proposition. At some point we would have to ford it, and we knew that just one more tributary could make the stream impassable. The ice bridge was a tempting route across, but when I looked downstream, the bushwhacking looked easier on our side.

"Let's stay on this bank for a little while longer," I suggested. "There has to be another place to cross further down." Leanne wasn't at all sure, but eventually agreed.

We went only three kilometres in the next three hours and by late afternoon we were so soaked and exhausted that we pitched our tent on a small, mossy cliff ledge. It was less than ideal, but it was the only campsite we'd seen all day.

"Better not sleepwalk tonight," Leanne muttered after she'd pegged out the tent. It took up almost the entire ledge. A misstep would mean a ten-metre plunge into the whitewater that swept past below.

I had been wrong about the snow bridge, I realized. It was a river we followed now, and it was running furiously, popping and boiling as far as the eye could see. To try to swim it would be suicidal, and to make matters worse, it was increasing in strength. The water had risen another twenty centimetres in the hour since we'd arrived. I filled the cook pot and climbed back up to where Leanne and Webster sat around a small fire, sheltered by a rock overhang from the incessant rain.

"I screwed up," I admitted. "When I said we should stay on this side I made a mistake."

In her usual style, Leanne remained optimistic.

"We'll keep going forward. We'll find something." Neither of us could bear the thought of spending all that energy just to return to where we'd started out. Hoping to get an early start, we crawled out from the overhang and climbed carefully to the perch that held our tent.

"Good night!" Leanne shouted beside me in the sleeping bag.

"Good night!" I yelled back. All night, the water roared, pounding at our nerves.

I was ragged without sleep the next morning, but impatient to find out what the river held in store. Within an hour of packing camp, we had found a place where all but a two-metre-wide channel was broken by a line of boulders. It was too wide to jump, too swift and dangerous to swim, but with the help of a rope, we thought we could wade it. We were wrong. After almost drowning, and almost losing Webster in the process, I returned to the shore and collapsed on the ground.

"We'll go one more hour," Leanne said. "After that, we turn around."

We were so sure we would have to retrace our steps, we could hardly believe it when we found a place to cross around the next bend. The river's main channel disappeared under a rock outcrop, leaving a metre-wide gap to a large boulder and then an ankle-deep wade to the opposite bank. After tightening our bootlaces, we made the jump, with Webster following gamely behind. The rest of the crossing was an easy hop across boulders and gravel shallows but we were still so shaken by our earlier attempt that we crept across on all fours.

Another hour of bushwhacking, and we came to another godsend: a well-defined horse trail led off in the direction of the Muskwa River.

"We might make it on time to meet Ted after all," Leanne mused.

"Maybe," I answered. I hoped she was right, but I wasn't counting on it.

One just never knew for sure.

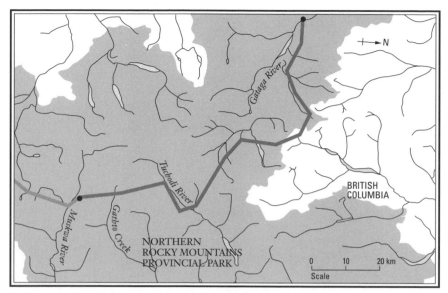

Muskwa River to Mayfield Lakes, British Columbia – 120 kilometres

11

The horse trail not only held, it improved as we neared the Muskwa, and, after a day of following it upstream, we crossed the river where its murky waters braided into a number of small, manageable, hip-deep fords. Once across, we found the old outfitter cabin where we'd arranged to meet Ted. It was empty and boarded up.

It took us about ten minutes to get inside the log cabin. Steel grates had been bolted over every window, and in front of the door lay a platform of upturned six-inch nails. Using a crowbar that sat hanging on an outside wall, we lifted the platform up off the porch, then set about working out the spikes that had been pinch-nailed from the walls into the door. Blond hairs sat crimped against some of the spikes, the door frame had been bitten away, and scratch marks were worn deep into the logs around the window. The place had attracted its share of curious bears.

Just as we started lighting the wood stove, we heard the engine. Leanne and I exchanged a dumbfounded glance and rushed outside. After hiking for thirty days across unknown country, we'd arrived within fifteen minutes of the plane.

There were the usual hugs and hand-shaking as we greeted Ted and the pilot, but I found myself at a loss for words. It had been almost a month since I'd been in a social situation. I left the chatting to Leanne and fetched Ted's gear from the plane – lenses, a heavy tripod, a whole box of film, and a bag of fresh vegetables and chocolate treats.

"So Glen, we'll see you next Sunday – the Gataga River – right?" said Ted. The pilot, we soon learned, hadn't flown on a Sunday in twenty-five years.

It would have to be Saturday then, they agreed, and with that Glen climbed back into the cockpit, flicked a few switches, and bounced the plane down the gravel bar before lifting into the air.

JULY 30 – *Gathto Creek, British Columbia – After three weeks of having seen or talked to no one, Leanne and I foresaw how the trip's energy would change with the sudden addition of a new person. The tough river crossings, bear encounter, interminable bugs, and cold, wet weather have forged a connection between us that often negates the need to talk. We were prepared to lose some of that intimacy when Ted arrived, but didn't expect his arrival to highlight the extent to which our own thinking has changed.*

"Now you're sure the trail isn't over there?" Ted asked, pointing to a grey line that wound across the top of a small ridge on the opposite side of the creek. After two days of good travelling, he was getting his first taste of bushwhacking, and he was fed up with wading through the chest-high birch and willow. "Are you sure we shouldn't have followed that other trail where it forked back there?"

"I'm never sure," I answered honestly, "but I'm following a good hunch."

After branching repeatedly, the game trail had deteriorated to little more than the occasional elk, grizzly, or moose track. It wasn't much to follow, but it was enough to keep me moving forward. Besides, the creek was getting big, and after what had happened the week before, Leanne and I were hesitant to risk getting caught on the wrong side of any watercourse again.

"You've got to have faith," I encouraged Ted over my shoulder, "faith that it'll improve." He sighed as I dived into another swale of willows, and reluctantly followed behind.

With most of his backcountry experience limited to following well-marked and maintained trails, Ted wanted clear lines to follow. I thought about trying to explain the whole notion of ghost paths to him, but realized I hadn't grasped it all myself. It wasn't easy to describe. It was a kind of instinct that defied words. The grain of a place could only be understood over time.

From the start, we'd been reluctant to have Ted along. The country was remote, lacked decent trails, and should anything go wrong, a rescue would take many days. But he'd convinced us. He worked for a magazine that would reach millions of people with the Y2Y message, and during a three-day trip earlier that spring, had proved to be a fit, friendly travelling companion. Besides, there were other advantages to having him come along, we soon realized. Although only in his early forties, he'd lived more than a lifetime of adventure while travelling on assignment and could spin story after spellbinding story. But even better than his jovial company was the good weather he'd brought with him. After almost a month of rain, the skies had cleared within hours of Ted flying in, revealing an abundance of wildlife that for the past few weeks had been hidden in the clouds.

There were the usual ptarmigans, grouse, and toads that we flushed from the undergrowth, but among the snowbanks that still fingered the alpine meadows were groups of caribou and elk grazing on the new green growth.

"See anything big, brown, and furry?" Ted asked as I sat glassing the slopes around camp one night.

"You mean elk?" The whole hillside was covered with big bulls chewing their cud in the soft evening light.

"No, no, something *really* big, brown, and furry," he teased.

I laughed, but just as I did, something else came into view. "Oh-oh. . . ."

"What, what?" Ted asked, sensing my sudden nervousness. By then we could both see it plainly with our naked eye, a grizzly coming towards us, its blond chest and silver-tipped shoulders glinting in the sun. It was only 200 metres away but unaware of our presence, pushing down leaves with an outstretched paw, snipping off fleshy stalks with its huge jaws.

"Well, at least it's alone," I said after scouting the surrounding area with binoculars. Almost immediately, though, something else moved a farther hundred metres away. "You're not going to believe this," I whispered. Upstream was another, much larger grizzly, lumbering down the creek towards us.

"Oh maaan!" Ted wheeled around, looking for an escape. "I can't believe it. Not one, but two grizzlies, and they're both headed this way!"

We got up slowly and made a smooth, fifty-metre-long retreat back to camp to get Leanne.

"What's going on?" she asked as I rushed to turn off the stove and grab the food bag.

"Bears, two of them, coming this way." She grabbed the rope and her headlamp, then followed us as we started up the slope.

It was probably the worst place to be visited by grizzlies. We were high in the alpine, and there wasn't a tree for hanging food within sight. So with darkness descending, we struck out for a cliff a kilometre away.

Leanne and I took turns carrying the heavy sack while Ted lagged a few steps behind, stopping every few minutes to look with the binoculars for the bears. Shadows had started to fill the small valley and it was getting difficult to make anything out in the dim light.

"They might still be where we last saw them," he reported, "or they could be in the meadow where we pitched camp."

We climbed quickly and were soon on top of the cliff, uncoiling the rope and lowering the food over the rocky edge. Once it was secured, we stopped to take one last look before figuring it was safe to descend back to camp.

The climb had helped to calm all three of us, and as we walked back down, Ted started into another one of his stories. It was about a friend of his, a renowned wildlife photographer from Japan who had lived and worked with wild bears around the world without incident until, one night in Alaska, he'd been mauled and killed in his tent. "No one knows exactly what happened," said Ted. "All they found was the grizzly feeding on him the next morning."

Ted was a good storyteller, but this was the wrong time to hear this one.

AUGUST 1 – *Headwaters of Tuchodi River, British Columbia – I always bring my bear spray into the tent, but tonight I bring in my six-inch-long knife and keep my clothes on as well. I feel vulnerable and exposed and want to be ready should I need to fight. This is what it feels to be mortal, to be prey, to be prepared and afraid. I listen, straining for a sound, but all is silent.*

I twisted off the light and thought back to what Otis and Kim had said about bears, even after their friend had been mauled to death back near Waterton: "You deal with the fear and, as a reward, feel more alive." That was almost a year ago, but for me, the fear was now worse than ever.

I slept fitfully that night, and was happy when the sun kept its promise of another day. There had been no sounds in the night, no nightmarish intrusions, and when we looked around, we found no sign of the bears. We retrieved the food, packed up, and set off for the next pass that would eventually lead to the Tuchodi River.

There was no trail as we started out but it didn't matter. The walking was open and easy across mats of alpine heather while a flawless blue sky stretched out overhead. We stopped to pick crow-berries and, when we moved again, inadvertently pushed a small herd of caribou ahead of us over the gentle pass. We followed a faint trail that led into the trees on the other side, merging with other trails until what lay ahead was a well-trodden path. Leanne charged ahead while Ted and I hung behind to take photographs, catching up to her only when she waited long enough to tell us about the wolf she'd spooked from a shrubby draw. An hour later we found its prints pressed into the mud fringing the blue waters of the Tuchodi.

There were tracks everywhere along the river – moose, elk, wolves, deer, black bears, and grizzlies had trampled every piece of flat ground. We waded the small river, and searched for a campsite away from all the activity, finally settling on a small island among the sand-banks of a dry flood channel. Within an hour of pitching our tents a large cow moose, lame in one leg, limped over the old riverbed and hobbled past. A few minutes later a black bear stole out behind it, then skittered away when our campfire popped like a gunshot.

"How do you feel being out here with all these animals?" Leanne asked after Ted had gone to bed. "Do you feel like an intruder?"

She knew I had felt that way farther south, in places like Yellowstone, Glacier, and the Bow Valley, places where the few remaining wildlife were being squeezed out by people.

"No," I answered after thinking a bit. "It's more equal up here. More elemental." I thought of how we were crossing the rivers just as they did, how we pushed through the same bush on their trails. We were conforming to how they lived, not the other way around.

Leanne nodded, and after scattering the dying coals into the sand, followed me to the tent.

The next morning, eager to get moving, I offered to scout out a shortcut while Leanne and Ted finished tearing down the camp. I was looking for a route I'd heard about from an outfitter. Shoving a canister of bear spray into my shorts and giving a whistle, I headed off.

Webster was uncharacteristically reluctant to follow right from the start, and not more than a kilometre from camp that reluctance turned to refusal. We had entered a small canyon by then, and although it didn't look promising, I wanted to check just a little further upstream.

"C'mon, buddy, let's go," I said, tugging at his neck. He was adamant, though, and a few seconds later, I understood why.

At first I was pleased to see the bear, thinking its presence suggested a trail did exist up the valley. But then I realized with a chill what was really happening – that I was being followed. Crouched low to the ground and slithering more than walking, the bear was stalking me, searching for an easy meal.

"Hey! Go on! Get!" I picked up a rock and tossed it, but the bear kept coming. I grabbed two more and banged them together, but still it came, unfazed by the sharp cracks that echoed down the canyon. Webster crowded against my feet as I continued throwing, all of the rocks bouncing uselessly while the bear continued to press forward. Fifty metres, forty, thirty. "Stay back," I yelled. No reaction.

When it stepped into the creek, I went crazy. The water was a boundary in my mind, and if the bear crossed it, I knew it would all be over. Other than the bear spray – which was useless beyond five metres – rage was the only weapon I had left. I went berserk, unleashing a torrent of screams, sticks, and stones, roaring while I tossed everything within reach. Finally the bear hesitated for a moment, standing on its hind legs, forefeet dangling in the water. There was a crack of uncertainty in its gaze, and I fought like something possessed to wedge it apart further. I threw more rocks, bigger rocks, harder and harder. Then, one of the fist-sized stones connected with a thud. It was enough to turn the bear's hesitation into a retreat. In one motion, it backed out of the water and streaked down the creek bank, disappearing into a triangle of trees. I shed a few tears of relief as Webster stood there beside me, watching where the bear had vanished. After a few minutes, I could hear the creek over the sound of my heartbeat again, and mustering up some nerve, shouted my way back to camp.

"What do you mean, the bear stalked you?"

"Let's just forget about the shortcut," I said, waving off most of Leanne's and Ted's questions. I wanted to keep moving.

> AUGUST 4 – *Sicily Peak, British Columbia – That bear has freed me. It has pushed me to a place where fear empowers rather than enslaves. There is none of the paranoia that followed the last aggressive encounter at Cypress Creek. I am quiet inside now, washed in a calm awareness. For the first time, I understand the risks and dangers for what they offer life, not what they threaten to take away. I see more, hear more, feel more. The fear of bears, wild rivers, and untamed storms strengthens the connections between a person and a place. Fear engages.*

It had been a long apprenticeship – about 2,800 kilometres long – but I had finally learned to accept misfortune, even death, as a condition for a richer life. I felt a new sense of belonging with the realization, and it was only heightened by the wildlife encountered over the next three days.

The first wolverine appeared the next afternoon, just below a staircase waterfall where Ted, Leanne, and I sat quietly eating lunch. A few rocks dribbled down, followed by the animal, jumping from ledge to ledge. It passed less than five metres away and it was everything I'd imagined from its tracks – broad and powerful, a sharp snout pushing ahead while a compact body hurried behind. Its yellow claws hardly touched down before lifting off each boulder, and it hopped from one to the next, the gold fur of its stomach brushing across the waterworn rocks. We sat in shocked silence while the rare animal raced past, unaware of our presence.

The next morning, after climbing steeply out of the treed Tuchodi Valley, Leanne spotted something moving across the meadow of rock and alpine flowers in front of us.

"What is it?" She pointed to a smudge of brown more than a kilometre away. The surrounding high peaks and glaciers made it difficult to grasp the scale of the scene, and for a moment the three of us thought that it was another bear headed our way.

"Another wolverine!" I whispered, looking through my binoculars. The steady, determined gait was unmistakable. I'd wondered many times over the course of the trip if we'd see a wolverine, but I had never dreamed of encountering two in as many days.

"Quiet!" hushed Ted as he readied his camera. "Stay perfectly still." We stood motionless, faces into the wind and watched the squat animal move in and out of the troughs of shadow, growing in size and detail as it came closer.

"Nobody move," Ted ordered after it had dropped into the final gully, bearing right towards us. Everyone tensed, and when the wolverine did bound into view, it was only a moment before it wheeled around and disappeared. Ted snapped off one picture, and then it was gone. I felt sorry for it as it doubled back, losing all the ground that it had gained. We watched for a while longer, until it was only a smudge again, then headed across the same uneven meadow and rocky slopes, taking an hour and a half to cover what the wolverine had traversed in minutes.

We were still talking about the two wolverines the next day when, halfway through our lunch stop, we were surprised by a grizzly. We had lingered a little too long at our last campsite – a high lookout of terraced meadows dotted with turquoise lakes – and as a result, had made the steep descent into the Gataga drainage in the blazing sun.

We pulled off our boots and socks after eating, and dozed in the shade while our feet aired in the breeze. Lazy with full stomachs, and deafened to other sounds by the roar of the nearby creek, we were as off-guard as we could be.

Fortunately, the bear happened upon us unaware, its head down, thoughts elsewhere, bumbling into the meadow after a refreshing swim. Still dripping wet, it was as surprised as we were and, after a few sharp huffs, it wheeled back into the creek while we scrambled for our socks. It didn't return, at least not before we'd gathered our wits, donned our boots, and continued down the valley.

Ten kilometres later, we came to the large, sandy flood plain of the Gataga River's south fork. Wolves howled as we crossed the large outwash, the almost comical high-pitched yelps of pups breaking around the steady, mournful notes of adults. We didn't see the pack, only their tracks among a multitude of prints that criss-crossed the river flats. It was a fitting finale to Ted's week with us, and after hugging him goodbye, Leanne and I walked into the whorls of seed and grit that danced along the windy river shore. It had been an amazing seven days together – good weather and more wildlife encounters than the previous five weeks combined. We hoped that Ted's photographs would help to bring the spirit of the place to a larger audience, and that the story that accompanied them would inspire readers to believe in Y2Y. We gave one final wave, then turned and waded across the river.

While Ted waited at the hunters' cabin for Glen's plane, Leanne and I pushed on for a rendezvous of our own. In three days we were scheduled to meet a floatplane carrying four friends, three canoes, and a cargo-hold full of fresh food. Our meeting place was a remote lake about thirty kilometres farther down the Gataga, but a steep canyon lay between us and our destination. We would have to travel twice as far, up and over another pass, then down a valley that, if we were right, would lead to the river's calm, lower reaches.

Although Ted had proved himself more than capable, it felt good to be responsible only for ourselves again. The trip was wearing both of us down to the point that we had little energy to spare. But where one worry left off, another quickly took its place. Webster had started limping the day before, and as we climbed along the rocky bank of the creek, he began to favour his right front leg more than ever.

There were many reasons for him to be limping. Perhaps the thousands of kilometres on the same leathery pads were finally taking their toll, or maybe it was a bruise or sprain from the tangle he'd had with a porcupine two days before. We relieved him of his pack and wrapped the tender paw, but the bandage didn't last long. There were too many creek crossings, and by the time we were halfway to the pass, it had come loose and was lost in the stream.

"Only three more days," I encouraged as he gamely limped behind. After that, he could rest in the canoe for ten straight days.

Ted had brought good weather when he arrived, and now he seemed to be taking it away as well. Within hours of his leaving, the sun disappeared and a dark, cold cloak of rain forced us to don our rain suits for the first time in eight days. We were miserable by the time we reached the pass. A week had been long enough to grow accustomed to being warm and dry, and being cold and wet once more was almost unbearable. "At least we're not bushwhacking," we said to each other. But we were soon doing that as well. The carpets of alpine heather leading to the pass gave way to snarls of willow, birch, and alder on the other side. Heads down and cursing, we plodded on, waiting for things to improve.

It was almost dark before they did. The rain was still coming down hard and both of us were soaked. But when we reached the valley bottom an unexpected sight greeted us: a log cabin, with blue smoke belching from its chimney.

Leanne and I looked at each other. Except for Ted and the pilot we hadn't seen anyone in thirty-six days.

"Hello!" I shouted out as we approached.

"What the . . . where'd you guys come from?" asked the stocky man who came to the door. He was tired and weathered-looking, unshaven and unabashed about greeting strangers in his long underwear.

"Wyoming," I deadpanned. "Along the mountains."

"What? Hah!" He looked back inside the cabin. "Hey, Stu! Come check these guys out. They claim to have walked from the States!" A second man, also clad only in long underwear, squeezed into the doorway.

"No really," I insisted, "from Yellowstone, beginning last year," and I launched into the reasons behind the trip.

"Well, I'll be," began the other man. "You're almost to the Yukon now, but you mean to say you actually *walked* from Yellowstone? Hang on, hang on," he said, reaching inside the cabin for a broad-rimmed Stetson. He gave a little bow as he stepped into the rain. "Well, I'm puttin' my hat on just so I can take it off to you guys!"

We spent a cozy evening in the cabin playing cards, drinking beer, and sharing stories with Ivan and Stu, two sheep hunters who had flown in from Fort St. John and were waiting to be picked up by a plane the next day.

"What barriers did you see along the way?" asked Stu, wanting to hear more about the trip and Y2Y after we'd shared a dinner of noodles and meat sauce.

"Well, surprisingly, only ten paved roads. All of them were highways, and about half were busy enough to make it difficult for wildlife to cross." I listed off a few more statistics: only five railways, and of the 3,000 kilometres I'd travelled so far, fresh signs of grizzly bear 85 per cent of the way. "But hundreds of oil, gas, and forestry roads too," I added, trying to paint a realistic picture. "At last count, there's a road, pipeline, seismic line, or railway in all but 28 of the 320 watersheds in the Y2Y region."

"Yeah," nodded Stu, "those are all the same reasons the two of us paid almost two grand to fly in here. Everything you're talking about –

especially the forestry and gas stuff – it's happening up north here as well. It's getting to the point where it's difficult for a guy to find a valley where his hunt isn't going to get spoiled by someone else riding in on a quad. But this Y2Y idea you're talking about, it sounds good," he said, reaching into a box and pulling out a bottle of Scotch. "Tell us more."

I told them about supportive and unsupportive landowners, about folks like Bryan Hilger and Ray Crone, and about the road restoration, conservation easements, and highway underpasses and overpasses. "More than half of my route was across public lands that are already protected in some way," I announced. "But even some of those areas have their problems," I added, mentioning how places like Glacier and Banff were being loved to death by tourists.

"I got a friend that lives down there, between Glacier and Banff," said Ivan, pulling a chair up to the table. "The amount of building that's going on there, he says he's never seen anything like it."

I took a swig of the liquor and coughed as it burned down my throat. "It is bad," I said, describing how forestry, mining, oil and gas exploration, along with the new recreational interest in the area, had resulted in a maze of roads, clear-cuts, open-pit mines, seismic lines, and housing developments that prevented all but the luckiest grizzly or wolverine from getting through.

Stu poured another round of drinks while I wandered outside to help Leanne finish setting up the tent. "Do you think it could ever get that bad up here?" I heard him asking Ivan as I closed the door.

I don't know if it was the Scotch or the meat sauce but something I ingested made my body revolt. No sooner had we left Ivan and Stu the next morning, than I had to stop, pull down my pants, and relieve my churning guts. For the next four kilometres, I had to stop every fifteen minutes.

"Are you okay?" Leanne asked as I caught up to where she waited.

"Not really, but hopefully this won't last too long." We needed to keep going to make our rendezvous the next day.

But it didn't get any better, and after more than fifteen stops, I finally had to admit that the stomach cramps were too painful to continue. Leanne pitched the tent while I retched up the last of my stomach's contents, then crawled inside and collapsed, shivering as I dropped into a fevered sleep. I was so skinny by this time, so robbed of reserves, that the sickness hit me hard.

"How are you doing?" Leanne asked when I opened my eyes.

"What time is it?" It was light out but she'd changed her clothes. "What day is it?"

"Same day, just a few hours later."

Hopelessness has always accompanied illness for me, and our remote location drove me deeper into despair. What if I didn't get better? We were a five-day walk from the nearest road. How would I get out to medical help? The same thoughts crowded Leanne's head, but she remained optimistic.

"You will get better," she reassured me. "Whatever this is, you will recover." I realized she probably was right. Like so many other things, it was only temporary.

I was up again four times that night, crawling through cold rain to the shelter of a small tree. There were no stars, and it was so dark that I couldn't be sure whether I squatted with eyes open or closed in the rain. I could hear things: water dripping off the spruce needles and, at one point, the deep beat of something running through the night. I was too miserable to really care though, and so I just stayed there, squatting, as the drumming grew louder then passed into a clatter of hooves striking hard rock. Whatever it was had reached the edge of the river. Silence, followed by a splash, and a wave of relief washed over me. Maybe I did care. Maybe I would be all right.

The next morning I felt well enough to try walking. Leanne lightened my pack by shouldering most of the weight, and we struck off with the hope that, by evening, we would make it to where we should have met our friends the previous day.

I was wobbly at first, too weak even to talk during the frequent rest stops, saving every scrap of energy I had for the task of moving forward. Walking seemed to help though. My head gradually cleared, and by midday, my stomach had settled to the point that I could begin to eat again. It wasn't a moment too soon. I needed the calories to negotiate the graveyard of trees that lay ahead, acres of angles, holes, and rolling traps where more than half the forest had been uprooted by windstorms a few years earlier. There was no easy way through, and I stopped every half hour to eat another few slices of dried fruit, some candies or chocolate, anything that would give me another fifteen-minute burst of energy to climb, jump, and crawl over the tangle of timber. By nightfall, we were still eight kilometres shy of our rendezvous point. Leanne, who had carried eighty pounds all day, was so exhausted that she hardly ate that night, only smiled as I'd gobbled down what would normally feed the two of us. It was good to see me eating, she said, and although we were discouraged by our slow progress, at least I was well enough to walk.

The next morning, we tackled the tangle of logs that still lay ahead with a new strategy.

"Stick to the low ground, the wetter the better!" joked Leanne, contrary to the rules that normally govern hikers. The poor travelling had given us no alternative, and I followed as she waded along the river shallows, through backwaters, and into swamps.

"Look at the bog bitch go now," I called as she forged ahead in a cloud of mosquitoes.

"C'mon, bush boy," she countered from beneath her headnet. "Let's see what you're made of!"

We left the water at one point and followed a faint game trail through a thick swath of alders. It was along that path, just a few minutes later, that we encountered the wolves.

There were three of them, the lead animal a dozen metres ahead of the other two, head down and trotting straight towards me.

"Hey," I called softly when contact seemed inevitable. It was a big wolf, more than three times the size of Webster, its back as high as my hip. For a second or two, both of us stood there, three metres apart, locked in a shocked, unwavering gaze. Then the wolf bolted through the alders, its two companions racing behind. Webster barked twice and lunged forward to give chase, but stopped short on a sharp command. Leanne, still working through the bush behind me, broke free in time to watch the last animal disappear.

By noon we were within one kilometre of the lake where we were to meet our friends, but were still on the wrong side of the river.

"That last crossing – the Gataga below the lake – it'll be a big one," Wayne Sawchuk, the part-time trapper and full-time conservationist, had said over the phone earlier that spring. "There'll be a good trail once you get across. Follow it up the hill for fifteen minutes and you'll come to the cabin at the lake."

He was talking about his cabin, part of a trapping concession he had bought from his uncle in 1988, and if all had gone according to plan, we would see him and his partner, Marcie, there. The two of them should have arrived a few days earlier after completing their own six-week trek on horseback from the west.

The Gataga at this point was big – more than twice as wide as the unwadable ford we'd tackled on the Akie – but we were hoping we wouldn't have to swim across it. In our last telephone conversation with Wayne, he'd offered to bring a dinghy across the river and leave it somewhere obvious on the bank where we now stood. Leanne and I searched for two hours, but didn't even see a horse track or a boot print on the dirt bank. We scanned the opposite side of the river with binoculars, looking for the canoes our friends might have carried down to the river, but saw nothing. We checked the map again, cross-referencing the lines and contours with the mountains and hills until we were certain we were in the right place. Slowly, the mind-wrenching doubts and second-guessing started to fill our heads.

"Maybe they ran into problems," I said, thinking about Wayne and Marcie's 400-kilometre-long route from Dease Lake. I couldn't imagine the work of slashing through tangles of forest so that a string of large animals could get through, much less find a place to camp where there was enough grass each night.

"And the weather has been pretty bad over the past few days," Leanne added, hinting that the plane carrying Jim, John, and the others might not have arrived yet with the canoes.

As a last ditch hope, we set off a couple of our last bear bangers and started a fire under the tarp. I tried to doze as we waited for someone – anyone – to walk down and rescue us from the river, but the bugs were so bad that even with my headnet on, it was difficult to sleep. Finally, after pulling my hands far up into the sleeves of my rainjacket and twisting them closed, I was able to steal a few minutes of rest.

"I think we're here alone," I said an hour later.

"It sure feels like it."

Both of us shuddered at the thought of having to swim. It had started to rain again, heavily enough to make the thought of stripping down unappealing, but still too light to dampen the bugs. We sighed across the fire at each other, and then started to move, stringing the packs into a nearby tree, stripping down to shorts and T-shirts, then stepping into the cold, muddy water.

AUGUST 8 – *Gataga River, British Columbia – There is no hesitation once we make the decision. There can't be. The mosquitoes and blackflies swarm our bodies and eyes. The water is cold but offers relief from the burning bites, and with no packs to haul, no rope to string across, we are free to swim together. Side by side we wade through the shallows, our feet touching down every second or third step, until the bottom drops away. It feels like flight this time, like two birds taking off, and we stroke through the currents as though our arms are wings. We are calm, relaxed, and laughing. In danger, but swimming with grace.*

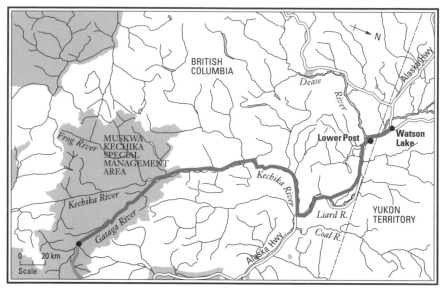

Mayfield Lake, British Columbia to Watson Lake, Yukon – 370 kilometres

12

I t was the beginning of the end of our journey when we saw all the fresh horse tracks on the far shore of the Gataga.

"They must be here!" Leanne exclaimed, already racing up the hill. I ran to keep up with her, a mix of excitement and disappointment racing through my mind. We were about to see friends, but would be leaving the remoteness behind.

Ten minutes later, the cabin came into view, and through its open door shadows moved as someone tended the wood stove inside. Another person read on the porch, and Wayne's familiar figure moved among the horses that grazed in the surrounding forest.

"Look who's here!" shouted Marcie, emerging from the kitchen to wrap her flour-covered arms around both of us. "Wayne, Wayne, it's Leanne and Karsten! They made it!"

"Well, I'll be . . ." began Wayne as he rounded the corner and shook our hands. He stood there in silence for a moment, drinking in the sight of our still-dripping bodies. Having travelled many parts of our route, he was one of the few people who could understand what we'd been through.

"You must have had one hell of a trip. All those river crossings, high passes. . . ." He paused as he looked us over. "It's no surprise the two of you look so skinny."

"We did lose a fair bit of weight," admitted Leanne. "Especially Karsten. He's been sick for the last three days. It's why we're so late."

"Well, the plane's late too," said the man who'd been reading. He introduced himself as Doug Chadwick, half of a writing and photography team from *National Geographic* that had accompanied Wayne and Marcie for part of their six-week horse trip. The other half lumbered through the bush towards us as we spoke, camera slung over one shoulder, rifle over the other, a silly grin on his face as he hoisted a freshly killed grouse above the bushes for us all to see.

"After two days of waiting and slowly running out of food, we had to send Ray off to shoot some dinner," Wayne explained.

I wanted to hear more about their trip. Wayne, in particular, looked tired and run down, but no sooner had Ray put the bird down and hung the rifle back in the cabin, than the sound of an engine drifted through the clouds. Leanne and I shook our heads. Despite the delays brought on by sickness and poor weather, a perfectly timed rendezvous was about to unfold once again.

For the next hour, the shore of Mayfield Lake was transformed into a bustling airport. Two floatplanes taxied in and out of the dilapidated dock, dropping off our four friends – John, Jim, Heather, and Dave – six boxes of food, and three canoes. Doug, Ray, and Marcie climbed on with their luggage. Somewhere in the rush we retrieved our belongings from the other side of the river, and Marcie found the time to give Leanne directions on how to finish baking the bread that was ready for the oven. An hour later, we were eating the browned loaves as we sat listening to stories from Wayne's trip.

"There was some rough country," he allowed, "and a time or two when we got a little disoriented and discouraged. But we never got lost. Confused once or twice maybe, but we always knew how to get back from where we'd started."

Despite looking a little exhausted, Wayne seemed healthier than when I saw him at a Y2Y gathering in the spring. He'd been a little rounder then, more portly from a winter of sitting in meetings with scientists, outfitters, and oil, gas, and forestry executives, negotiating the future of British Columbia's Northern Rockies. Because of Wayne and other hard-working citizens, most of what Leanne and I had walked through that summer, an area larger than Switzerland was going to be conserved, along with an estimated 4,000 caribou, 15,000 elk, 22,000 moose, 5,000 goats, 7,000 Stone's sheep, and the thousands of predators that called it home.

"You have to understand not all of it is fully protected," Wayne explained. "Most of the connections are what we call 'Special Management Zones,' not parks. There will be some development and resource extraction in those areas, but only under very strict restrictions."

"What kind of restrictions?" asked John.

"We're still working out some of the details," explained Wayne, "but I'm talking about things like cutting narrower seismic lines on foot instead of with bulldozers, using helicopters to fly in oil drilling equipment instead of building roads, making small-scale selective cuts instead of clear-cutting. The odd road will still be built," he admitted, "but before it is, an existing one will have to be deactivated."

John nodded his head. "Sounds pretty progressive."

"In theory, but there's a lot more work to do before industry will agree to all these things. More negotiating, more committees, more sitting around more getting fat." Wayne sighed and gave his flat stomach a pat. "If it weren't for these summer trips, I'd probably have died of meetings by now."

Wayne wasn't used to sitting around and being indoors. The next day, while helping him with a few repairs around the cabin, I watched, fascinated, as he chainsawed an old log into two square beams with a series of swift and exacting cuts.

"Why did you give up logging?" I asked, holding one of the beams as he nailed it into place.

"As a logger I went into a lot of valleys," he said. "Then, as a hunter, I'd return to those same valleys a few years later. Too many of the trees were gone, but I was bothered by other things too. I ran into more people, saw less wildlife. It took me a while, but I finally realized I liked the 'before' a whole lot better than the 'after.'"

Wayne helped us portage all the canoes and gear from the cabin to the river, checking on the horses as he did so. Because of them, he'd never done the paddling trip we were about to embark on, and although a part of him wanted to come along, I sensed that he was looking forward to being alone as well. After a week's rest, he would embark on the final five-day section of his summer trip, walking the horses out to the nearest road.

"Thanks for everything," I said when it came time to say goodbye. "Have a relaxing week and a safe trip out."

"Don't worry. The only sound that'll be coming from that cabin will be the sound of snoring and turning pages." He untied our canoe and gave it a gentle shove into the current. "You guys try to get some rest too. And good luck."

AUGUST 13 – *Gataga River, British Columbia – Sliding into the flow of this river is like pulling onto a freeway. Bogs, blowdowns, raging creeks, and vein after vein of impenetrable bush passes by without effort. For Leanne and me, every mile is a gift.*

Webster also appreciated our new mode of travel. Day after day he lay on top of the packs, his chin resting on the gunwales, dozing as the river pulled us north through the high peaks. He seemed to snap alert at all the right times – when a pair of caribou wandered to the riverbank, when a cow moose and her calf looked up from an adjacent swamp, when a wolf trotted up the shore, and when we passed a dead black bear, rotting in the sun.

"What do you think happened?" asked Jim, a sixty-three-year-old friend from Canmore who, despite two artificial hips, ventured out in his canoe at every opportunity. We pulled up beside the carcass and I prodded it with a stick. Everyone jumped back when a wave of beetles and maggots seethed out of the festering flesh.

"I don't know, disease?" Leanne guessed. The fact that the head, paws, and hide – parts coveted by poachers – were still intact suggested that foul play wasn't involved. Besides, we were days away from the nearest road or well-used trail.

"Old age?" someone else ventured. "Maybe a deadly fight for territory?"

Whatever the calamity, it had happened a while ago. Lines of silt striped the dark coat, high-water marks from when the rain had swelled the river a few weeks earlier. The mystery unsolved, we climbed back into the canoes and left the beetles and maggots to do their work.

There were other animals for which Webster didn't even lift his head as we continued northward: tiny toads and frogs swimming past the boat, a huge black bear watching us from atop a high cliff, and one morning, a young bull moose that casually walked through our camp. Webster was asleep in the tent when that happened, soaking up the luxury of another late-morning start as the rest of us dawdled through a long breakfast.

It was a lazy river trip. Except for one short portage there were no rapids, and except for the odd sweeper or submerged log, no real danger. So we relaxed, floating more than paddling, spending more time in camp than on the river, napping between taking makeshift saunas and eating extravagant meals. For Leanne and me, it was the perfect end to a memorable summer.

"I sure am going to miss you," I said, lying in the tent beside her as she wrote in her journal. Once we reached the Liard River, she would catch a ride south with the rest of the group while Webster and I walked the last 150 kilometres to the Yukon along the Alaska Highway. We would be apart for at least two months. I had a sixty-day presentation tour planned for the Yukon and western British Columbia, while Leanne needed to get back to her job in Vancouver. Neither of us could say exactly how or when we would be back together again, only that it would happen. After everything we'd been through, it would be impossible to stay apart.

Two days short of the Liard River and the inevitable goodbye, the Gataga spilled out from its narrow, steep-sided valley and poured into the Kechika, a looping, bowing, braided river that wandered back and forth across the Rocky Mountain Trench. Wide, low, and rich with alluvium, the Kechika was one of the few drainages in the 1,400-kilometre-long trench that still supported vast populations of fish and wildlife. Farther south, along the Fraser and Columbia rivers, for instance, the Trench was compromised by roads, bridges, railways, towns, and dams. Only the Kechika remained free.

For all its charm, our time on the Kechika was short-lived. No sooner had the muddy Gataga melded with its clearer waters than Terminus Mountain – the most northern peak in the Rocky mountain chain – came into view. Beyond lay the forested hills of the Liard Basin, and farther still, another mountain chain – the Mackenzies – which stretched along the Yukon–Northwest Territories border for another thousand kilometres to the Arctic Circle and the northern edge of Y2Y.

Terminus was a beautiful mountain – a line of grey slabs that pointed skyward in a 2,400-metre-high milepost. It marked the end of the Rockies, and the end of our canoe trip. After bumping down one last riffle, we merged with the Liard River and paddled across a shallow canyon of boiling water to where the Alaska Highway paralleled its course.

"Okay, let's get these boats loaded," said Jim after he'd backed the truck and trailer down to the river.

"How far do you think we'll be able to get tonight?" John asked as he and Heather lifted one of the canoes out of the water. With a vehicle and a road ahead everyone but Leanne and I was suddenly discussing schedules, timetables, and deadlines. We had scarcely been off the river for an hour and already the modern life was taking over.

It was a difficult moment for Leanne and me. We hadn't set foot on a road, much less seen or heard a car, in more than fifty days. And now, in the midst of all the rush and hurry, we struggled with our farewells.

AUGUST 24 – *Alaska Highway, Coal River, British Columbia – The jar and grind of road walking is no different here than it was farther south, but now I have to contend with the loneliness as well. Part of it is because Leanne is gone, but there is something else, a kind of emptiness that I remember from the city. Webster and I are passed by thousands of cars, and yet none stop. I talk to no one. Despite all the remote country I've walked, I am more lonely now than I have been all trip.*

The loneliness was interrupted a day later when Erica pulled up. Knowing that I'd made it to the highway, she drove down from Whitehorse where she was preparing the presentation tour that would soon begin.

I'd had hesitations about hiring her as the project's publicist because I wasn't sure it would be easy for a brother and sister to work together. But no sooner had she pulled the van onto the shoulder and hopped out than those doubts began to fade. The hug she gave me was uncharacteristically brief, and with little time wasted, she sat me in the front seat and brought me up to date.

"Karst," she began, "there are lots of good things happening, but lots of bad stuff as well."

I sank into the comfort of the front seat. I could handle any news, no matter how bad, as long as I was seated there. "Okay, start with the bad stuff."

"The Forest Alliance," she said. "The propaganda machine is up and running again and you won't believe some of the comments I've had to deal with in western British Columbia. In Quesnel, a number of talk-show hosts sat down and gave *me* a lecture on Y2Y. And none of it was true! Then, someone in Williams Lake left a death threat on our answering machine, warning us not to come and talk there."

"What else?" I asked, holding back my anger.

"Well," Erica continued, "there are a lot of people who are buying the lies, and other groups that are helping to spread them."

"Groups? Like who?"

"Fording Coal."

An image of Fording Coal's PR person, the woman who had gone on a rant at the Fernie Chamber of Commerce meeting more than a year ago, surfaced like a photograph in my mind.

"Somehow, Fording convinced the municipality of Elkford to pass a motion against Y2Y," Erica continued, "and a movement for other communities to do the same has been slowly spreading across British Columbia. Next month, the entire Union of B.C. Municipalities will vote on an anti-Y2Y motion at their annual general meeting in Vancouver, and all they're going to be basing their vote on is a bunch of lies."

"Union of B.C. Municipalities? What's that?"

"An association of town governments. The motion probably doesn't mean anything from a legal perspective, but it's very symbolic.

It hasn't even come to the vote yet and already it's meant a lot of bad press for Y2Y."

I was furious. It had been made clear to both the Forest Alliance and Fording Coal what Y2Y was really about, and yet they were continuing to depict it as a huge national park that would cause tens of thousands of jobs to be lost. I knew from my own on-the-ground experiences that when people heard the truth about Y2Y, they usually supported the proposal – even if they worked in forestry or mining.

"So what's the good news?"

"Well," Erica smiled proudly, "you're going to have plenty of chances to set the record straight. I've arranged interviews with national radio and television, newspapers up and down both sides of the Rockies, and I've set up presentations in almost every forestry stronghold in western British Columbia." She handed me the schedule for the next two months, a list that made me both excited and fearful. I would be far busier than I wanted to be. There would be hour upon hour of talking on the phone, lengthy shoots in front of television cameras, late-night drives, early-morning meetings, and a perpetual rush to get from one interview to the next. I'd only been near a road for two days, and already the duty of promoting Y2Y was pulling my mind from the land.

"What's this?" I asked Erica, pointing to the top of the list. I only had sixty kilometres left to walk to Watson Lake, but the schedule showed me arriving at the hike's endpoint in eight days.

"I had to pick a date so that the media could plan to cover your arrival," she explained. "Without knowing exactly where you were and when you'd get out to the road, I scheduled something far enough ahead so I'd be sure you'd make it." Her shoulders shrugged as she flashed me an apologetic smile. "Sorry, Karst, but for these last few days, you're going to have to conform to someone else's schedule."

After all the freedom of the past few months, it was hard to be told to hike at a pace that suited others. But as I set off again the next morning, I realized that the extra time would allow me to do two important things along the way: visit the Kaska Dene at Lower Post, and have a few more nights to camp and sit alone before the intense work of the next few months.

After walking among soaring peaks and gleaming glaciers, the Liard Basin seemed drab and boring. Green forests and brown meadows rolled off in all directions, giving way to nothing but a low and uninviting grey horizon. There were no jagged ridges as I hiked north, no shining waterfalls, no arresting blue lakes, nothing to tease and command the eye.

But the Liard Basin was one of the most important connections in the entire Y2Y region. With the Rockies rising to the south, and the similarly rugged Mackenzies looming in the north, the area was a critical link for wildlife between the two mountain ranges, and a low-elevation oasis as well. The Liard's rolling hills were warmer than the surrounding mountains and, in winter, held less snow. Wildlife wandered freely from river to forest, from beaver pond to willow meadow, from favourite feeding to resting spot. There was more useable habitat than in the mountains, and, as a consequence, more animals.

The Kaska Dene had long known these things. For thousands of years they had fed and clothed themselves from the Basin, and although they'd grown less dependent on furs, hides, and wild meats in recent years, many of them continued to trap, hunt, and fish through the range of their traditional territory. It spanned a huge area – from Williston Lake in British Columbia to the tiny community of Ross River in the Yukon – and many of the old trails that crossed it were still well used. Travellers themselves, they welcomed someone with a story of walking the land.

It was a good time to visit the community of Lower Post. Nearly all the Kaska nation's leaders – from Fort Ware in north-central

British Columbia to Ross River – were gathered for a meeting to discuss their outstanding land claim with the federal, provincial, and territorial governments. While the tribal council met behind closed doors, I talked to young students about the trip, periodically checking on Webster who lay on the school steps, enduring the playful mob of local dogs. Then, after a feast of moose stew and freshly baked bannock, everyone packed into the school gymnasium for the evening presentation.

Despite having stood in front of almost a hundred crowds by then, I was nervous that night. This wasn't like any other audience I had talked to. Sitting in the dark silence were native elders and chiefs, many of whom understood the cycles and rhythms of animals and plants more deeply than I did. Much of the science that I talked about was nothing more than common sense to them. And so I made a few changes. While talking about the travels of wide-ranging animals, I didn't describe them as recent knowledge; and while discussing the ebb and flow of fire, disease, and other disturbances, I didn't mention what was obvious to them – that animals needed to move. And when it came time to share a few personal insights, I felt silly and self-conscious talking about "humility," "respect," and "reverence." For the first time, the words sounded empty and hollow. My once-in-a-lifetime experience, I suddenly realized, was a part of the culture of almost everyone in that room.

But there was applause at the end, heavy applause, and unlike the stiff, often awkward discussions that had followed many of the presentations I'd made in other communities, the Kaska wasted no time relating my trip to their own travels. Within minutes of the lights coming up, a number of the chiefs had pulled me over to the maps taped to the wall.

"Here, this is where I still trap," said one man, brushing his thick, weathered hand over a corner of the paper. I glanced to where he pointed, an area west of where Leanne and I had hiked, but still days from any road. "I walk there too," he beamed.

"This is where my grandfather's trail still runs," said the chief from Ross River. She was a small woman, and she could hardly reach the green curving lines towards the north end of the map. "We still hunt moose in those valleys every year."

I wanted to hear what people thought about the idea of Y2Y as well.

"What about a system of reserves and connections?" I asked. "What do you think about a plan so that everyone – Kaska and other people – can work together to conserve wildlife?"

A few of the chiefs looked at one another, then back at me. Finally, one man cleared his throat.

"It's a good idea," he answered carefully, "but I'm not sure it's relevant. We already take good care of the land. But maybe something needs to be done, something like you suggest, something more official. For now, though, we need to wait." The waiting, someone else explained, was for the land claim to be settled. Until that happened, no new initiatives or documents would be signed.

There were other guests in the room that night, pushing other agendas. Two businessmen from one of Canada's largest oil and gas drilling firms sat in the crowd, there to strike a deal with the Kaska over the region's rich petroleum reserves. They too were treated to hedging and noncommittal answers.

"We need to develop the economic opportunities that are already benefiting others around us," began Dave Porter, the Kaska's business manager, in a final speech to close the evening. "But like Karsten illustrated so well in his talk tonight, we need to do it in a way that will keep everything that's important to our culture."

I knew of some of the "others" he spoke of. In the nearby community of Fort Liard, for example, the Deh Cho First Nation were enjoying the benefits of the gas reserves on their land. More than 200 of them now had well-paying jobs. And less than 100 kilometres to the north, the Yukon government had just granted a company the right to start logging some of the Liard Basin's biggest trees.

I mulled Dave's words over as I struck out again the next morning. The dilemma facing the small native community of Lower Post was the same one I'd encountered everywhere: how to balance short-term economic benefits against long-term environmental costs. The difference for the Kaska was that their decision-makers lived in the community and viewed any impact as a personal cost. A new seismic line might lead the wolves to their prized moose hunting area, and the washouts from roads and clear-cuts might ruin the spawning beds of the fish they netted each fall. Unlike the large multinational corporations that roamed the globe in search of good deals and high profits, the Kaska would always live with the consequences of their decisions.

When I left Lower Post, I still had two days before I needed to arrive at Watson Lake – plenty of time to hike the remaining twenty kilometres. I walked just long enough to pass the Yukon boundary marker, and then, leaving the final few kilometres for the next morning, veered off the highway and into the trees. I had decided my last night would be away from vehicles and roads, under the stars. After bushwhacking for a half-hour, I emerged at a white sand beach and dropped my pack on the bank of the Liard.

SEPTEMBER 5 – *Six kilometres from Watson Lake, Yukon – Tomorrow, when the crush of interviews and presentations begins, it will be harder than ever to remember the turns and twists of wild rivers and valleys. I will need to remember how this stillness and simplicity feeds me, how the humility and awareness evoked by bears and wild swims feeds into my everyday life. I will need to remember the good that inevitably follows the bad, the warmth that follows the cold, the calm that returns after the storm, and the quiet patience of animals that endure these cycles day after day, year after year. I need to remember that everything, including life, is only temporary.*

Webster had curled up next to me, his weight and warmth a comfort as I wrote, his paws twitching against my legs. Maybe he was thinking back on the trip as well, dreaming about the wolves, bears, and river crossings, reliving each wild valley through a tapestry of scents and smells. I put down my pen and ran my fingers over his sinewy body. He was still an inspiration: always happy, always accepting whatever came his way, and although the walk of a lifetime would end abruptly the next morning, I knew he would adjust to that change as well. He would sleep and loaf as though it was all he had ever known, and then spring to his feet when called again, not knowing if he was going for a walk around the block or across the continent. Regardless, he would trot gamely out the door.

I picked up my pen and added one last line to the journal entry: *Always remember Webster.*

A chill roused me from my thoughts. The sun had disappeared and the campfire was nothing but a few burning coals. I pulled on a jacket, then looked up at the night's first stars with a shiver. Early September was cold in the Yukon, colder than it had been in Banff the year before, and although it was still early, I headed for bed.

They came just as I was zipping the tent door closed, flying from the north in strings and waves, every wingbeat flashing in the day's dying light. For ten minutes they flew overhead, dozens of snow geese, Canada geese, and big white swans. Rare trumpeter swans, I thought. Nothing would be more fitting: them starting their migration south, me ending mine north, crossover journeys from Y to Y.

I lay back and imagined myself flying with them, the Mackenzies in my wake, the Rockies a crinkled skin ahead, the lakes of the Liard Basin glittering below like silver stones. In two weeks the birds would cover the same distance I had trekked in eighteen months, seeing in a glimpse what had filled my eyes for more than a year.

For the first few days, they would fly over pristine forests and mountain peaks, and then, somewhere north of Williston Lake, the first signs of clear-cuts and seismic lines would come into view. There would be more and more scars on the land as they birds flew south over the Bow, Crowsnest, Elk, and Gallatin rivers. Even there, where roads and towns clutter the valleys, there would be patches of healthy forest and alpine meadow, linked in places, separate in others, and still capable of being reconnected to the big wild. Farther south still, amid a confusion of roads, lay an island of wilderness familiar to the swans. Now the birds descended as they and their ancestors always have, breaking formation as they swooped down, followers overtaking leaders as they splashed down on the marshes of their winter range in Yellowstone Park.

I rolled over in the tent, comforted by the idea of the swans being in the place where I'd started hiking. It seemed so long ago, so far away. How many other animals had shared the mountain corridor with me since then, I wondered as I drifted off to sleep. Must have been millions.

Threading, always threading their way. Their lines holding the wilderness together.

It is mid-November 1999, two weeks since I finished the post-hike presentation tour, and it feels good to take a seat at the back of the rustic conference room. I'm tired from all the talking. Today, I am happy just to be in the audience rather than on the stage.

Twenty-seven people file into the dimly lit room – all of them top scientists in their field. Stephen Herrero, one of Canada's foremost grizzly bear experts, chats with wolf specialist Paul Paquet. Lance Craighead, the man who mapped the best remaining wildlife corridors in western Montana with Rich Walker, nods a quiet hello as he shuffles to where Dave Mattson and John Weaver, two top-level carnivore experts from the United States, sit on the other side of the room. Beside them, Dave Schindler, Canada's most celebrated aquatic scientist, talks to an expert on forest birds.

It's prestigious company that has gathered in this draughty log building on the outskirts of Jasper, and I hope the elk-dotted meadows and snow-covered mountains that surround us inspire the ambitious meeting to unfold as planned. By the end of the weekend, the assembled brain trust will have begun to address questions such as which species to focus on while mapping the Y2Y reserve network, and at which scales the mapping needs to occur.

Fortunately, there is someone in the room who has been through this whole process before. The lights go down, people settle into their chairs, and a retired, grey-haired professor from California bounds to the front of the room. Michael Soulé, the man everyone calls "the grandfather of conservation biology," fiddles with the slide projector and launches into his presentation.

We are toured quickly through some examples where reserve network designs are already underway: the mesa butte country of Sky Islands in New Mexico; the Klamath rainforest region of the Oregon Cascades; and the Everglades and Big Bend areas of Florida. Soulé pauses for a moment, pointing out how Florida, one of the most densely populated of all the states, is the furthest along in the effort. Spurred on by the rapid decline in endangered panthers (there are fewer than fifty left in the wild), a $2.7-billion program has been launched to purchase and restore some of the cats' most vital connections.

My mind stays in Florida as Soulé goes on to talk about other places where similar ideas are beginning to emerge. I hear the names but not the details: Algonquin to Adirondacks; Manitoba to the Mountains; Rainforest to the Rockies; and a Wildlands Project that, someday, will connect the networks together. It is inspiring stuff, but the image of Florida panthers, trapped and isolated on a few remaining chunks of habitat, lingers in my head. Many males are being born sterile, I later learn, leaving everyone wondering if the rescue effort will happen in time.

Soulé's voice pulls my thoughts back to the screen. A wolf flashes across and then a bear. He is listing the focal species that have been used to map some of the reserve networks now, naming predators with large habitat requirements that, if accommodated, will benefit the smaller plants and animals that share their range. He lists the panther in Florida, the red wolf in Sky Islands, the black bear and lynx in Algonquin and the Adirondacks – and when he finishes I'm almost certain that it will be the grizzly for Y2Y. I'm wrong. A passionate discussion ensues. The area is simply too big for a single land-based animal to capture the full breadth of its diversity, argue the scientists, and in the end it will be the grizzly, along with a number of key bird and fish species, that will be used to map out the area's habitats and important connections.

Two years later, in January 2002, I'm starting to understand that even the simplest kind of science – gathering and summarizing existing data – takes a long time to complete for such a vast area. Only one of the three Y2Y-wide habitat maps – the one for grizzly bears – has been completed, and the others aren't scheduled to be finished for several more months. Even at that, the maps will provide only a general overview of the reserve network design. To bring it down to the ground, a host of regional and local biologists, First Nations, hunters, trappers, landowners, and others with intimate knowledge of the land will need to fine-tune the design. Slowly, the mountain of data, research, reports, traditional knowledge, existing land-use plans, and maps will be analyzed, compared, and overlaid until an increasingly clear picture emerges: cores, corridors, and transition zones, running from one Y to the other.

How long will such a process take?

If all goes well, the first cut of the Y2Y "Conservation Areas Design" will be finished by 2005. It won't be perfect, but it'll be better than anything that exists today. And it will help land trusts, municipal governments, enlightened forestry companies, and others who have previously worked in isolation to coordinate their conservation efforts.

This kind of coordinated work is urgently needed. In the two and a half years since the hike ended, the Y2Y region has experienced tremendous change: an additional 100,000 people have moved into the area and more than 300 million tourists have visited. As well, another 1,800 square kilometres of trees have been cut; approximately 500 more oil and gas wells have been drilled; an estimated

3,300 kilometres of seismic line have been cleared; and 1,500 kilometres of road have been built. All of this has happened piecemeal and haphazardly, cutting once-contiguous valleys, watersheds, and ecosystems into smaller and smaller pieces.

But all the science and coordinated mapping can only take us so far. The Conservation Areas Design will show us where, how, and why corridors need to be conserved, but not when. When will be up to us.

When will we adopt sustainable forestry practices instead of clear-cutting? When will we live in towns instead of on acreages? When will we end our love affair with roads? We need to ask these and other questions now, before it's too late. And as we search for the answers, we must remember that it isn't how much we can get away with that's important, but how much the world, and its wildlife, can still absorb. Nature has its thresholds, and for an experiment such as Y2Y to succeed, we need to find the generosity, even the love, to keep places where those thresholds will never be tested.

ACKNOWLEDGEMENTS

Thank you to editors Dinah Forbes and Tom Howell, who provided the objectivity that helped turn a manuscript into a book. Erica Heuer, Joe Obad, Bart Robinson, Justin Thompson, and Harvey Locke also provided useful comments on earlier drafts, as did Mike McIvor, who wisely prodded me to think and write further. Conversations with Joan Dunkley, Don Gardner, Peter von Tiesenhausen, Julian Norris, Mark Hebblewhite and Whip Funk helped this process, as did the inspiring spaces to write offered by Betty Anne and Don Graves, Hugh and Shirley Pepper, Bert and Marilyn Dyck, and Don Gorrie. Thanks to Ron Larsen, Bob Haney, and Ian Syme of Parks Canada for granting me the time from work to do the trip and write the book.

I would also like to thank all the organizations and individuals who made the hike possible. The TD Canada Trust Friends of the Environment Foundation, along with TransAlta Utilities, Mountain Equipment Co-op, Endswell Foundation, the Banff Centre for Mountain Culture, the Bear Society, and Friends of Banff and Yoho National Parks funded all our community and media outreach efforts. Wayne Sawchuk, Brian Churchill, Bryan Pate, Ken Forrest, Ross Peck, Roy Howard, Dustin Lynx, Dave Higgins, and Walkin' Jim Stoltz offered helpful hints for route selection. Soft Path Cuisine and Community Natural Foods of Calgary, as well as Marra's Grocery, Nutter's, and Sylvia McAllister at the Veterinary Hospital in Canmore, all made sure human and canine hikers were well fed. Mountain

Equipment Co-op and Patagonia provided some of our clothes and camping equipment.

A special thanks to Maxine Achurch who, after becoming deeply involved in the project, was forced to step away at a difficult time. I am grateful to Justin Thompson for weathering that awkward period, and to my sister, Erica, for capably assuming his position the following year, as well as providing logistical and moral support throughout the project, along with her incredible partner Cameron Johnson.

Thanks to the dozens of conservation groups and activists in communities across the Y2Y region who not only opened their homes and offices to us, but inspired me with their hopes and dreams as well.

Finally, thanks to my wife Leanne, whose beauty and wisdom grounds me in time and place.

FURTHER READING AND RESOURCES

Brooks, T., and S. Jones. *The Hiker's Guide to Montana's Continental Divide Trail.* Falcon Press, 1990.

Lynx, Dustin. *Hiking Canada's Great Divide Trail.* Rocky Mountain Books, 2000.

MacArthur, R.H., and E.O. Wilson. *The Theory of Island Biogeography.* Princeton, N.J.: Princeton University Press, 1967.

Newmark, W.D. "Mammalian Extinctions in Western North American Parks: A Landbridge Perspective." *Nature* 325: s430-32.

Noss, R.F. "The Wildlands Project: Land conservation strategy." *Wild Earth* (special issue) 1: 10-25, 1992.

Noss, R.F., and A. Cooperrider. *Saving Nature's Legacy: Protecting and Restoring Biodiversity.* Washington, D.C.: Defenders of Wildlife and Island Press, 1994.

Paquet, P., and A. Hackman. *Large Carnivore Conservation in the Rocky Mountains; a long-term strategy for maintaining free-ranging and self-sustaining populations of carnivores.* World Wildlife Fund Canada, 1995.

Soulé, M.E., and J. Terborgh. *Continental Conservation: Scientific Foundations of Regional Reserve Networks.* Washington D.C.: Island Press, 1999.

Willcox, L., B. Robinson, and A. Harvey (eds). *A Sense of Place: An Atlas of Issues, Attitudes and Resources in the Yellowstone to Yukon Ecoregion.* Canmore, Alberta, 1998. (Also available on the Internet at <www.y2y.net>).

For more information on Y2Y:

Yellowstone to Yukon Conservation Initiative
710 9th Street, Studio B
Canmore, Alberta
T1W 2V7 Canada
(403) 609-2666
www.y2y.net